POWER & GREED

A SHORT HISTORY OF THE WORLD

POWER & GREED

A SHORT HISTORY OF THE WORLD

PHILIPPE GIGANTÈS

CARROLL & GRAF PUBLISHERS
New York

Carroll & Graf Publishers
an imprint of Avalon Publishing Group, Inc.
161 William Street
New York
NY 10038 2607
www.carrollandgraf.com

First published in the UK by Constable,
an imprint of Constable & Robinson Ltd 2002

First Carroll & Graf edition 2002

ISBN 0-7867-1077-2

Printed and bound in the EU

Library of Congress Cataloging-in-Publication Data is available on file.

To the memory of my brilliant,
kindly, loving brother Terry,
who so wanted me to write this book

CONTENTS

ACKNOWLEDGEMENTS

My thanks to my daughter Claire who made me write this book and kept a professional editor's eye on the text during its gestation.

John Saunders and Adrienne Farrell Jackson scrutinized this book to make sure it had no errors of fact, grammar, syntax, vocabulary or form. I can't thank them enough.

My thanks also to my daughter Eve-Marie, the lawyer, who did a forensic editing, to see that the research was sound and conclusions warranted.

Above all, I have a huge debt of gratitude to David Blomfield who edited the book for the publishers. He is perfect. Other authors should have the luck to have him improve their work.

ABOUT THIS BOOK

This is a short book. Purposely.

A rock smashes through plate glass. Tear gas drifts through the streets. Police in riot gear skirmish with demonstrators, mostly young, waving a crop of angry placards denouncing corporate rapacity. Inside an elite hotel, men in £2,000 suits discuss the world and wealth and power. Their world. Their wealth. Their power.

This book is about that power: human power. It is not a history of human culture, nor of human knowledge, but it does attempt to explain why history happened as it did, to give an historical lineage of events, to highlight powerful, often extravagant, men and women who marked their times and ours.

Whatever their culture and epoch, mankind has sought to acquire what it takes to satisfy five basic desires: security, shelter, sustenance, sex (for pleasure or progeny) and self-expression. To avoid chaos, society needs rules that limit the freedom of its members to pursue their desires.

Many thinkers have addressed the conflict between freedom for individuals to pursue their desires, and the rules society uses to contain this freedom. Among them, a handful of giants stand out: Moses, Solon, Plato, Jesus, Muhammad, Lao-tzu,

Confucius, the founders of Brahminism, and the Buddha. They are giants because their rules have had the greatest following, their teachings have marked human societies. They are the subjects of the book's first part.

The second part focuses on those who insist on breaking or circumventing society's rules. These are the grand acquisitors.* Grand acquisitors always want more, and hence they disturb the social order. They are Manichaean, creators as well as destroyers; among other things they have given us the industrial revolution, railroads and mass-produced automobiles. They can be compared to the dominant male in a pride of lions. The rest of the pride does all the work to get a kill; the dominant male gets the best share of the meal, all the sex, and he does the serious roaring. The dominant lion has the power, and he has the greed.

Very few of us know how to get and keep power – the best instrument for satisfying our desires. Throughout human history power has come in different forms: owning more slaves, or more domestic animals, or more land to exploit, or more subjects to tax, or more followers to lead through changing the faith or conquering the lands of others, or having more money to rival their power. So this is the theme of the book: grand acquisitors, in their need for freedom to achieve their desires, wage war on society's need for order – a war that often has a determinant effect on history.

In so short a text, selecting events to illustrate the theme of the book must be arbitrary. Here I have deliberately focused on the development of what we know as the western world, the greatest predators in history. By this I am not suggesting that the West is more important than its neighbours in the east

---

* There is no such word as acquisitor in the dictionary. I think it is a permissible invention to say that those who are acquisitive are acquisitors.

and south, but its history provides a broader choice of well-documented case studies.

I have been equally arbitrary over the choice of my grand acquisitors. I could, for instance, have written a chapter on Augustus rather than Agrippina. Augustus, the first Roman emperor, acquired absolute power, which led inevitably to absolute corruption. Augustus was an effective military commander. He was a good administrator. He was also extraordinarily dull. Agrippina is certainly more fun to study than Augustus.

There is no rule that says history should not be fun.

P.G.

PART 1

The Rules of Engagement

1

MOSES

(c. 14th – 13th century)

We have in our hands today a short, hugely important, text called Moses' Ten Commandments.*

There is a tender story about Moses: he was a baby, set adrift on the Nile, in a reed basket; an Egyptian princess found him and adopted him. He grew up in the palace, in gilded splendour, somehow discovered his Jewish relatives, and led all the Jews out of Egyptian bondage.

Was Moses an historical person? Were the Ten Commandments dictated by God to whoever Moses was, or were they compiled by others but attributed to a mythical figure called Moses? These are important questions. The answers that are advanced are matters of faith which deserve respect. But whatever the answers, let us follow the tradition that Moses inspired, if he did not write, the first five books of the Bible.

We *think* that *maybe* we can date the Ten Commandments back to the fourteenth century BC.† Here is the

---

* Others, like the Babylonian King Hammurabi, gave some similar commandments. But, in our western minds, the ideas in such commandments are associated with Moses.

† References are listed at the end of the book on p. 231. All dating of Moses is an uncertain approximation. See Will Durant, *The Story of Civilization*, New York: Simon & Schuster, 1980, vol. 1, pp. 301–2.

text, compressed and translated into contemporary English:*

1. I am the only God. You must not worship any other gods. You must not worship pictures or statues. If you disobey me I will punish you and your descendants for four generations.
2. Do not use the word God in vain.
3. Work six days and rest on the seventh. On the day you rest, your family, your guests, your slaves and your animals should also rest.
4. Look after your father and your mother, so that you in your turn will be looked after by your children.
5. You must not murder.†
6. You must not commit adultery.
7. You must not steal.
8. You must not give false testimony harmful to your neighbour.
9. Do not covet your neighbour's house.
10. Do not covet your neighbour's wife; do not covet your neighbour's slaves, male or female, his ox, his donkey, or anything else that belongs to him.

These commandments are brilliant in their brevity: in a few words Moses prohibits the behaviours that disrupt society. He prescribes limits on what the individual can do to increase

---

* *Exodus* 20: 1–17; *Deuteronomy*, 5: 1–21, from the King James Version. The Jews, the Catholic Church and Luther differ on which part of the commandments comes under which number. Are there ten commandments, or more, or less? This does not really matter. Everyone agrees on what the commandments say.

† In the original Greek the verb can be translated both as 'kill' and 'murder'. The God of the Old Testament, as we shall see, approved the killing of enemies, and even of disobedient Jews.

his share of sustenance, shelter, safety, and sex: do not steal, murder, or commit adultery. He sets boundaries to self-expression: do not calumny, do not use the word God in vain and, more importantly, do not dispute the existence of God or his Commandments. He goes to the very motive for the bad behaviour he prohibits – greed or covetousness: do not covet your neighbour's wife, nor his slaves, nor his house, nor his animals. He establishes the principle of social security – look after the old – as well as the principle of statutory holidays – a day of rest each week.

A great shortlist on how to stay out of trouble in society, the Ten Commandments are the basis for modern legal codes in the western world.

Moses elaborated on his Commandments. In a long passage of the *Septuagint*,* we learn of the limits he imposes on sexual gratification. He tells the Jews:

> You are forbidden to uncover the sexual organs of your father; of your mother; of your father's other wife – her sexual organs belong to your father; you are forbidden to uncover the sexual organs of your sister; of your son's daughter; of your daughter's daughter; of your father's sister; of your mother's sister; of your father's brother; and you should not penetrate his wife, because she is your aunt. You are forbidden to uncover the sexual organs of your daughter-in-law; of your brother's wife.

---

* The text of the Old Testament in Ancient Greek, the *Septuagint*, is a translation into Greek of Hebrew or Aramaic texts, done under the sponsorship of Ptolemy II Philadelpheus (308–246 BC). The Hebrew texts of the third century BC translated for the *Septuagint* were older than the oldest currently available Hebrew manuscripts – which started, possibly, as translations of the *Septuagint*.

You are forbidden to uncover the sexual organs of a woman of your household and of her daughter also; you must not uncover the sexual organs of a woman while in bed with her sister, to make them jealous. You must not have sex with your neighbour's wife. You must not masturbate. A man must not have sex with another man or with a beast. Nor may a woman have sex with a beast.[2]

We should remember that life expectancy was not what it is now: it might have been thirty-five years, high testosterone years. One's aunt might have been no older than fifteen. In Moses' conversation with the Lord about these prohibitions, the Lord says these practices were common among the other nations which inhabited Palestine, nations that the Lord allowed the Jews to slay: 'thou shalt smite every male thereof with the edge of the sword.'[3]

Moses also elaborated on his other commandments. In amassing wealth and power, the rich should not oppress other people.[4] In Moses' view, acquisitiveness should not result in the poor being ground down by the rich. The land which was bought by the rich should periodically be redistributed to those who presumably had sold it to repay money they owed to the rich.[5]

When things went wrong, Moses had conversations with God, which he relayed to the Jews. He told them how God would punish them if they disobeyed. The punishments were truly frightening. The earth opened up and swallowed those who disobeyed the Lord or his spokesman Moses.[6] When Moses caught the Jews dancing naked around a golden statue of a calf and worshipping it, he ordered the Levites, the priestly caste, to kill the dancers. Three thousand were killed.[7]

However, despite their fear of punishment by God or by Moses, the Jews did not obey the Ten Commandments as much as they obeyed their instinct to acquire more. The grand acquisitors restrained themselves the least. The prophet Isaiah described it: 'The rich have taken all the vineyards; taken all the land for their houses . . . The poor had their faces ground underfoot by the rich. The rich denied justice to the needy, preyed on widows and robbed the fatherless.'[8]

To propitiate God when the Babylonians besieged Jerusalem, the rich Jews emancipated poor Jews they had turned into slaves. When the Babylonians lifted the siege, the rich caught and re-enslaved those whom they had released.

The constant, brutal fighting against the other occupants of Palestine was hardly designed to teach compassion, consideration, abstinence from rape and pillage to the Jews. Let us make no mistake: the conquest of Palestine by the Jews was a holy war ordained by God, a *jihad* as the Muslims call it.[9] Moses sent 12,000 Jews against the Midianites, killing all adult males. The Jewish troops returned with their booty and the Midianite women and children. Though Moses did say 'love your neighbour as you love yourself',[10] it obviously only applied to Jewish neighbours. He ordered that all the male Midianite children be killed. Of the females, only the virgins were to be spared for use by the Jewish soldiers. Non-virgins he ordered to be killed.[11] When Joshua, Moses' immediate successor, took cities, his army killed every living human: men, women, and children.[12]

Moses said that Abraham was the first to be told by God that there was only one God. In a patriarchal, tribal society, such as Abraham's, the concept of one patriarchal God ruling over his children made sense. Moses went further. He told his followers *how* God created the universe. The common sense of Moses' teachings is breathtaking when compared with what others thought at the time. God, he said, created the heavens; then the earth; then divided the water from the dry land on earth; then plants; then the creatures that live in the sea; and those that came to the land from the sea; then the birds, and the animals that live on land; then the mammals; and finally man. This sequence is very close to what contemporary science tells us. Paleontology, the science of ancient bones and fossils, confirms most of Moses' sequence for the appearance of various species on earth. How did he figure it out?

One is left with the image of this protean man, leading his bedraggled, insubordinate, oversexed tribesmen out of slavery, through famine, lack of water, hostile enemies, finally to the fertile crescent, the land promised by God to his chosen people, the Jews.[13] And through these titanic tribulations, Moses' mind came up with lasting legislation, the sequence in which the universe was created, the correct sequence of how life evolved on our planet and, above all, the watershed theological concept of one God who created the universe and everything in it.*

Human beings have long searched for the causes of what was happening to them and around them. The polytheistic answer was to assign one god to one happening and other gods to other happenings, gods of rain, gods of thunder, wind, harvest, etc. The assumption that one superior power accounted for everything was a huge step in human understanding. It posited one single scheme of things imposed by one single power. The quest for understanding would have been much harder if one assumed that there were myriad gods each with a different scheme of things. After monotheism, humans only had to understand the one God's single scheme.

The first question about the single scheme of things may have been: why? This led, among the Greeks, to other questions: when? how? who? The Greeks asked: is God the answer to everything we do not understand? If not, how do we explain

---

* The husband of Nefertiti, Amenhotep IV (Pharaoh c. 1380–62 BC) who changed his name to Ikhnaton, tried to introduce monotheism in Egypt but failed against the concerted opposition of the priests, who had a commercial interest in the popular festivals for the deities they served.

what is around us? Is it perfect? Does it change? By imposing monotheism, Moses took the first step in this major intellectual exploration.

To sum up, Moses made rules he said came from God, to restrict exploitation by the grand acquisitors. Those who broke the rules, Moses said, would be punished dreadfully by the Lord. But the fear of God did not always deter the grand acquisitors; for they were not always seen to be punished when they enriched themselves excessively by grinding down the poor and straining the fabric and cohesion of society.

As we shall see in the next chapter, Solon, the Athenian, tried another way. His constitutional reforms gave power to the poor, so they could protect themselves against the rich.

2

SOLON

(c. 630–560 BC)

God is mentioned nowhere in Solon's legislation. Among Greeks, his was not a time for much belief in gods. Their intellectual leaders were more concerned with scientific and philosophical explorations.

Some two centuries before Solon, the Greeks had made a momentous invention – the vowel. Until then, none of the alphabets had vowels. This meant that only a Phoenician knew how to pronounce written Phoenician words. In a modern analogy, try the three letters CST. Do they spell cost or cast or caste or cyst? Imagine yourself being a foreigner and trying to read such a language. The Greeks adopted the Phoenician alphabet and added vowels to it. Having an alphabet with vowels, the Greeks could transcribe foreign words, know how these were pronounced and ask what they meant. They probably made glossaries of foreign words and thus learned foreign languages. This contributed largely to their becoming major traders in the Mediterranean.

Their geography also helped the Greeks. Their sea, the Aegean, was dotted with islands, no more than a day's rowing one from the other, an important factor in those days when sailing techniques were not yet advanced. These 'stepping stones' were used by the Greeks to visit their neighbours: in what is now Turkey – the Phrygians, the Paphlagonians, the Lydians, the Cilicians, the Mysians, the Capadocians; in what is now Iraq – the Babylonians; in what is now the Lebanon and Israel – the Phoenicians and the Jews; in Africa – the Egyptians; along the shores of the Black Sea – the Scythians.

The Greek traders became intellectual burglars. They brought back to Greece the ideas and the knowledge of others and then took them many steps further. The renowned classicist John Burnet says:[1]

We are far more likely to underrate the originality of the Greeks than to exaggerate it; and we do not always remember the very short time they took to lay down the lines scientific enquiry has followed ever since. By the early part of the sixth century BC, the Greeks had learnt the rough and ready system of measuring which was all Egypt could teach them. And a hundred years later we find in Greek cities the study of arithmetical and geometrical progressions, plane geometry and the elements of harmonics firmly established on a scientific basis. Another century saw the rise of solid and spherical geometry and the sections of the cone (the parabola, the ellipse, the circle) were soon added. The Greeks learned, directly and indirectly, from Babylon that certain celestial phenomena recur in cycles and may, therefore, be predicted. Within fifty years, the Greeks had discovered that the earth swings free in space and the knowledge of its spherical shape soon followed.

There were similar Greek achievements in the study of living organisms, for example, the flux and reflux of the blood between the heart and the surface of the body. Further, the Greeks always tried to give a rational explanation of the appearances they had observed. They were also quite conscious of the need for verification, that every hypothesis must do justice to all the observed facts. That is the method of science, as we understand it still.* Many consider what the Greeks did in those days to be an intellectual miracle.

Solon, who was born sometime around 630 BC, and died around 560 BC, lived through the beginnings of the Greek intellectual miracle. This may be one explanation for his willingness to challenge the traditional, and for his attachment to reason over passion. His motto was *meden agan*, which means 'nothing in excess'. Solon was possibly the greatest lawgiver of all time. His thought still dominates the democratic systems of western civilization. American democracy and British-style parliamentary democracies are his intellectual children. It is astounding to see how close to successful contemporary democratic constitutions is what he prescribed 2,600 years ago. He truly understood the nature of man and legislated accordingly.

In his time, the gods had already been totally discredited by the poets Homer[2] and Hesiod[3], who described most Greek deities as adulterers, murderers, thieves, liars, cheats, creatures full of envy, jealousy and vengefulness – in fact much like not very nice humans. Greek intellectual – if not popular – thought had moved towards the conclusion of Xenophanes (570–484 BC): there was only one God – the universe itself.[4] Had some Greek trader, returning from a voyage to Palestine, brought back to Greece Moses' idea of monotheism?

---

* Burnet adds that the only eastern people who 'bear comparison with the Greeks in science and philosophy are the Indians'. However, he says, no Indian works were written in the fields of philosophy or mathematics, before Greek science and philosophy reached India with Alexander in the fourth century BC.

Solon came from the most noble of the Athenian families. His father had brought the family fortune to ruin; so Solon became a shipowner in a small way. He was considered one of the Greek world's seven wisest men – the other six being Bias of Priene, Chilon of Sparta, Cleobulus of Lindos, Periander of Corinth, Pittacus of Mitylene and Thales of Miletus, who said that all things come from water,[5] and was generally considered the earliest of the Greek philosophers.

On his sojourns home, Solon talked at length of what he had seen and heard. People admired the good judgement he acquired in adapting to different cultures. He also was a brave warrior. He was generous and compassionate. Unlike many of his peers, he never enslaved nor sold into slavery people who could not repay money he had lent them.

The other nobles of Athens, who owned all the good land, did enslave any man who did not repay the money they had lent him. These slaves had mostly been peasants cultivating a rich man's land for a small share of the crop. If the crop was bad, the poor peasant's share would be too small to feed his family. He then had to borrow money from the landowner, usually under unforgiving conditions: if the borrower did not repay the loan, he, his family and descendants would belong to the lender. Such was the inevitable consequence of two bad crops in a row. Enslaved families could be split up and sold separately, even to masters living in far-off lands.

By the end of the seventh century (700–600) BC, revolt was brewing in Athens – not only among the poor peasants and manual workers who rented their muscle to the rich, but also among well-off people who were not *eupatridae*, i.e. well-born. Indeed, the nobles excluded everyone else, even rich merchants, from any role in running the state. They controlled the armed forces and the courts. Laws then were not written:

the *eupatridae* made them up to suit their interests, in trials before judges who were fellow *eupatridae*.

By 621 BC, revolt was so likely that the nobles mandated one of their own, Dracon, to write a code of laws. In this code he prescribed the death penalty even for minor offences. When asked why his penalties were so severe, Dracon answered that even minor offences deserved death, and that, for greater crimes, he unfortunately knew of no more severe penalty. Hence the word 'draconian' to describe excessive penalties. Dracon's reform did not keep things quiet for long. By 594 BC, the non-nobles were in revolt against the nobles. The nobles had horses and wore armour. The non-nobles had bows, arrows and slingshots, but were much more numerous.* In an act of profound political wisdom – seldom seen in history – the two sides agreed to appoint Solon as their arbitrator, with full powers to settle the dispute. They also made him *archon*, the head of the government.

The nobles thought of Solon as one of them, by kinship and by class. They felt he would side with them. The non-noble prosperous merchants also thought of him as one of them – he was a merchant. The poor trusted him because he had never ground any of them down. His fellow nobles expected him to find a solution that preserved all their privileges, powers and wealth. The poor wanted him to confiscate the land of the rich and distribute it to the poor peasants. No group got what it wanted from him. In poems that have survived, Solon recounts that, before he proclaimed his constitution, every one loved him.[6] Afterwards, he says, everyone hated him because he did not give the factions everything they wanted

---

* Men armed with bows and slingshots were called *peltasts*. Many times in Greek history *peltasts* tore armoured infantry to pieces by staying at a distance and hurling stones and arrows at their less mobile foe.

but found a middle solution that protected each faction from the other.

He abolished Dracon's harsh laws, which were applied by the noble judges mostly to non-nobles. He abolished all debts. He freed the men and their families who had been enslaved for not repaying their debts. Those who had been sold abroad, he bought back and repatriated. He made it illegal to lend on the security of the person: people would never again be enslaved for not being able to pay their debts.

But Solon did not make the mistake the Communists would make in 1917 Russia: he did not expropriate the land of the rich. He let them stay rich and continue using their talents to make the economy grow. However, as we are about to see, he gave political power to the poor who could thus protect themselves from oppression. This is the very essence of modern democracies.

High state offices were no longer reserved for the nobles. In fact, under Solon's reform, people were no longer divided into nobles and non-nobles. He established four classes based not on heredity but on income:

> the *pentakosiomedimnoi*, who had incomes equivalent to 750 bushels of corn or more;
> the *hippeis*, who had incomes between 450 and 749 bushels;
> the *zeugitai*, who had 300–449 bushels;
> and the *thetes*, who had less income than the first three classes.*

The classes were taxed on their income. Members of the fourth class, the *thetes*, were not taxed at all. The third class,

---

* The *medimnos* was a measure equal to one and half bushels of corn. *Pentakosia* meant 500; so 500 *medimnoi* (plural) was equal to 750 bushels. *Hipperis* means horsemen. *Zeugitai* means people who owned a pair of cattle to pull their plough. *Thetes* were paid a wage to work.

the *zeugitai*, paid the basic rate. The second class, the *hippeis*, were taxed at twice the basic rate. Members of the first class, the richest, the *pentakosiomedimnoi*, were taxed at 2.4 times the basic rate. Solon, clearly, was no partisan of the flat tax: he introduced the first graduated income tax in history.

Solon reserved the highest offices for the *pentakosiomedimnoi*, the very rich. However, this class now included not only nobles by birth, but rich merchants and rich artisans. Members of the lowest class, the *thetes*, could hold no offices but they were members of two important new institutions: the *Ekklesia*, and the *Heliaea*. The *Ekklesia* was the assembly of all the citizens. At its peak, Athens had 25,000 voting citizens. For major state decisions, the constitution required a minimum quorum of 6,000. The *Heliaea* was a body of 6,000 jurors to which one could appeal regarding the decision of any office holder. The *Heliaea* also heard appeals against decisions of the Supreme Court, the *Areopagus*, whose seats were reserved for the members of the richest class. Members of the *Heliaea* were not permanent. They were picked by lot from the citizens present at the *Areos Pagos*, a hillock where votes and trials took place. All 6,000 members only met for the most important cases. For routine cases, juries were limited to 500.* Another important institution, the *Boule*, was composed of 400 elected members. This chamber deliberated on issues and submitted them for a decision to the people – to the *Ekklesia*.[7]

As things evolved, the real power was soon wielded by the *Ekklesia* where each citizen, rich or poor, had one vote. The

---

* For a trial, jurors were chosen at dawn and a decision had to be rendered by sunset. No trial could last more than one day. There was thus no way to 'fix' a jury, especially since verdicts were taken by a majority vote.

poor, far more numerous, easily outvoted the rich. The *Heliaea* was also inevitably dominated by the poor.

All deliberations of these institutions took place in public, in the open. Every citizen could watch and hear everything.* This was an essential aspect of Solon's democracy. Only recently has such universal public scrutiny been made possible, through television, for our much larger contemporary democracies.

Solon's laws were much milder than those of Dracon. He had them carved on wooden columns, so people could read them. He wanted the Athenians to have a strong sense of civic duty: in times of serious political discord, he decreed, a citizen who did not actively support one or the other side would be disfranchised.[8] A citizen who saw another citizen wronged had the legal obligation to indict the wrongdoer. The best city to live in, Solon said, 'was that city in which those who are not wronged, no less than those who are wronged, exert themselves to punish the wrongdoer.'[9]

Before Solon's laws, if a man died without heirs, his fortune reverted to his clan. Solon gave the individual the right to bequeath his property to people outside his clan, provided he was of sound mind and had not made a will under duress.[10]

Solon's legislation strongly supported the family and the begetting and education of children. He decreed that sons not taught a trade by their father need not support him in his old age.[11] The sons of those who died in battle were to be brought up and educated by the state. Solon forbade dowries. Marriages should not be for money but for passionate love that leads to begetting children, he said.[12] A bride need only bring

---

* The *Boule* could vote to deliberate in secret. But then its decisions or suggestions would have to be submitted openly to the *Ekklesia*.

three changes of clothes and small personal items to her husband's house. Solon forbade marriages between old men and young women, for they might not lead to passionate love. He also prohibited marriages or even sex between old women and young men. The young man should be taken away from the old woman 'who was fattening him like a partridge' and given as husband to a young woman who could have children.[13] By law, if a man incapable of having sex married an heiress, she would have the right to sleep with any man of his clan she fancied. Thus, impotent men would have to desist from marrying heiresses or submit to the shame of seeing their wife copulate with whomsoever she fancied in the clan.[14]

Solon not only abolished debt. He wanted to encourage economic activity other than agriculture. People who migrated to Athens with their whole families, to ply a trade, were given citizenship.[15] Olive oil was the only export Solon allowed – there was a big foreign market for it.[16] Many Athenian fields were less suited to producing grain than olives; but, it took years before the trees grew large enough to produce oil. Solon established and taxed state brothels,[17] boosting Athens' tourist industry, not unlike several cities today. The monies collected subsidized farmers waiting for their olive trees to grow. To make imports cheaper, Solon devalued the currency by adding 30 per cent lead to the Athenian silver coins.[18] People who willingly did no work or led a life of debauchery lost their right to address the *Ekklesia*. This amounted to losing their citizenship.[19]

Not surprisingly, some citizens tried to circumvent Solon's legislation from the very beginning. When preparing his constitution, he told his most intimate friends, Conon, Cleinias and Hipponicus, that he would not expropriate the lands of the rich but would abolish all debts. The three 'trusted friends', grand acquisitors all, immediately borrowed huge sums of money. When the decree abolishing debts was published, they refused to pay their creditors. Thus were founded the three greatest Athenian fortunes. Nasty rumours circulated that Solon had colluded with his friends, probably to make money. But it was soon discovered that Solon himself was owed large sums of money which he was not able to collect because he had cancelled all debts.[20]

Solon was asked whether he had given the Athenians the best laws. No, he answered, only the best they would accept.[21] To which he added: 'Make no law you cannot enforce.' This still is the essence of democracy today. The people choose their laws. Legislators know their legislation will not stand long if the people eventually vote against it.

Solon clearly understood another fundamental truth about democracy: there are always at least two views of what constitutes perfection. What is perfection for one group may very well be oppression for another. True democratic solutions must therefore always lie in compromise. The nobles wanted the continued right to oppress the poor. The poor wanted the oppressive dispossession of the rich. He gave neither side what it wanted. He let the few rich keep their wealth, instituted several measures to encourage economic growth, and gave political power to the many poor – power to tax the rich and pay for public services that benefit the poor. In contemporary terms, Solonian democracy meant taxing the rich to give the poor free education and health care. Solon's ideas are the ancestors of modern *progressive* democratic capitalism.

Solon was the first to strike at the political power of the nobility and the clans. He did so by giving political power to non-nobles; by changing inheritance laws; by giving room for merchants and artisans to develop their talents and control their destiny. He pioneered the concept that the individual is more important than his clan; that the citizen has rights and power, but also the responsibility to prevent wrongdoing. By affording all male citizens equal voting power, his political system tended to exclude extremes from governance. As is still the case today, extremists are generally not given office, but are relegated rather to the role of advocating the ideas between which the democratic pendulum oscillates, from the left to the right.[22]

Through the ages, there have been seeds of early democratic thought in other societies – tribal councils, for instance. But Solon is unique in that he understood the importance of *institutions* to nurture democratic power and freedom. The greatness of Solon's law-giving is best affirmed by how lasting his effect has been. Five centuries later, Cicero could say that Solon's reforms were still in force in Athens.[23] His institutions and principles clearly influenced our western democratic societies: the 'one man one vote' rule; a government of laws not of men, and an elected legislative chamber (the *Boule* being the ancestor of the US Congress and Anglo-Saxon Parliaments).

His abiding influence may be due to the fact that he was a deeply democratic man himself. He was urged by some of his friends to take the position of dictator for life, but he refused. Solon did the job for which he was elected and then returned to private life, *de facto* establishing the principle of the *revocability* of power. It is not voting by citizens to *confer* power that really defines democracy but the voting which takes it away.

However, though Solonian democratic principles and institutions govern the political thinking of today's western democratic societies, his principles and institutions were buried by their enemies for long centuries. These enemies used the ideas of another Athenian, Plato, considered by most philosophers who have followed him as the greatest mind humanity has known.

3

PLATO

(c. 428–347 BC)

'The whole of western philosophy is a footnote to Plato,' Bertrand Russell, British philosopher, mathematician and Nobel prize winner, used to say in lectures.

Professor Paul Shorey of the University of Chicago, and an eminent translator of Plato, wrote: 'As a thinker for all time, Plato, in logical grasp and coherency of consecutive and subtle thought stands apart and above.'[1] Plato's philosophy is far too encompassing and complex to be examined in depth in this short book. Our focus will be limited to his ideas on social governance – which radically diverged from Solon's. Nevertheless, it is important to appreciate the unequalled impact of his intellectual and political thought on western civilization.

Plato* founded a university, the Academy, that lasted 900 years – longer than any other university in history. It was finally shut down by the Christian Church. Students he personally taught were the first to study conic sections (parabolas, ellipses, and hyperbolas, crucial to, among other things, contemporary space mathematics). One of them, Theatetus,

---

* Plato's real name was Aristocles which means the 'best and famous'. Plato is a nickname meaning 'broad'.

invented solid geometry. Eudoxus, created the study of proportions (that apply to metal alloys, statistical sampling, opinion polling). Another, Archytas, invented mechanical science.

It is universally accepted that early Catholic thought was largely shaped by St Augustine (AD 354–430). His major work, *De Civitate Dei* (*The City of God*) owes a great deal to Plato's writings.[2] Later, St Thomas Aquinas, according to Bertrand Russell, 'follows Aristotle so closely that [Aristotle] has among Catholics almost the authority of one of the fathers.'[3] Aristotle was Plato's major pupil.

Plato influenced some of the most important philosophers of the last centuries. Oxford Professor Gilbert Ryle wrote of the

affinities between Plato's enquiries in [his] dialogues and Hume's [1711–76] and Kant's [1726–1804] account of assertions of existence; Kant's account of forms of judgement and categories; Russell's [1872–1970] doctrine of propositional functions and theory of type; and, perhaps, more than any other, the whole of Wittgenstein's [1889–1951] *Tractatus Logico-Philosophicus*.[4]

In other words, Plato gave impetus to mathematics and inspired the greatest theological and philosophical minds of the western world. The argument can also be made that he prefigured Communism.[5] Further, he wrote impressively on education and music, as means for training people to run society the way he wanted. Karl Raimund Popper, the Austrian-born British philosopher, said cattily:

even now Plato has many musicians on his side, possibly because they are flattered by his high opinion of the importance of music, i.e. of its political power. The same is true of educationists, and even more of philosophers since Plato demands that they should rule.[6]

Karl Popper, along with many reputable and learned scholars, accused Plato of being the greatest enemy of freedom and democracy. Several critics deem Plato responsible for the philosophical underpinning of endless tyrannies such as the Catholic Church with its blood-soaked Crusades and its Inquisition before the Reformation; the similar excesses of the Greek Orthodox Church and its persecution of 'heretics' in the Byzantine Empire; the relegation of peasants to the status of serfs by the nobilities of Europe; the massacres committed by the Communists in Europe and Asia; as well as Hitler's genocides. Should Plato really be blamed for these horrors? Was he that evil?

In his writings, one discovers evidence of decent sentiments: friendship, loyalty, respect for others, deference to justice. Plato refutes the Greek rule which said help your friends and harm your enemies. The rule cannot be right, Plato says, for it is not the task of the good man to do harm.[7] But, then, Plato also states that slaves are subhuman, incapable of thought.*

Trying to analyse Plato's psyche amounts to pure speculation. At best, psychoanalysis is uncertain exploration, even when patient and analyst are in the same room, let alone when the subject lived twenty-four centuries ago. There is, however, a sort of consensus that Plato's personal history contributed to shaping his thought, especially his relationship with his

---

* Plato was in favour of slavery, as was his student Aristotle who repeats his teacher's view that 'some are by nature free and others slaves; for the latter, slavery is fitting as well as just. The slave is totally devoid of any faculty of reasoning.' Aristotle, *Politics*, 1252a to 1260a. Late in life, Plato softened his attitude towards slaves, at least those of Greek blood, *The Laws*, 777.

beloved teacher Socrates (c. 469–399 BC). So it is essential to place his writing in context.

Socrates, a carver of tombstones, spent most of his time enquiring about the right conduct of life, about what is good, what is just. He would cross-examine fellow citizens and highlight the contradictions in their thinking. He stressed that to be good citizens, to vote laws that were just, people had to understand truly what is good and what is just. He doubted most of them did.

Socrates was a highly moral citizen, totally indifferent to luxury. He had shown bravery in battle for his country. Ugly but genial and humorous, he attracted many devoted followers, including several young members of influential families, such as Plato. These pupils would walk with Socrates as a group or, occasionally have a symposium, or put in simple terms, have a drink together. He would ask them questions and point out the contradictions in their answers. Plato first joined the group possibly because older relatives of his – Critias, Charmides – had joined. Socrates' tutoring had such an impact on his pupils that a number of them eventually founded philosophical schools of their own.

Most of what we know of Socrates' discourse emanates from Plato's written 'dialogues' which are like scripts for a theatrical play.* Plato had a profound admiration for his teacher. Was Plato genuinely reporting Socrates' thoughts or was Plato putting words in Socrates' mouth? Classicists, historians and philosophers have long debated the issue

---

* Aristophanes poked fun at Socrates in his comedies. Xenophon was one of his disciples and wrote about him. However, Bertrand Russell writes that: 'there has been a tendency to think that everything Xenophon says must be true because he did not have the wit to think of anything untrue. This is a very invalid line of argument. A stupid man's report of what a clever man says is never accurate because he unconsciously translates what he hears into something he can understand.' *A History of Western Philosophy*, p. 101.

but the truth of the matter is that we shall never know. For the purposes of this book, our true concern is not how much of Plato's writing is owed to Socrates, but rather the writings themselves, and their lasting influence on the western world.

At the time of Plato's birth, many Greek states regarded Athens as an imperialist bully. In 431 BC, Sparta led an attack against Athens, and the ensuing battles, called the Peloponnesian War, lasted twenty-seven years. During the war, Athenian citizens voted for many sound strategic decisions, but made one fatal mistake: they voted to conquer Syracuse and the whole of Sicily. In this they accepted the advice of a young noble demagogue called Alcibiades, one of Socrates' most brilliant pupils.

The Syracusans totally destroyed the Athenian expeditionary force. Athens, the great naval power, besieged from land and sea, surrendered in 404 BC. Victorious, undemocratic Sparta picked thirty Athenian aristocrats to write a new constitution for their city. History remembers them as the Thirty Tyrants. Their leader, Critias, a student of Socrates, was a cousin of Plato's mother. Charmides who served under him was Plato's uncle. Critias declared that 'all changes of constitution involve bloodshed,' and that 'the finest constitution is that of Sparta.'[8] The Thirty Tyrants 'proceeded to kill their opponents without the formality of a trial.'[9] They exterminated some 1,500 people, including the leader of the moderate nobles, Theramenes.

A few months later, in early 403 BC, the Athenians successfully overthrew the tyranny and re-established democracy. The Thirty Tyrants and their principal followers were hunted down and put to death, including Critias and Charmides. They died in complete dishonour, punished for the lawless and brutal assassinations of fellow citizens.

Yet, Plato praised his two relatives Critias and Charmides, even after their dreadful deeds.[10] Should we assume that Plato approved the vile acts of his relatives? Was he blinded by pride in his aristocratic family?

In analysing Plato, one must consider that his beloved teacher, Socrates, was condemned and executed by the common citizens of the restored Athenian democracy. This execution has occupied a central place in western thinking. For many intellectuals, the tragedy bears comparison with Christ's crucifixion. In both instances, an exceptionally good and just man was condemned and executed in an indisputable miscarriage of justice. Neither victim grovelled.

In 399 BC Socrates was brought before the court accused of two crimes by two citizens, Anytus and Meletus. He was charged with introducing new gods into Athenian society. The accusation referred to what Socrates called his *daimonion* (literally, his 'private god'), by which he obviously meant his conscience, a very personal *daimonion* who spoke only to him. This charge played no great role at the trial. The most serious accusation against Socrates was that he was corrupting the minds of the young. That charge stemmed from the fact that many of Socrates' students had contributed to overthrow the Athenian democracy (Critias and Charmides, among others).

As for any other trial, 500 jurors were picked by lot at dawn. Proceedings started immediately, to ensure that the trial would end by sunset. The accuser made a speech and produced witnesses. Both sides had exactly the same amount of time to present their cases – measured by a water clock. Socrates defended himself. He stood his ground. He had taken the risk of criticizing the lawlessness of the Thirty Tyrants while they were in power. He had risked his life in battle for his country, in obedience to its generals. How could he disobey his god who had ordered him to fulfil the philosopher's task and search within himself and others for what is good and what is just?

Men of Athens, he said, I honour and love you, but I shall obey my god rather than you. And while I have life and strength I shall not stop practising and teaching philosophy. Men of Athens, either acquit me or not. But whatever you do, know that I shall never alter my ways, not even if I have to die many times.[11] He also taunted the jurors. 'You shouldn't condemn me: Athens is like a large horse that moves slowly. It needs me as a gadfly.'[12]

It was time for the jury to vote on whom they believed, the accuser or the defendant. The accuser had brought no evidence that Socrates had in any way suggested or encouraged the dreadful acts of his students. Nevertheless, probably because of the monstrous murders committed by his pupils, the jury voted for the accuser.

In an Athenian trial, the accuser proposed a penalty, and the defendant submitted a lighter counter-proposal. These had to be thoughtfully calculated suggestions, because jurors could not deviate from the two penalties before them. They were bound by law to vote for one or the other. If the accuser proposed too harsh a penalty, he risked seeing the jurors vote for the defendant's. On the other hand, if the defendant proposed too light a penalty, he risked having the jurors vote for the accuser's.

The accuser proposed death. Socrates insolently suggested he pay a minute fine. Had he counter-proposed exile, such would pro-bably have been the sentence. But, for Socrates, exile was worse than death.[13] The jury could not vote for a sentence that mocked their verdict: they voted for the death penalty. Socrates, last words were: 'The hour of departure has arrived and we go our ways – I to die and you to live. Which is better, God only knows.'[14]

The ordinary citizens of democratic Athens had not only killed Plato's noble relatives, but also his beloved teacher, a good and just man who did not deserve death. Is this what turned Plato against democracy?

Against democracy, he certainly was. James Adam, renowned editor of Plato's work, summarizes a famous passage of *The Republic* where Plato explains how one 'degenerates' into supporting democracy:

> Let us now return and explain the genesis of the democratical man. An oligarchical father has a son whom he brings up on narrow and parsimonious principles. The young man tastes the honey of drones [unnecessary pleasures, that is, including sex] and sedition is engendered within his soul. A struggle ensues, the unnecessary desires prevail and the young man becomes an impartial devotee of pleasure in all its forms and consequently a follower of democracy.[15]

In its entirety and its style, this passage has impressed many. James Adam says of this passage:

> Plato's description of the genesis of the democratical man is one of the most royal and magnificent pieces of writing in the whole range of literature, whether ancient or modern. No better example will ever be discovered of that full tide of lofty thoughts and images and words.[16]

This is but one more instance of Plato mesmerizing thinkers through the ages, inducing many to accept his condemnation of democracy.

Probing Plato's anti-democratic thinking further, we must also consider the social and political context of his upbringing. Paul Shorey writes:

> The background of Plato, the experience that ground to devilish colors all his dreams and permanently darkened

his vision of life, was the war that made shipwreck of the Periclean ideal* and lowered the level of Hellenic civilization.[17]

The Greeks had gone through their world war – a small war by today's standards, but the Ancient Greek world was a small world. All sides had seen their share of horrors, hecatombs, and moral disintegration. Athens, the ideal democracy of Pericles, was not only defeated, but also corrupted.† And under what regime had Athens' descent taken place? Under the rule of politicians democratically elected by the ordinary citizens. Hence, Plato could not trust democratically elected politicians.

In Plato's view, there was a single root cause for the decline of Athens: acquisitiveness. Even in an ideal state, he says, if the rulers acquire their own houses and land and money, they will oppress and exploit their fellow citizens. In other words, they will become grand acquisitors. We are back to Moses, and Isaiah – money is the root of all evil.[18]

What is Plato's ideal state? He described it at length in his *Republic*. It is a society in which there are three classes.

At the very top, the Golden Ones, or Guardians, dominate. Plato clearly states that women, too, can be Golden Ones, with absolute power over everyone else.[19] These men and women

---

* Pericles was the leader of Athens for many years before the Peloponnesian war and is considered by most major historians as the exemplar of a democratic leader. He won yearly elections for fifteen years straight; he gave jobs to demobilized sailors and marines by hiring them to build the Parthenon; and he knew when to compromise – he even traded land for peace.

† In 416 BC Athens attacked the small island of Melos which wanted to stay neutral, killed all its men and enslaved its women and children. Euripides, the famous Athenian playwright, wrote a play exposing the brutality of the Athenian forces. He pretended that he was talking about the sacking of Troy and called his play the *Trojan Women*. This fooled no one and some Athenians wanted to lynch him. He left town.

know what is good, what is just, and they will decide accordingly. They will live in common. The state will provide them with houses and the necessities of life, free of charge. They will share mates, and their children will be brought up by wet-nurses and nannies. The Golden Ones will own no property. Doing the bidding of the Golden Ones will be the Silver Ones, soldiers who will defend the state against outside attacks and see that the third class, the Bronze Ones, obey the Golden Ones. The Silver Ones will live in a kind of military Communism, also sharing children, wives or husbands, owning no property, but well provided for. The Bronze Ones will be the drudges: they will cultivate the land, be the artisans, the merchants, the labourers. The Bronze Ones will have absolutely no say in how the state is ruled or administered.

The Golden Ones will study advanced mathematics and philosophy. The Silver Ones will receive a military and administrative education. For economic reasons, the Bronze Ones will be taught reading, writing and arithmetic. Much literature will be censored, Homer for instance.

All citizens would breed eugenically, under the control of the Golden Ones: the best males with the best females, as often as possible. Lesser people should breed as little as possible. Only the offspring of the best would be reared. Not the others.[20] 'The offspring of the inferior and any of those of the (best) who are born defective, will be disposed of in secret so that no one will know what has become of them. That is the condition of preserving the purity of the race.'[21]

The Golden Ones would have absolute claim to bed any partner they thought best for breeding among the three classes. All the children, boys or girls not put to death would be given an equal chance. Preferment would not be hereditary. The children would be brought up by the state and given the same education initially. A series of tests would determine whether they would be bronze drudges, silver soldiers, or the very best – the golden guardians.[22] The Golden Ones would pick their own successors.

Paul Shorey, commenting on Plato's ideal state writes:

> By subtle artifices of style, the cumulative effect of which can be felt only in the original Greek, the reader is brought to conceive of the social organism as one monster man or leviathan whose sensuous appetites are the unruly mechanic mob; whose disciplined emotions are the trained force that checks rebellion within and guards against invasion from without; and whose reason is the philosophic statesmanship that directs each and all for the good of the whole. And conversely, the individual man is pictured as a biological colony of passions and appetites 'which swarm like worms within our living clay' – a spurious compound of beast and man which can attain real unity and personality only by the conscious domination of the monarchical reason.[23]

'Plato's Republic, unlike modern Utopias was intended to be actually founded,' wrote Bertrand Russell. 'This was not so fantastic or impossible as it might naturally seem to us. Many of its provisions, including some that we should have thought quite impracticable, were actually realized at Sparta.'[24] Plato tried hard to 'sell' his system to young Dionysius, tyrant of Syracuse. Had Dionysius accepted, Plato would have become the philosopher king, with guaranteed shelter, sustenance, safety, sex and self-expression. In that sense, despite his vast intellectualism, Plato had all the instincts of a grand acquisitor, motivated by a strong ambition to acquire power.

It is not surprising that through the centuries, his writings, such as the following, were quoted as justification for the absolute power of autocratic rulers:

> The greatest principle of all is that nobody, whether male or female, should be without a leader. Nor should the mind of anybody be habituated to letting him do anything at all on his own initiative; neither out of zeal, nor even playfully. But in war and in the midst of peace – to his leader he shall direct his eye and follow him faithfully. Even in the smallest matter he should stand under leadership. For example, he should get up, or move, or wash or take his meals only if he has been told to do so. In a word, he should teach his soul never to dream of acting independently and to become utterly incapable of it.[25]

These words of Plato describe the ethics of Stalin, Hitler, and every other dictator, brain-washer, megalomaniac, self-adulatory human who thinks he is so much better than others that they must obey him blindly.

Fortunately for its citizens, Athens did not follow Plato's advice.

4

JESUS

(c. 5/1 BC–AD 30/33)

Some 2,000 years ago, a man came to earth who went by the name of Jesus. He preached forgiveness and love, for neighbours as well as enemies. The Scriptures tell us that he died on the cross for the redemption of our sins; that he was resurrected on the third day; and will come back on the last day and take to paradise those who have repented, but not those still unrepentant for the one unpardonable sin – lack of faith, which can also be construed as 'denial of Christ'.[1]

Did Jesus really say that lack of faith is an unpardonable sin? Jesus, on the cross, said: 'Father, forgive them; for they know not what they do.'[2] In the Gospels, Jesus constantly advocates forgiveness. One can easily suspect later Christian leaders of wrongly attributing to him the statement that lack of faith in Christianity was 'the one unpardonable sin'. After all, these Christian leaders wanted to keep their flock from straying.[3]

The official Christian Churches, both Catholic and Greek Orthodox, certainly made malevolent use of the 'unpardonable sin' doctrine, justifying mass murder, torturing heretics whose only crime was faith that varied from the official version.* One can also argue that the doctrine also lies at the root of the anti-Semitism that has been the shame of the Christian Church, which condemned the Jews throughout the centuries for killing Jesus, and so killing God himself, an accusation of a metaphysical dimension, and as absurd and malevolent as condemning today's Greeks for killing Socrates in 399 BC.[4]

Was Jesus a revolutionary? He openly criticized the establishment (the Pharisees and the Sadducees). To be saved, the rich must share their wealth with the poor, Jesus said. He overturned the tables of the money-changers at the temple, saying that it is easier for a camel to go through the eye of a needle than for a rich man to enter the kingdom of heaven.[5] As one historian wrote:

Jesus does not seem to have thought of ending poverty: 'the poor ye have always with you.' He takes for granted, like all ancients, that a slave's duty is to serve his master well. He is not concerned to attack existing economic or political institutions; on the contrary he condemns those ardent souls who would take the kingdom of heaven by storm.[6] The revolution he sought was a far deeper one without which reforms could only be superficial and transitory. If he could cleanse the human heart of selfish desire, cruelty and lust, [the Kingdom of heaven] would come of itself, and all those institutions that rise out of human greed and violence would disappear, and the consequent need for law would disappear. Since this would be the profoundest of all revolutions, beside which all others would be mere coups d'état of class

---

* The Inquisitors would torture someone until he declared he believed the official Church doctrine. Then they would kill him so he would not again risk eternal damnation by changing his mind.

ousting class and exploiting in its turn, Christ was in this spiritual sense the greatest revolutionary in history.[7]

Did the Romans see him as a revolutionary? Was Jesus one of the militant Jews who wanted to shake off the rule of Rome? Hardly: he said people should 'render to Caesar the things that are Caesar's, and to God the things that are God's.'[8] And he also said we should love our enemies. The militant Jews fought with their swords against the Romans whom they surely did not love.[9] Apparently, Jesus was not concerned with who governed whom. He was defining a code of conduct for the individual.

Few Christians have abided by his code of conduct. He tried, but did not succeed in changing human nature. Not many have lived the way Jesus said they should. Christian Churches have monstrously exploited the teachings of Jesus. Nevertheless, to this day, some 1,970 years or so after his death, the western world – Europe, North and South America – is still under his spell.

For those who do not believe in the divinity of Christ, the question remains: why are so many under his spell? Of course, such questions disappear if we believe he was indeed divine, and not merely human.

Are there reasons for not being under his spell? Here we run into questions impossible to answer. If we had stuck to faith, as he recommended, and neglected doubt, would we have pursued the scientific enquiries of the Greeks with the same zeal? If the grand acquisitors had not accumulated vast wealth, not sharing with the poor, would the financing of technological advances have been possible, raising the standard of living of the poor in much of the western world, far above what it was 2,000 years ago? We cannot answer such questions with certainty.

Why was it Jesus who captured the imagination of so many humans? What about Isaiah, the great Jewish prophet? Surely, his preaching was as exalted as that of Jesus:

> The Spirit of the Lord God is upon me; because the Lord
> hath anointed me to preach good tidings unto the meek;
> he hath sent me to bind up the brokenhearted, to proclaim
> liberty to the captives, and the opening of the prison to
> them that are bound . . . to comfort all that mourn . . . to
> give unto them beauty for ashes, the oil of joy for
> mourning, the garment of praise for the spirit of heaviness
> . . . everlasting joy shall be unto them.[10]
> . . . and they shall beat their swords into ploughshares,
> and their spears into pruninghooks: nation shall not lift
> sword against nation, neither shall they learn war any
> more.[11]
> . . . The wolf also shall dwell with the lamb, and the
> leopard shall lie down with the kid; and the calf and the
> young lion and the fatling together; and a little child shall
> lead them.[12]

These are some of the Bible's most beautiful passages. Isaiah
preached much of what Jesus preached centuries later. True,
Isaiah himself said that he was not the one who would lead the
people to a better life:

> 'The Lord himself shall give you a sign. For unto us a child
> is born, unto us a son is given: and the government shall be
> upon his shoulders. Behold a virgin shall conceive* and
> bear a son and shall call his name Immanuel.[13]

---

* The language of Isaiah in the *Septuagint* cannot be interpreted to mean
that a virgin would conceive without being impregnated by a man. It
simply means that a virgin shall get a child in her womb, an expression
used for getting pregnant.

And the Prince of Peace shall suffer for the atonement of
our sins. Surely he hath borne our griefs, and carried our
sorrows . . . he was wounded for our transgressions, he
was bruised for our iniquities: the chastisement of
our peace was upon him; and with his stripes we are
healed.[14]

Isaiah never pretended to be the Messiah; but there is no
clear evidence that Jesus ever claimed to be the Messiah either.
On this, the texts of the Gospels are uncertain and contradictory. So why did Christianity catch on? Here is Will
Durant's explanation:

Christianity arose out of Jewish apocalyptic–esoteric
revelations of the coming Kingdom; it derived its impetus
from the personality and vision of Christ; it gained
strength from the belief in his resurrection, and the
promise of eternal life; it received doctrinal form in the
theology of Paul; it grew by the absorption of pagan faith
and ritual; it became a triumphant Church by inheriting
the organizing patterns and genius of Rome.[15]

Jesus lived at a time when the vast majority of people
subsisted in misery, oppressed by secular power they could
not overthrow. His peers – the masses, not the grand acquisitors – had no realistic hope of bettering their lives on this
earth. It was a time when people were eager to believe in the
supernatural, if only because the natural was so bleak.

In the years after Jesus's death, the masses were told that
the centuries-old prophecies about the son of God coming to
earth had finally come true. The Apostles efficiently spread
the Word, reminding the masses how Jesus, the son of God,
preached forgiveness and love for enemies as well as neigh-

bours. They told that he died on the cross for the redemption
of sins; that he was resurrected on the third day. They
promised that he would come back on the last day and take
to paradise those who have repented. It had been prophesied
for centuries. He died to save you. He rose from the dead. Is
there a more wondrous miracle? Believe and there is hope. St
Paul was particularly efficient in 'pressing the right buttons',
as contemporary political strategists might say. He preached
that everyone could hope to benefit from the same miracle, to
be resurrected and go to heaven where all the wrongs would
be righted. *Salvation*. The path was faith. 'Faith is the
substance of things hoped for, the evidence of things not
seen.'[16]

There was something more. Jesus, the Gospels say, was 'one
of us'. He moved among the people; talked with publicans,
customs officers, whores, lepers, fishermen. He had worked as
a carpenter. He was not a standoffish prophet. He had first-
hand knowledge of the people's lives and sufferings. He clearly
felt sympathy and pity. There was tangible sweetness in what
Jesus preached. A person forgiven by a neighbour feels the
sweetness of this forgiveness. So does the person who forgives.
A person treated with neighbourly love feels the sweetness of
this love. Such behaviour, be it rare, does exist. Such behaviour is occasionally reciprocated. It was there to be believed;
whereas the Mosaic threat that the grand acquisitors would be
punished was not so easily believed – God was not often seen
punishing grand acquisitors.

Compared with the pagan gods, Jesus gave more hope, more
comfort, more inspiration. These aspects of his preaching, plus
the promise of eventual resurrection were used skilfully by the
clergy that St Paul, not St Peter, organized. Consequently the
adherents of Christianity multiplied so much that the Roman
emperor Constantine (c. AD 274–337) made Christianity the

state religion and painted Christian symbols on the shields of his Christian legionaries.

For many centuries, among the endless multitudes of the poor and helpless, reciprocal kindness and forgiveness as preached by Jesus did occasionally work and felt good, surely. Moreover, Christianity held the promise of an eventual ascent to heaven. And the most important thing of all: Christ said on the cross: 'Father forgive them for they know not what they do.' These words may explain why he has such a hold on us, even if so few of us have lived according to his precepts. Unlike other gods, he is not a god of vengeance, but a god of forgiveness. We are not afraid of him.

5

BRAHMINISM, THE BUDDHA, LAO-TZU, CONFUCIUS, MUHAMMAD

(3102 BC–AD 632)

In the past 500 years, Europeans and their offspring in the Americas, have been the world's greatest predators. That is why this book will inevitably appear to be Eurocentric, focusing on the effect of western Helleno–Judaeic rules for dealing with human nature. But other societies on the Asian and African continents have their own ways of dealing with the conflict between the individual's need for freedom to satisfy his or her desires and society's need for rules to curb individual freedom.

In the world, there are currently an estimated 1.95 billion Christians and 13 million Jews of the Helleno–Judaeic group. But there are also 700 million Hindus, 300 million Buddhists and 1.3 billion Muslims who only numbered 400 million in 1960.[1] The Muslims are growing faster than any other religion at 3 per cent a year, mainly because of their high birth-rate. Forty-nine countries have Muslim majorities and they cover vast expanses of the globe.

All these religions have rules of ethics. Some rules differ, from religion to religion; others are remarkably similar. This comparison is interesting on two levels. First, it highlights how similar are the codes of ethics that most organized human societies adopt. Secondly, it highlights the differences between the various codes. What is acceptable in a given society may be utterly immoral in another. These differences have been, and continue to be, at the origin of innumerable conflicts. If human beings have any chance of not repeating history, it is not by knowing history; it is by mutually knowing, then understanding, and ultimately accepting the differences in their respective codes of behaviour.

Brahminism (3102 BC)

The Hindu religion is polytheistic and has thousands, perhaps millions, of gods and goddesses, many with four arms or more; phallic worship; erotic sculptures and customs that can best be read in the Abbé Dubois' *Hindu Manners, Customs, and Ceremonies*, published by the Oxford University Press. The good Abbé repeatedly says that a particular ceremony was so 'risqué' that he had to cover his eyes: nevertheless he describes its every detail.

This section is about castes, the social system brought about by the Hindu religion.* Three quarters of India's population still live in villages, dominated by the Hindu caste system, defined in the *Bhagavad Gita*, the Hindu holy book.

---

* To learn more about Hinduism I recommend J. H. Hutton's *Caste in India*, Cambridge: University Press, 1951. On the same subject, there is an excellent little pamphlet called *The Hindu Jajmani System*, which describes the obligations of the higher castes to the lower castes (minimal) and the obligations of the lower castes to the higher castes (huge).

According to tradition, the god Krishna himself 'spoke' the *Bhagavad Gita*, in 3102 BC.* There are some 3,000 castes, subdivided into 25,000 subcastes – for example, a limousine driver is of a higher subcaste than a truck driver who, therefore, is not good enough to marry the limousine driver's daughter. The castes (*jati* which means 'race' in most Indian languages) are grouped into four categories called *varna* (which means 'colours'). There is a fifth group of people who are too polluted to belong to the caste system; they are the outcastes or untouchables, now called *dalit*, which means 'the broken people'. Here is what the *Bhagavad Gita* says about the four varna.

> The works of brahmins, kshatriyas, vaishyas, and shudras are different, in harmony with the powers of their born nature. The works of a brahmin (priest, thinker, teacher) are peace, self-harmony, austerity, and purity, loving-forgiveness and righteousness, vision and wisdom and faith. The works of the (nobleman warrior) Kshatriya are: a heroic mind, inner fire, constancy, resourcefulness, courage in battle, generosity and noble leadership. Trade, agriculture and the rearing of cattle is the work of a vaishya (commoner). And the work of the shudra (serf) is service.[2]

The more impure the substances a Hindu works with, the lower his or her varna. Blood, menstrual flow, saliva, dung, leather, corpses are so polluting that those who handle them as a part of their work are themselves so polluted that they cannot belong to a varna. They are untouchables. They cannot

---

* For a complete translation of the *Bhagavad Gita* and commentaries, look in the Internet's search engine, Google: keyword: bhagavadgita. The complete text was written some time between the fifth century BC and the second century AD

even be shudra. However, though female *dalits* are polluting, men of superior castes are still prepared to rape them.

Here is an episode from a *Human Rights Watch* 1999 investigation of India's caste system:

> I am a twenty-six-year-old Dalit agricultural labourer. I earn 20 rupees [35p] a day for a full day's work. In December 1997, the police raided my village. The Super-intendent of police called me a pallachi, which is a caste name for prostitute. He then opened his pant zip. At 11 a.m. the 'Collector' (the Superintendent's boss) came. I told the Collector that the Superintendent of police had opened his zip and used a vulgar word. The next morning the police broke all the doors and arrested all the men in the village. The Superintendent of police came looking for me. My husband hid under the cot. The police started calling me a prostitute and started beating me. The Superintendent of police dragged me naked on the road. I was four months pregnant at the time. They brought me to the police station naked. I begged the police officers at the jail to help me. I even told them I was pregnant. They mocked me for making bold statements about the police the day before. I spent twenty-five days in jail. I miscarried my baby after ten days. Nothing has happened to the officers who did this to me. (*Guruswamy Guruammal*, Madurai, Tamil Nadu.)

How did these social divisions come about? Historians speculate that as Aryan tribes from the north invaded the Indian subcontinent in about 1500 BC, they pushed previous populations further south. The defeated earlier races were darker than the conquerors who came later, hence the classification into varna or colours. The lighter your colour, the higher your social status.[3] And it was decreed, as we saw, that people 'are different, in harmony with the powers of their born nature.' In other words, you are born to be the highest, a brahmin, or the lowest, an untouchable, and there is no escaping this fate. (Notice the similarities with Plato's scheme, as described in Chapter 3. Plato gave a scholarly formulation to a system of brutal discrimination that has no boundaries in geography or epoch.)

For centuries, the brahmins in alliance with the next caste, the warriors, grand acquisitors all, lorded it over the rest of the population. This is the oldest political alliance of all time: very early in human history, the autocrat with the big club and the witch doctor with his potions and maledictions, became natural allies. The one with the big club organized the hunt and the defence of the territory. The sorcerer took care of the uncontrollable, the unpredictable and the inexplicable – he took care of God, in other words. The two, king and priest, in modern parlance, ran the tribe through the fear of violence and the fear of 'God'. In that tribal system, they each took a much bigger share of everything. In Hinduism too.

In its 1949 constitution, independent India abolished the term untouchable and all the ill-treatment associated with the term. But the abolition has not had much effect yet. Such changes take time.

There are 160 million *dalit* in India and they are constantly oppressed. They are not alone. The other oppressed people of India are now called OBC – Other Backward Classes. There are no reliable census figures by caste; however, we are talking of hundreds of millions if we add the OBC to the *dalit*. But there is hope. India is, after all, a democracy. One of the best observers of recent Indian developments is John Stackhouse who has won the Canadian equivalent of the Pulitzer Prize more than once. Here is what he says in his book:[4]

Corruption and abuse are common, to be sure, but there are checks and balances in the form of courts, autonomous media, an active Parliament, increasingly powerful state government, elected local councils and an independent Elections Commission that gives people an absolute weapon over those who rule them. The people can no longer be duped, at least not all the time. In India where democracy has long been ridiculed as an encumbrance to economic development, the political system with free votes and free speech is fundamental to social change.

In other words, the votes of the oppressed have brought down many a politicians who paid no attention to their fate. Other politicians have noticed. There is hope.

The Buddha (6th or 5th century BC)

The Buddha's mother, Mahamaya, a queen, dreamed that a beautiful silver elephant entered her womb.[5] She asked the sixty-four brahmins assembled by the king, her husband, what the dream meant. They said that she would have a son who would either conquer the world or become the Buddha, which means 'the enlightened one'. Two hundred and eighty days later, while she was travelling, she had to stop in the middle of a field to give birth. Today a stone pillar marks the spot in what is now Nepal.

At the moment of the Buddha's birth, the night sky was bathed in a great light, the deaf heard, the dumb spoke, the lame walked, the gods bent down to the baby and kings came to welcome him.

The little boy was named Siddartha. In the palace 40,000 dancing girls entertained him, tradition says. When the time came for Siddartha to marry, they brought along 500 noble Kshatriya maidens for him to choose a bride. He married and had a son. But he saw how the ordinary people suffered, left his palace, lived the ascetic life. Then, one day, he understood it all. Why was there a succession of births and deaths? It made sense only if births were reincarnations – rebirths – to atone for one's sins in a previous life. So, if one lived a virtuous life, suppressing selfishness, one would have nothing to atone for; then there would be no need to be reborn for more earthly suffering: there was no doubt in the Buddha's mind that living meant suffering.

He put on a saffron-coloured robe and wandered from place to place, preaching in the evenings. He said: 'if a man foolishly does me wrong, I will return to him the protection of my ungrudging love.'* Pain is the constant in life, the Buddha said, not pleasure. Pain is unending. Pleasure is fleeting. Therefore one should renounce *tamba*, selfish desire, especially sexual desire because it leads to reproduction and therefore to pain for new human beings. So the Buddha's five moral rules were:

Let no one kill any living thing.
Let no one take what is not given to him.
Let no one speak falsely.
Let no one drink intoxicating drinks.
Let no one be unchaste.

In fact, the Buddha said, it is best not to see women nor talk with them.[6] The Buddha also said we should overcome our anger with kindness; respond to evil with goodness. Victory breeds hatred in the vanquished. Hatred can only be ended by love.[7]

The Buddha would not talk of God, or eternity, or immortality, or the infinite.[8] He refused to speculate on the beginning or the end of the world; of the soul as distinct from the body.[9] And he urged his disciples to preach everywhere

---

* Lao-tzu and Jesus said the same thing.

that 'the poor and the lowly, the rich and the high, are all one, and that all castes unite in this religion as do the rivers in the sea.'[10] The Buddha totally rejected the caste system and the brahmins' claim that their Vedas, their sacred books, were inspired by the gods who, thus, endorsed the caste system.[11]

In the brutal Hindu society, the Buddha's message of love attracted disciples who followed him; they eventually wrote down his teachings. His disciples tell us he lived in accordance with his preaching, that he laughed a lot and urged them to be happy.

But Buddhism remained a small sect for about three centuries until a powerful ruler of India, the Emperor Ashoka, adopted it. He reigned from 273 to 232 BC over an empire that covered what are today India, Pakistan and Afghanistan. Early in his reign he conquered what is now the Indian state of Orissa. He was a great warrior. He was even reputed to have gained the throne by cruelly murdering his brothers lest they claim it. But when he saw the destruction he had wrought in Orissa, he decided to forswear violence. He adopted Buddhism and declared that he would rule by the precepts of the Buddha.[12] And he did not just adopt the precepts for himself. He sent Buddhist missionaries to all countries around him, to what we now call Sri Lanka, and to Burma.

Alas, after Ashoka, Buddhist precepts were no longer policy, anywhere. Many sects developed whose monks had the defects of established clergies everywhere. The Buddha's followers came to think of him as a saint, even a god, which was against everything he stood for. However, the whole world feels for him deep respect, the same sort of respect accorded to Lao-tzu and Jesus. All three preached kindness, forgiveness, love and a rejection of rapacity. Multitudes think life would be sweeter if we listened to those three. Few if any live by those rules.

Lao-tzu (c. 604–517 BC)

Recompense injury with Kindness. To those who are good I am good, and to those who are not good I am also good; thus all get to be good. To those who are sincere, I am sincere, and to those who are not sincere I am also sincere; and thus all get to be sincere.[13]

So said the Chinese sage Lao-tzu in the sixth century BC.

Lao-tzu means 'the old sage'. His real name is supposed to have been Li. We do not really know whether he ever lived or not. There is a book he is supposed to have written. We have that; it is called *Tao-Te-Ching*, which means 'The Book of the Way and of Virtue'. Some scholars think the book is genuine, others say it is merely a collection of sayings by various sages.

There is a legend that Lao-tzu was a librarian. Tired of crooked politicians and fed up with his job, he decided to leave China. At the border, the man-in-charge asked Lao-tzu to write a book first, which he did. That is all we know about Lao-tzu, apart from the contents of 'his' book.[14]

Anything else about Lao-tzu is a collection of legends, among them one that he came down to earth again and again to teach virtue to rulers.

What was Chinese 'philosophical' thought before him? It was all about divination, astrology and magic. There may have been some sages who were exploring avenues that appear in *Tao-Te-Ching*.

Beyond that we know Lao-tzu lived in turbulent times. His country was full of competing grand acquisitors: warlords or 'dukes'. The people were oppressed, often tortured if they protested.[15] They could not easily escape their misery. So Lao-tzu said, as Jesus did several centuries later: let us be good and forgiving towards one another. He also said that there was nothing the little people could do except withdraw from progress and big government.*

> In the kingdom, the multiplication of prohibitions increases the poverty of the people. The more implements to add to their profit the people have, the greater disorder is there in the state and clan; the more acts of crafty dexterity men possess, the more strange contrivances appear; the more display there is of legislation, the more thieves and robbers there are. In a little state with a small population I would so order it that though there would be individuals in it with the abilities of ten or a hundred men, there should be no employment for them. Though the people had boats and carriages, they should have no occasion to ride in them; though they had weapons, they should have no occasion to use them. They should think their coarse food sweet, their plain clothes beautiful, their poor dwellings places of rest. Should there be a neighbouring state, I would make the people not have any intercourse with it.[16]
>
> When we renounce learning, we have no trouble. The difficulty in governing the people arises from their having too much knowledge. He who tries to govern a state by his wisdom is a scourge to it, while he who does not do so is a blessing.[17]

Notice the connection in Lao-tzu's mind between lots of legislation and thieves and robbers, between government and grand acquisitors. So, like Jesus, he favours the humble,

---

* Which has some resemblance to Jesus saying 'Render therefore unto Caesar the things that are Caesar's, and unto God the things that are God's' (*Matthew*, 22: 21). Or, in other words, we cannot do anything about the power that governs us; we can behave in the way God wants us to behave.

counsels retreat from public affairs, being satisfied with one's spare possessions, and being good and forgiving to one another.

Lao-tzu is still respected in China. Ordinary people long thought of him as a saint or a god. Was he influential? Those who ruled China did not act as he prescribed. Like Jesus later, Lao-tzu represented an unworldly, kindly ideal that many admired but very few observed. Confucius took a different view.

Confucius (c. 551–47 BC)

Confucius, the most respected sage of China, was born in a cloud of legends.[18] There were apparitions to tell his young mother that his birth would be illegitimate (his father was seventy-two when Confucius was born). Dragons watched. Spirit ladies perfumed the air. She delivered him in a cave. He had the back of a dragon, the lips of an ox and a mouth like the sea. The Chinese still believe today that he came of the oldest family in the land, and that by about AD 1830, he had 10,000 descendants through his one son. He had married at nineteen, divorced at twenty-three and never married again.

He began teaching at twenty-two. The pupils came to his house and paid what they could afford. It is what these students remember of his teachings and wrote down that became the book called Confucius' Analects.

We are told, 'he had no foregone conclusions, no obstinacy, no arbitrary predeterminations, and no egoism.'[19] He shunned any discussions of theological matters. Modern commentators have called him an agnostic. However, he was so moral a man that few rulers were prepared to accept his view on how they should behave: so Confucius spent many years without being employed by rulers.

He was also particular about which master he would serve. One grand acquisitor warlord, the Duke of Wei, offered

Confucius the leadership of his administration but Confucius, disapproving of the Duke's character, refused the appointment.[20] 'My children', said Confucius to his students, 'oppressive government is worse than a tiger.'[21] But on the rare occasions when he did agree to serve, Chinese tradition has it that everything went unbelievably well, crime and dishonesty disappeared, as did deficits and poverty, and the people trusted their government.[22]

His world was at war, Confucius taught, because its constituent parts were badly governed. For governments to be at peace, one had to make sure they governed well, through properly trained and wise senior bureaucrats. The knowledge of these senior public servants became complete after they had thoroughly

> ... investigated things. Their knowledge being complete, their thoughts were sincere. Their thoughts being sincere, their hearts were rectified. Their hearts being rectified, their own selves were cultivated. Their own selves being cultivated, their families were well regulated. Their families being well regulated, their states were rightly governed. Their states being rightly governed, the whole empire was made tranquil and happy.[23]

We have here not a philosopher-king, but a philosopher-bureaucrat who gives his master the following advice:

> The ruler should preside over the people with gravity, then they will reverence him. Let him be filial and kind to all, then they will be faithful to him. Let him advance the good and teach the incompetent, then they will eagerly seek to be virtuous.[24]

Further, the ruler should reduce the luxury of the court and seek a wide distribution of wealth, for the centralization of wealth is the way to cause disunity among the people; while letting the wealth be distributed among them is the way to unite the people.[25]

Confucius also believed that if the people have no faith in their rulers, the rulers would lose 'the mandate of heaven' and would be overthrown.[26]

Deservedly, his sayings are still considered nuggets of wisdom:

The whole purpose of speech is to be understood.[27] In regard to what he doubts about, the good man is anxious to question others. When he is angry, he thinks of the difficulties this might cause him. When he sees gain to be got, he thinks of righteousness.[28]

Not to do unto others as you would not wish done unto yourself.'[29]

However, when he was asked whether he agreed with Lao-tzu that injury should be recompensed with kindness, Confucius replied: "With what, then, will you recompense kindness? Recompense injury with justice, and recompense kindness with kindness.'[33]

Wisdom is 'to give one's self earnestly to the duties due to men, and while respecting spiritual beings to keep aloof from them.[31]

He was immensely influential. From the Han dynasty that started in 202 BC, to the fall of the Manchu dynasty in AD 1912, for more than 2,000 years, the doctrine of Confucius was China's doctrine. His philosophy promoted peace; but those bureaucrats who had to know his sayings by heart, and not deviate from them, did not have his genius. Eventually they produced too rigid a system.[32] It allowed no freedom, no initiative, not enough flexibility for China to compete economically with other powers. It became a system hostile to progress. And it shackled women into a position of inferiority. Confucius is still respected but is not a part of the modern, increasingly entrepreneurial China.[33]

Muhammad (c. AD 570–632)

Six hundred years after the death of Jesus, Muhammad, an itinerant caravan merchant travelled the desert sands of the Middle East. Once, according to an uncertain tradition, he went to Syria and Palestine, 1,000 miles from Mecca as the crow flies. He came from a distinguished family, was orphaned early and inherited only five camels and a slave who had looked after him when little.

At twenty-five, Muhammad married Khadija, a rich forty-year-old widow. Tradition says he lived monogamously with her till her death twenty-six years later. Subsequently, he had ten wives, each with her own house in a compound surrounding his. (He prescribed four wives for others but felt he deserved an exception. He loved women.)

Muhammad, we are told by his adopted son, Ali, was very handsome, with a white and pink complexion, black eyes, lustrous black hair and a beard which flowed down to his chest.[34] He associated with Jews and Christians in Arabia and talked theology with them.

One day, when he was forty and sleeping in a cave up the mountain, covered with a cloth that bore some writing, he had a vision. The Archangel Gabriel appeared and ordered him to read what was written on the cloth. I do not read, replied Muhammad. 'Read', shouted Gabriel. And Muhammad read, 'Muhammad, you are the messenger of Allah.'* Muhammad

---

* It was the Archangel Gabriel who told the Virgin Mary she would give birth to Jesus.

had other visions during which Allah dictated to him the Koran which became the holy book of Islam, the Muslim religion. Allah means 'the one God'. Islam means 'total submission to God'. A Muslim is he or she who submits totally to God.

Muhammad began preaching his religion, which much resembled Judaism. He preached for ten years but the notables in the city of his birth, Mecca, did not convert. In AD 622, they drove him out. They had profitable pagan religious festivals in Mecca and did not want them disturbed. Muhammad took refuge in Medina, another city of the Arabian peninsula. In 628, leading 10,000 believers in his creed, he took Mecca. Then he dictated to his pupils what he had heard from Allah and they wrote it all down – he was illiterate. What he dictated was the Koran. The dictation took four years, then he died – in AD 632.

Like other religions, Islam is much misunderstood, by believers and non-believers alike. The more a religion spreads, the more interpretations arise, often deviating from the original intent. For his time, what Muhammad said God dictated to him was tolerant and civilized, as the following text from the Koran shows:

> Righteousness is that one should believe in God and the Book.* And, for the love of Him, give away wealth to the near of kin, and to the orphans and the needy and to the wayfarer and the beggars and for the emancipation of the captives, and keep up prayer, and pay the poor rate,† and pay those who keep their promises, and give to the patient in distress and affliction and in times of conflicts. Those (who do all this) are true to Islam and guard against evil (ii, 177).

---

* The word 'Book' refers to the Koran or Qu'ran in this discussion of Islam. References will be in Roman numerals for the chapters and Arabic numerals for the line. This is from line 177 in the second chapter.
† Two and a half percent of one's income donated to the poor.

Those who follow these rules will go to heaven. Those who do not will burn in hell. God, however, is merciful.* Allah knows everything, says the Koran (i, 15). He knows the past and the future, whom he will send to paradise, and whom he will send to hell (xxxv, 8; lxxvi, 31). So a Muslim warrior can't do anything about his death: the warrior will die at the time appointed by God, neither later nor before. No matter what a believer has done, if he dies for the faith in a *jihad* – a holy war – he will go to heaven (iv, 74). In heaven, he (any believer who dies in *jihad*) will be for ever young and potent. He will be given seventy virgins forever young, beautiful and libidinous. The food and the clothes will be splendid. There will be wonderful fruit, rivers of milk, honey and wine which he will be able to drink with no hangover (xlvii, 15; lxxvi, 14–15; lv, 56–8).

> In a holy war, if those you defeat are prepared to convert to Islam, they must be spared. They are to acquire all the privileges of a Muslim, regardless of race. Slay the idolaters wherever you find them; and take them captive; and besiege them; and lie in wait for them in every ambush; but if they repent and keep up prayer and pay the poor rate . . .

In other words, if they become Muslims, they are safe (ix, 5; see also ii, 90; li, 191 and 193). And that goes whatever their race because 'all people are a single nation' (ii, 213).

Conquered Christians and Jews do not have to convert to Islam because the Koran recognizes Abraham, Moses and Jesus as prophets. But Jews and Christians must pay a tax. 'Those who are Jews and the Christians, whoever believes (in the one) God, they shall have no fear nor shall they grieve' (v, 69. See also xxxi, 15).

---

* Nearly every chapter of the Koran begins with the words 'In the name of God, the compassionate, the merciful.' The text I use here is a translation by M. H. Shakir. It can be found on the Internet at http://www.hti.u-mich.edu/k/koran/

Islam is a virile creed – colloquially we would call it macho. A man is not expected to turn the other cheek: 'Whoever acts aggressively against you, inflict injury on him according to the injury he had inflicted on you' (ii, 194). Man need not be forgiving, but God is: 'Repentance is only for those who do evil in ignorance then turn to Allah. So these are to whom Allah turns mercifully' (iv, 17). However, 'repentance is not for those who go on doing evil things and then repent just before death. Nor for those who die as unbelievers' (iv, 18).

Mohammad's immediate successors, who had known him and heard him, the Caliph* Abu Bekr and the Caliph Omar, believed the Prophet favoured a frugal life.† But Muhammad had no objection to people making money: 'There is no blame on you in seeking bounty from your Lord' (ii, 198). But not in any way whatever. The Koran says that God punishes businessmen who lie, cheat and 'hoard grain to sell at a high rate' (xvii, 35). And all men who leave a heritage should bequeath part of it to the poor (iv, 8).

Women may inherit. However, if there also are male heirs, women will inherit half what the males inherit. The Koran makes it clear that 'the men are a degree above women' (ii, 228). 'Men have charge of women because God has made men to excel' (iv, 34). 'A man's wives are a field for him to plough at will' (ii, 223). A man can divorce a wife; a woman cannot divorce a husband. However, if a blameless wife is divorced, there are consequences. The husband may have to

---

* The word Caliph means successor.
† Sir William Muir, *The Caliphate, Its Rise and Fall*, London: The Religious Tract Society. 1892, p. 198, tells us that Omar visited his victorious troops that were besieging Jerusalem. His clothes were patched. He saw that his officers were luxuriously dressed and he threw gravel at them, scolding them for their fineries. Abu Bekr's and Omar's puritan views did not generally prevail.

return the dowry he received. A husband, who could afford to, could divorce one of his four wives but keep her in his household even though he has replaced her; he would thus have five or more women in his household, four wives and some former wives (ii, 227–37).

'The good women are obedient; as to those on whose part you fear desertion, admonish them, and leave them alone in the sleeping places and beat them' (iv, 34). 'Those who are guilty of an indecency [fornication]* from among your women,' according to four male witnesses, 'confine them to the house until death takes them away' (iv, 15).

Though men are given predominance, the Koran affords women a degree of protection. The Koran gives equality with men when it comes to dealings with the law. They are allowed to follow any legitimate profession, keep what they earn, and dispose of their property as they wish (iv, 4, 32). Women cannot be disposed of against their will (iv, 31–2; lv, 10). The Koran does not prescribe that women be veiled, only that they dress modestly.

Like other religions, Islam has many facets, many sects. In some areas, its observance is as relaxed as some Anglican Christians are relaxed. In other areas, Islam is fervent. This fervour frightens many westerners because we are centuries away from Christian martyrs, from Daniel in the lions' den. In a military era when westerners wage war but hardly accept the prospect of losing combatants, the Muslim who festoons himself with dynamite sticks and dies for his faith is terrifying and paranormal. To his people he is a heroic martyr.

Muslims consider they have been, and are, unjustly

---

* Some Arab translators of the Koran do not use the euphemism 'indecency' and come right out with the word 'fornication'.

oppressed and exploited by the West. They accuse the West of denigrating their religion. These feelings cannot be ignored. It may well be the hardest problem of what comes next in history.

PART 2

The Grand Acquisitors

6

THE DECLINE OF
THE ROMAN EMPIRE

(1st century)

Agrippina (AD 15–59)

Europe, as we know it today, has defined itself by its languages. It is the land of the Aryan language group. In long struggles, people speaking Aryan languages successfully defeated attempts at conquering Europe by people of the Semitic and Altaic language groups. The Aryan language group includes Greek, Celtic, Roman, German, Slavic, and such modern descendants as English, French, Swedish, Russian. The Semitic language group includes Hebrew and the various dialects spoken by the Arabs who attempted to conquer Europe. The Altaic group includes the languages spoken by the Turks and the Mongols who also tried to take Europe. This is a major pattern to keep in mind when reading what follows: Aryan, versus Semitic and Altaic, to see who possessed Europe.*

There were similar struggles for possession of lands elsewhere. Great numbers of people, races, tribes, nations, call

---

* Conversely, as the following chapters will illustrate, the Europeans invaded the lands of others in the past five centuries.

them what you will, looked across a river, or from the crest of a mountain, at greener pastures to invade, under the leadership of grand acquisitors. Among them, the Egyptians of the Nile and the Sumerians, of what is now Iraq, appear on the stage of history in 3000 BC;* the Phoenicians, of what is now Lebanon, in 2750 BC; the Babylonians, of contemporary Iraq, the Chinese and the seafaring Minoans of Crete in 2200 BC; Aryan tribes poured south from the north into India and into Greece in 1500 BC; again, in what is now Iraq, we have the Assyrians appearing at about 1400 BC; shortly thereafter, the Celts appear in Europe and the Jews in Palestine; the Germans, 1000 BC; the Persians, in Iran, around 800 BC. They all behaved aggressively towards whoever occupied the lands they invaded. They fought and conquered one another. Each new wave was dubbed 'barbarian' by the previous wave of 'barbarians'.

Under the command of Alexander the Great, nearly all of the above were conquered by the Aryan Greeks. Alexander started his conquests in 338 BC as a teenager and died at the age of thirty-three. His generals divided his conquests among themselves. Their kingdoms were called 'Hellenistic'. They were administered in the Greek language which became, for that part of the world, what English is today around the globe: the indispensable second language.† These Hellenistic kingdoms lasted until they became provinces of the Roman Empire

---

* The dates at which various nations appear on the stage of history are, of course, approximate: the evidence is equivocal.

† St Paul was born in Tarsus, home of noted Greek Stoic philosophers. For more than two centuries Tarsus had been part of a Greek-speaking Hellenistic kingdom. Consequently St Paul spoke good enough Greek to speak publicly in Athens. It was a Greek Pharaoh of the Hellenistic kingdom of Egypt, Ptolemy Philadelpheus, who had the Jewish Holy Books translated into Greek for his Jewish subjects who spoke only Greek at the time: see, Chapter 1 p.5, footnotes above.

some two centuries later. West of the Adriatic Sea the Romans governed in Latin, their own Aryan language; east of the Adriatic they governed in Greek – Romans in the higher administrative echelons had often studied Greek which carried the prestige of Greek philosophy; Romans from rich families studied in Athens.[1]

The Roman Empire was a terribly unwieldy structure to govern, full of different nations, cultures, languages, religions, customs and historical resentments at having been repeatedly defeated, conquered and exploited. The government of Rome in its empire was an autocracy. The Roman governors who administered the provinces were corrupt autocrats. It was understood that they would enrich themselves at the expense of the conquered people whom they ruled. Corruption and oppression would eventually lead to the conquest of the Aryan-speaking empire's European possessions, by 'barbarians', German tribes, who spoke various forms of German, another language of the Aryan group.

The times of Jesus provide striking illustrations of rule by corrupt, brutal, grand acquisitors whose excesses eventually felled the Roman Empire. One such was Agrippina (AD 15–59). She rose to power by marrying Claudius, the ruler of the Roman Empire. She is depicted as a cunning, stunning, seductive, courageous, promiscuous, incestuous, rapacious and murderous woman. She ran the empire for only a brief time, but was good at it. In short, she was the grandest grand acquisitor type, and a sort of poster girl for timorous antifeminist males.

Agrippina's father was the famous general Germanicus, revered by the Roman soldiery. Her mother was also called Agrippina. Most of this we know from Tacitus, by common consent the greatest historian who wrote in Latin.[2] He was born two years before Agrippina's death and lived to be sixty-three years old. He claims to have read Agrippina's memoirs: '*Id ego repperi in commentariis Aggrippinae filiae*' (I spotted this in the commentaries written by Agrippina, the younger.)[3] Suetonius, a contemporary of Tacitus, is another source.[4]

Agrippina grew up in terror. The Emperor Tiberius had probably starved her mother to death. One never knew whom Tiberius would strike next. He was a great military commander and administrator. But the last ten years of his reign were grotesque in their blood-steeped cruelty. 'In Rome the carnage was continuous,' says Tacitus;[5] 'I have compressed the events of two summers to give the reader some relief from horror. Not time, nor prayers, nor satiety that soften other breasts, could mollify Tiberius or change his policy of avenging' crimes, real or imagined.

Tiberius died in AD 37. Weak and helpless, he was suffocated by Macro, the commander of the Praetorian Guard, who wanted to put Agrippina's twenty-four-year-old brother Gaius on the throne.[6] Gaius had been nicknamed Caligula, 'little boot', when his father, Germanicus, displayed him to the troops in miniature uniform.

Caligula brought his three sisters, Agrippina, Livilla and Drusilla, to court and associated them with his glory.[7] Agrippina, the eldest, was twenty-two at the time. He made a show of his very intimate affection for them: at a formal banquet he fornicated with each of them publicly. His favourite was the youngest, Drusilla. He violated her when she was still a little girl. When she died of an unspecified illness in AD 38, Caligula had her deified and ordered a season of public mourning, during which it was a capital offence for anyone to laugh, have a meal with family and friends or wash.[8] In AD 38 he married Caesonia, who was between fifteen and twenty years his senior. They had a little girl he named Drusilla. In a fit of anger, Caligula exiled his sisters Livilla and Agrippina to small islands, reminding them that he didn't just have islands, he also had swords.[9]

Caligula kept Agrippina's little son Nero at court. When she was twelve, the Emperor Tiberius had given Agrippina in marriage to a nasty, violent, rich man called Gnaeus Domitius Ahenobarbus.[10] For ten years, the couple had no child. But nine months to the day after Caligula became emperor, Agrippina gave birth to a boy, Nero.* Her husband, Ahenobarbus, apparently thought Caligula was the father and said that any child by those two would be a danger to the world.

Caligula, who reigned a mercifully brief four years, turned out to be a kinky, homicidal maniac. Suetonius gives us a long list of Caligula's horrifying acts, beginning this section of his text with the words: 'So much for Caligula as emperor; we must now tell of his career as a monster.'[11] Here are samples:

Caligula killed Tiberius Gemellus, grandson of the Emperor Tiberius.[12] Though bisexual himself, he had male prostitutes tortured to death.[13] He saw himself as a god: he had sculptors substitute his head for those of various gods on sacred statues.[14] He killed his cousin Ptolemy.[15] Though Macro had helped him gain the throne, Caligula killed him and his wife.[16] Because he thought it was too costly feeding cattle to the wild beasts kept for gladiatorial shows, Caligula fed prisoners to the animals instead. Many men of honourable rank whom he thought possibly disloyal, he disfigured with branding irons before throwing them to the lions; or he would put them in cages where they could only be on all fours, like animals;

---

* This little Nero grew up to be the emperor who fiddled while Rome burned.

and in those cages he had them butchered. Some of his victims were guilty of nothing more than criticizing one of his shows (he fancied himself as performer). And he forced their parents to watch the executions. One of those he threw to the lions loudly protested his innocence. Caligula brought him out of the arena, cut out his tongue and threw him back to the beasts. And if he saw handsome men with a fine head of hair, Caligula had the back of their heads shaven – Caligula was bald.[18]

His spending was so extravagant that he emptied the well stocked treasury he inherited from Tiberius. So Caligula began imposing tariffs on everything and used his army as tax collectors. He annulled wills that did not mention him or his predecessor as an heir and he confiscated the inheritance.[19] In particular, he did this to the military officers he had appointed. Not mentioning him as heir, he said, was ingratitude.[20]

Despoiling the officers of his bodyguard is not a wise move for a tyrant. On 24 January 41, Caligula was twenty-nine and had been emperor for three years, ten months and eight days. Cassius Chaerea, a tribune (colonel) of the Praetorian Guard, struck Caligula from behind and gashed his neck. Another tribune, Cornelius Sabinus, stabbed the Emperor in the chest. The next sword stroke split Caligula's jaw bone. He was writhing on the ground, still alive. Other conspirators stabbed him thirty times – some thrust their swords into his genitals. They also killed Caligula's wife Caesonia and dashed his little daughter's brains out against a wall.[21]

The Praetorian Guard found Caligula's uncle Claudius cowering behind a curtain. They took him to their camp. There he paid each of the 4,500 guardsmen 15,000 sesterces, a substantial sum. So, the members of the Praetorian Guard imposed him as emperor. The Roman Senate had no military force of its own to resist the guards, who were largely 'barbarian' mercenaries. For the first time ever, someone had bought the imperial throne.[22] This was also a harbinger of things to come – of the 'barbarians' becoming the real power behind the throne and eventually the real power on the throne.

By the time Caligula died, Agrippina was twenty-six and she had seen every possible horror. She had experienced first-hand that life near the sovereign was unspeakably dangerous. As Tacitus says, '*arduum sit eodem loci potentiam et concordiam esse*' – it is hard for power and concord to cohabit.[23] Better be the sovereign herself and make sure no one killed her, seems to have been Agrippina's conclusion.

When he ascended the throne, Claudius was married to his twenty-one-year-old cousin Messalina. He had a son by her, Britannicus, and a daughter, Octavia. Messalina was the kind of person who gives wives a bad name. She was astonishingly selfish and let nothing stand in her search for personal gratification. She had scores of lovers and she would not put up with any rivals. She had Claudius wrapped around her little finger. That is, until she went too far. She fell for Gaius Silius, the handsomest man in town. She planned to kill Claudius, replace him as emperor with her son Britannicus and marry Silius. One day, when Claudius was on a trip, she had a marriage ceremony with Silius. It wasn't valid, she knew, but she thought it would be fun.[24] It wasn't kept secret. Claudius had Silius killed. On her mother's advice, Messalina tried to slash her own throat before Claudius' executioner came. She didn't quite succeed, and the killer sent by Claudius ran her through with a sword.[25]

This was Agrippina's big chance. Her Greek lover, Pallas, the minister of finance, was the richest man in the Empire.[26] Everybody was advising Claudius to remarry: an emperor must have an empress. The eligible women of sufficiently high rank and wealth were strutting their stuff, showing off their looks, boasting of their noble lineage. The two favourites were Lollia Paulina and Agrippina.[27] Pallas had much influence with the Emperor – ministers of finance usually do. He pushed Agrippina's candidacy – after all, she was his mistress. Agrippina had 'access' to Claudius, for he was her father's brother. She sneaked into his bed.[28] Claudius, intoxicated by her expert love-making, pledged that he would marry her. But their marriage would have been incestuous under Roman law.[29]

Arguments were put before the Senate, arms were twisted, votes were bought.[30] When Claudius appeared before the august body and asked them to pass a law allowing marriages between uncles and nieces, they did so. Three months after Messalina's death, Claudius married Agripinna.[31] Here is how Tacitus describes the immediate result:

> in the state, all things happened in obedience to the bidding of a woman, but not a lascivious one like Messalina who had treated the Roman Empire as her toy. It was a tight and almost manly tyranny. In public [Agrippina] appeared austere and often arrogant. At home there was no unchastity, unless to increase her power. And she had an immense love for gold, on the grounds that it would serve as a support for the monarchy.[32]

The besotted Claudius did anything she asked. He gave her unprecedented honours, the title 'Augusta' which no wife of an emperor had had before.[33] Her features appeared on the imperial coinage. Her outings became a grandiose spectacle: she travelled in an ornate carriage, covered in sparkling jewels, dressed in magnificent embroidered dresses and wearing a cloak of golden threads. The city where she was born was renamed

Colonia Agrippinensis, or 'the Colony of Agrippina'.[34] That city is now Germany's Cologne. She was openly involved in the official business of ruling the Empire, receiving embassies on a raised dais, just like Claudius.[35]

Agrippina realized that her position ultimately depended on the aging Claudius. If her power was to survive his passing, she would have to pick his successor. At the time of her marriage to Claudius in 49, the imperial family included Agrippina's twelve-year-old son Nero and the Emperor's two children by Messalina: Britannicus, almost nine and Octavia, ten. The trick was for Agrippina to make Nero, not Britannicus, heir to the throne, step by step.

She could convince Claudius to rescind his decisions. He had exiled Seneca, a distinguished, popular writer and philosopher. At Agrippina's urging Seneca was brought back to Rome as tutor for her son Nero. Agrippina calculated that Seneca would feel beholden to her and would help her make Nero emperor.[36]

In 50, Pallas, as minister of finance, convinced Claudius to adopt Nero.[37] Then, because Agrippina asked it, Claudius named Nero *Princeps Iuventutis*, or Prince of the Youth, heir to the throne.[38]

The Empress was determined to concentrate as much power as possible in her own hands. She used her agents to accuse and ruin potential rivals and conspired with Pallas to undermine the Emperor's other advisers, making the Emperor ever more dependent on her.[39] She had Claudius remove Lusius Geta and Rufrius Crispinus, commanders of the Praetorian Guard: she did not think they would help her secure the throne for her son. The two were replaced by Afranius Burrus who became Agrippina's supporter because she had given him this choice appointment.[40]

Power over the Emperor but also power over her son Nero mattered to Agrippina. So when Domitia Lepida – beautiful, rich, sexy and a member of the Imperial family – started charming the boy, Agrippina had her assassinated.[41] Then, in 53, Nero was married to Claudius' daughter by Messalina, Octavia. He was sixteen, she was fourteen. Agrippina's plan seemed to be working.

Suddenly there was chilling news. One day, Claudius, in his cups, was overheard saying that it was his destiny to suffer the infamy of his wives and then punish them.[42] The Emperor had learned the details of his wife's torrid love affair with Pallas. Would he execute them both? Would Claudius change his mind and appoint Britannicus rather than Nero as his successor? There was a faction which wanted just that.[43]

Agrippina acted swiftly. She hired Locusta, a woman famous for her expertise with poisons. Locusta provided a deadly powder.[44] Some, says Tacitus, maintain that the powder was sprinkled on a particularly fine mushroom fed to the Emperor. Claudius felt sick but wasn't dying. He was struggling to vomit. Xenophon, the imperial doctor, in the pay of Agrippina, dipped a feather in an even faster poison and tickled the Emperor's throat, allegedly to induce vomiting. At the age of sixty-three Claudius died an agonizing death.[45]

The death could not be revealed before all the arrangements were in place to have Nero proclaimed emperor. So health bulletins were issued throughout the night, saying the Emperor was ill but recovering. Agrippina had his corpse swathed in hot blankets so it would not feel cold should anyone touch it after his death was announced. At last the death was revealed. Nero stepped out of doors accompanied by Afranius Burrus, the commander of the Praetorian Guard. Nero promised the soldiers 15,000 sesterces each, as Claudius had done, and was acclaimed emperor. The powerless Senate gave its assent, and voted divine honours for Claudius; and his funeral was splendid.[46]

Agrippina had done it. She had reached the top. She controlled her sixteen-year-old son. For the first time in Roman history, a woman was the dominant political force in the Empire. Nero's first watchword for the military was 'Best of Mothers'.

But Nero did not tolerate Agrippina's dominance for long. He was the emperor, after all. When Armenian ambassadors came to present their country's views to Nero, Agrippina was all set to go and sit beside him as a co-equal on his dais. Seneca advised Nero to walk down and greet his mother affectionately, thus keeping her from mounting the dais.[47]

Agrippina's control of Nero first collapsed when in 55 he fell in love with Acte, a former slave.[49] Agrippina ranted about her competitor, 'the freed slave', her 'daughter-in-law, the serving maid.'* But the more Agrippina made scenes, the more Nero's infatuation with Acte grew, till he totally abandoned his filial obedience to his mother. Agrippina changed tack. She said she no longer objected to Acte, gave the young lovers her bedchamber and offered to give Nero all her private wealth. Nero, in response, gave his mother a bejewelled dress from the imperial collection. Agrippina flew into a rage, screaming that he was giving her what was already hers.[49] Exasperated by these maternal scenes, Nero struck at Agrippina's power: he fired her lover, Pallas, from his position of finance minister.

Agrippina became reckless. She threatened to present the late Claudius' son Britannicus to the Praetorian Guard as a better candidate for the throne than Nero.[50] Nero went into a hysterical panic and poisoned Britannicus at a family dinner. Tacitus says: 'A flash of terror passed over Agrippina's

---

* Nero would have nothing to do with Octavia, Claudius' daughter, whom he had wed for political reasons.

features. She saw that her last hope had gone, that the precedent for matricide had been set.'[51]

She didn't give up. She worked to increase her influence among the officers of the Guard. Rumours circulated that she was raising vast amounts of money to put someone other than Nero on the throne. Nero took away his mother's personal bodyguard and forced her to leave the imperial palace.[52]

It was clear to everyone that she had lost all power. Her enemies grasped at the chance to bring her down totally. They reported that she and her supporters were about to make a move against the Emperor.[53]

Nero went into a panic again and demanded the immediate deaths of his mother and the other conspirators. Afranius Burrus, commander of the Praetorian Guard, told the Emperor he would lose the support of the army if he killed his mother, the daughter of the great general Germanicus, idol of the soldiers.[54] Agrippina escaped that time, but to be safe she had to regain power: she decided to seduce Nero. She started visiting her son after lunch when he was usually in his cups. She was dressed alluringly, they kissed lasciviously and had sex, reported Acte, the freed slave. The girl was alarmed at the danger she herself faced if Agrippina regained her hold on Nero. Acte reported (to Seneca?) that the incest was known by everyone and that the troops would not submit to so profane an emperor. So Nero (on Seneca's advice?) stopped having private meetings with his mother.

But then Nero fell in love again, this time with Poppaea Sabina, the wife of a senator. She chided Nero for being a dependent boy, submitting to his mother's orders. 'To these and similar attacks, pressed home with tears and the adulteress' art, there was no retort,' says Tacitus, adding: 'all men yearn to break their mother's power; however no one believed that the hatred of the son would result in murder.'[55]

It did result in murder. Anicetus, an admiral who had tutored Nero, suggested that a special ship be constructed for Agrippina to go to the city of Baiae, near Naples, for the festival at the temple of the goddess Minerva. A section of the upper deck was designed to fall on Agrippina's bed and she, would thus be killed.[56] However, the headboard and the footboard of the bed were too solid and Agrippina was not crushed. Agrippina knew she had survived an attempt to assassinate her – her servants had been killed by the crew. Being a strong swimmer, she dived into the sea. A fishing vessel picked her up and brought her ashore.[57] But what could she do? She could only pretend she suspected nothing, since there was no appeal from a decision of her son, the Emperor. So she sent one of her servants to assure Nero that she was safe. Nero dropped a sword at her servant's feet and claimed that the servant had been sent by Agrippina to assassinate him.[58] Then he despatched his assassins to finish off his mother.

She was alone in her bedroom when they came. One of them hit her on the head with a club. She pointed to her womb where she had carried Nero and told her killers: 'Strike here.'[59] An officer's sword killed her. She was forty-three. She had been the sister of an emperor, the wife of an emperor and the mother of an emperor.

Legend has it that a diviner had told her she would have a son who would be emperor and who would kill her. She had replied, 'Let him be emperor and he can kill me.'

Could she have behaved differently? She was born into a family of grand acquisitors who accepted no ethical limits in their search for the power that allowed them to satisfy any desire. At any moment a father, an uncle, a son, a grandson, a cousin, a stepmother, even a mother could kill you, even if you demonstrably had no designs on power. The ambitious relatives would not believe you if you said you supported them fully. The only guarantee of survival was to hold the power yourself, and for a woman, in those days, that could only be through a husband or a son. Even that proved no guarantee of survival at all for Agrippina.

In the following centuries, there were some Roman emperors who did not like corruption but they could not really abolish it. They still had to plunder the Empire to maintain their armies; and they needed their armies to retain the Empire. The armies lived off the land. The soldiers, from the lowliest private to the generals, tried to make a fortune, small or large. Those at the top, the emperors, held unimaginable power, and most of them would do anything – as we have seen – to seize this power and retain it. Torture and murder of rivals were commonplace.

Agrippina was a product of the system. It almost seems that, in such systems, there is hardly any way for those in power – whatever their sex – to be moderate. They had to be corrupt acquisitors.

7

THE BYZANTINE EMPIRE

(6th century)

Theodora (AD 497–548)

The times of Agrippina illustrated the reasons why the empire of the Romans (the Aryan linguistic group) began to decline. This process of decline lasted more than 400 years. Piece by piece, other Aryans – the Germans – took the Roman possessions west of the Adriatic Sea. By 439, the Vandals, a German tribe, had captured North Africa. Rome itself fell to the Ostrogoths, another German tribe, in 476. Yet other Germans, the Visigoths, ended up conquering Spain in the next century. We shall come back to the doings of these Germanic tribes in a later chapter and now skip to what happened in the eastern part of Roman Empire.

By the sixth century AD, the Roman Empire was left with only its possessions east of the Adriatic Sea. Not only did its geography change but its name changed. It came to be called the Byzantine Empire. Its capital was Constantinople. It was a considerable and rich dominion which functioned in Greek. Christianity was the state religion. The patriarch of Constantinople far outranked the pope in those days.*

The Byzantine Empire controlled the Balkans, Asia Minor, Iraq, Syria, Lebanon, Palestine and Egypt. It controlled the trade with Asia in spices and fine cloth. It could have been satisfied with what it had, and probably was, until Justinian became emperor.

Justinian reigned from 527 to 565. He tried to reconquer the western parts of the old Roman Empire, which were firmly in German hands by the time he came to rule in Constantinople. Although the Byzantine Empire lasted for almost nine centuries after Justinian's death, his attempt to retake Europe and North Africa from the Aryan Germans so weakened the Byzantine Empire that the Arabs, of the Semitic language group, were able to begin their remarkable conquests (detailed in Chapter 8).

Justinian had a remarkable consort, Theodora. She was born in 497 and died fifty-one years later. She started life as the most spectacular whore and stripper of the Empire, and then became Justinian's most trusted adviser. Her superior intelligence and deft handling of political affairs caused many to think that it was she, rather than Justinian, who ruled Byzantium. In 532, she saved her husband, as political factions in Constantinople had united to overthrow him, rioted and set up a rival emperor. Justinian's advisers urged him to flee. Theodora said: 'Stay and fight.' Justinian's general Belisarius herded the rioters into the Hippodrome and cut them to pieces.

---

* Constantinople had been called Byzantium until the Roman Emperor Constantine the Great renamed it Constantinople, after himself, in the fourth century AD. Renamed Istanbul by the Turks in the fifteenth century, it sits on the north shore of the Bosphorus Straits, which lead from the Mediterranean into the Black sea.

Theodora is remembered also as one of the first rulers to recognize the rights of women, altering the divorce laws to give greater benefits to women, and passing strict laws to prohibit the traffic in young girls. She also set aside a palace in which she housed 500 prostitutes she wanted to save from life on the streets. Some of them, bored with chastity, prayer and penitence, jumped to their death from their bedroom windows.

Historians are unanimous in recognizing Theodora's skills in statesmanship. Will Durant says of her: 'Sometimes she countermanded her husband's orders, often to the advantage of the state.'[1] 'The prudence of Theodora is celebrated by Justinian himself; and his laws are attributed to the sage counsels of his wife,' wrote Edward Gibbon,[2] referring to the Justinian Code that still indirectly influences lawmakers in Europe, Latin America, Quebec and Louisiana.

What then do we make of the historian Procopius, our main source for what we know about Justinian and Theodora? He wrote books published while Justinian was alive in which he said all the good things stated above about Theodora and her husband. But he also wrote another book published after his death called *Anekdota*, which means 'unpublished', and not 'anecdotes'. This book, generally referred to as *The Secret History*, is vitriolic in its attacks on the imperial couple. Did Procopius write *The Secret History*, or is it a libellous tract by someone else?

According to Professor Paul Halsall of Fordham University, 'it is generally accepted that *The Secret History* was, indeed, written by Procopius.' Edward Gibbon wrote of Procopius' *The Secret History*: 'Even the most disgraceful facts, some of which had been tenderly hinted in his public history, are established by their internal evidence.'[3]

Selected Excerpts from *The Secret History*

'It was impossible, during the life of certain persons, to write the truth of what they did, as a historian should. If I had, their hordes of spies would have found out about it, and they would have put me to a most horrible death. I could not even trust my nearest relatives. That is why I was compelled to hide the real explanation for many matters glossed over in my previous books. These secrets it is now my duty to tell.

'Theodora was born to a man called Acacius who trained bears at the hippodrome of Constantinople. He died leaving three daughters named Comito, Theodora and Anastasia. Their mother put them on the local stage, for they were beautiful.

'As soon as she reached puberty, Theodora became a whore. She gave her youth to anyone she met, in utter abandonment. She was very funny and a good mimic, and immediately became popular on the stage. In the theatre, in the sight of all the people, she removed her costume and stood nude in their midst, except for a girdle about the groin: not that she had any reservations about being totally nude; but there was a law against appearing altogether naked on the stage.

'Often she would go picnicking with ten young men or more, in the flower of their strength and virility. She fornicated with them through the night. After she tired them out, she would approach their servants, perhaps thirty in number, and fornicate with each of these; and even that did not satisfy her. She conceived frequently, but she immediately had abortions.

'Justinian fell violently in love with her. At first he kept her only as a mistress. Through him Theodora was able immediately to acquire an unholy power and huge wealth. She seemed to him the sweetest thing and he would stop at nothing to please her. It was illegal for a man of senatorial rank to make a courtesan his wife. However, Justinian took Theodora as his wife after convincing his uncle, the Emperor Justin, to create a new ordinance, permitting the marriage. When Justin died of an illness, after a reign of nine years, Justinian and Theodora ascended the imperial throne.

'The Emperor Justinian, Theodora's husband, was deceitful, devious, false, hypocritical, two-faced, cruel, skilled in dissembling his thoughts. He was never moved to tears by either joy or pain, though he could summon tears artfully at will when the occasion demanded. He was a constant liar. Even when he swore sacred oaths to his subjects in their very hearing, he would immediately break his agreements and pledges. A faithless friend, he was a treacherous enemy, insane for murder and plunder.

'He had no scruples about appropriating other people's property. He did not even think any excuse necessary, legal or illegal, for confiscating what did not belong to him.

'Theodora received the ambassadors of the Persians and other barbarians and gave them presents, as if she were in command of the Byzantine Empire: a thing that had never happened in all previous time.* Thus it was that Theodora, though brought up as a whore, rose to royal dignity over all obstacles. For no thought of shame came to Justinian in marrying her. He might have taken his pick of the noblest born, most highly educated, most modest, carefully nurtured, virtuous and beautiful virgins of all the ladies in the whole Byzantine Empire: a maiden, as they say, with upstanding breasts. Instead, he preferred to make his own one who had been common to all men.

---

* Procopius is wrong, Agrippina received ambassadors.

'What Theodora and her husband did together must now be briefly described: for neither did anything without the consent of the other. The churches of so-called heretics, especially those belonging to the sect of Arius, were incredibly wealthy.* As none of the previous emperors had molested these churches, many men, even those of the Orthodox faith, got their livelihood by working on their estates. The Emperor Justinian, in confiscating these properties, took away what for many people had been their only means of earning a living.†

'The persecution of the so-called heretics filled the Roman realm with blood. Justinian accused some of polytheism; others of heresy against the Orthodox Christian faith; some of paederasty; others of love affairs with nuns; some of starting sedition, or treason against himself, or anything else; or he made himself the arbitrary heir of the dead and even of the living.

'The Emperor also exerted himself to destroy the traditions of the Jews. For whenever in their calendar Passover came before the Christian Easter, he forbade the Jews to celebrate it on their proper day, or perform any of their customs. Many of them were heavily fined by the magistrates for eating lamb at such times, as if this were against the laws of the State.

'Publicly in the Forum, and under the management of palace officials, the selling of court decisions and legislative actions was carried on. Justinian licensed many monopolies, as they are called, selling them to those who were willing to

---

* The followers of Arius (250–336) were Christians but rejected the divinity of Christ.
† This is one among countless examples of grand acquisitors using the pretext of religion to steal other people's property.

undertake this reprehensible traffic. Of course, he exacted his price for the privilege. To those who made this arrangement with him, he gave the power to charge whatever they pleased. He sold this privilege openly, even to magistrates. And since the Emperor always got his share of the plundering, these officials and their subordinates did their robbing with impunity.

'It was easier to count the grains of sand in the sea than the number of men Justinian murdered in his wars. Libya, vast as it is, he so devastated that you would have to go a long way to find a single man. Yet 80,000 [German] Vandals capable of bearing arms had dwelt there. Who could guess the number of their wives and children and servants?

'As for Theodora, her palace had an underground cellar, secure and labyrinthine, in which most of those who gave offence to her were eventually entombed. Accused of disloyalty, Buzes [a high official Theodora distrusted] was thrown into this dungeon. There the man remained and no one knew what happened to him. Neither, as he sat there in darkness, could he ever know whether it was day or night; nor could he learn from anyone else, for the man who each day threw him his food was a mute, and the scene was that of one wild beast confronting another. Everybody soon thought Buzes dead. No one dared to mention even his memory. But after two years and four months, Theodora released him. Ever after he was half blind and sick in body.

'Basanius, a prominent young man, incurred Theodora's anger by making some uncomplimentary remark. Basanius, warned of her displeasure, fled to the Church of Michael the Archangel. She immediately sent the prefect after him, charging Basanius not with slander, but paederasty. And the prefect, dragging the man from the church, had him flogged in public. The populace cried loudly to let Basanius go.

Whereupon the Empress had him castrated so that he bled to death. She confiscated his estate, though his case had never been tried. Thus, when this female was enraged, no church offered sanctuary; no law protected; no intercession of the people brought mercy to her victim; nor could anything else in the world stop her.

'She had accidentally become pregnant by one of her lovers, when she was still on the stage. She tried all the usual measures to abort but nothing worked. So she gave birth. The father of the baby saw that Theodora was at her wit's end and vexed because motherhood interfered with her usual recreations. He suspected with good reason that she would do away with the child; took the infant from her, naming him John, and sailed with the baby to Arabia. Later, when he was on the verge of death and John was a lad of fourteen, the father told him the whole story about his mother. So the boy, after he had buried his father, went to Constantinople and announced his presence to the Empress' chamberlains. They reported to Theodora that her son John had come.

'Fearing the story would get to the ears of her husband, Theodora ordered that her son be brought face to face with her. As soon as he entered, she handed him over to one of her servants who was ordinarily entrusted with such commissions. And in what manner the poor lad was removed from the world, I cannot say, for no one has ever seen him since, not even after the Queen died.'[4]

Theodora could be as ruthless as Agrippina. But Theodora was much luckier. She had a husband who loved her constantly. She did not have to fear for her life every day. She died in her bed. Were Justinian and Theodora as rapacious, unscrupulous, treacherous and murderous as *The Secret History* says? Evagrius, a historian who wrote a generation later, a moderate man, and Zonaras who wrote in the twelfth century and cites documents, do not seem to disagree with *The Secret History*.[5] Edward Gibbon wrote:

> A lover of truth will peruse with a suspicious eye *The Secret History* of Procopius. This book represents only the vices of Justinian. Ambiguous actions are imputed to the worst motives; error is confounded with guilt; accidents with design and laws with abuses. The Emperor alone is made responsible for the faults of his officers, the corruption of his subjects; and even the calamities of nature, plagues, earthquakes and inundations are imputed to Justinian.[6]

But Gibbon believes and cites much that is in *The Secret History*.

Justinian had a superhuman job to do. He wanted to reclaim all the parts of the empire which had been lost by his predecessors. He wanted one united realm again stretching west to the Atlantic – and with a common set of laws. He had inherited a full treasury but it was not equal to the task. From the 'barbarian' Germans Justinian's generals reclaimed North Africa, Dalmatia, Italy, Corsica, Sardinia, Sicily and Spain. It was a hugely expensive undertaking. To finance this reconquering, he taxed heavily. And the burden on the taxpayers was made worse because Justinian's tax collectors were extortionist crooks. The war of reconquest, moreover, destroyed cities, decimated populations, left fields empty of farmers. The nations his armies 'liberated' hated the suffering this liberation brought.

Justinian's code of laws was admirable but it was savage towards 'heretics' and, thereafter, these had no love nor loyalty towards the empire. The Arab Muslim conquerors who would soon swarm all over the Middle East, North Africa and Spain proved to be kinder to these heretics than was the Byzantine Empire.

8

ISLAMIC INCURSIONS INTO EUROPE

(711–1603)

It is now time to consider the impact Islam has had on Europe. This chapter covers the Islamic incursions while Chapter 9 looks at the European counter incursions: the Crusades.

So what happened in Europe after the Romans left? Exactly what had always been happening before – as in Africa, Asia and in the Americas before the Europeans arrived there: grand acquisitors made grabs for the land wealth of other grand acquisitors, slaughtering and plundering, often their own tribes, their own close relatives. Christianity did not soften these people.

The Germanic tribes – of the Aryan language group – settling in western Europe, pushed out the Celts who had been there before and who moved west and north. One such Germanic tribe, the Franks – who became the French – dominated. Our main source for these years is Bishop Gregory of Tours, who wrote towards the end of the sixth century. So here are a few typical passages from the reverend Bishop.

'Clovis who founded the kingdom of the Franks, was baptized a Christian along with 3,000 of his army. He killed many close relatives who might challenge him for the throne; he killed many kings, took their realms and became ruler of all the Gauls.[1] After reigning thirty years, he died aged forty-five, in Paris, in 511.[2] His four sons Theodoric, Chlodomer, Childebert and Clothar, divided his kingdom among themselves.[3] They and their descendants followed Clovis' example, slaughtering neighbours and murdering relatives.

'Theodoric reminded the Franks that the Thuringians, another Germanic tribe, had attacked them, plundered them and tortured them: "They hung youths by the sinews of their thighs to trees; they cruelly killed more than 200 maidens, tying them by their arms to the necks of horses, which were then goaded in opposite directions, and tore the maidens to pieces." So the Franks retaliated. There was such carnage that the bed of a river was filled with Thuringian corpses, and the Franks crossed upon them to the farther shore as if on a bridge.[4] The king of the Thuringians was promised safety; but Theodoric pushed him off a city's walls and killed him.[5]

'Another of Clovis' sons, Chlodomer died leaving two little boys. Childebert and Clothar, brothers of Chlodomer, slaughtered the little boys lest they later claim part of the kingdom.[6] A descendant of Clovis, King Chilperic, invaded the region around Tours, burned and laid everything to waste. He did not even spare Church property. He stole whatever he got his hands on. Why was this Frank ravaging the land of the Franks? Because he was looking for Merovech, a son he considered disloyal.[7] Despairing of evading his father, Merovech asked one of his slaves to kill him. The King found his son dead. Merovech had thus avoided torture, which was commonplace. A high official the King suspected of indulging in sorcery,[8] was stretched on the wheel and beaten with triple thongs until his torturers wearied. Then they put splinters under his finger and toe nails.

'King Childebert commanded his army to march into Italy and to conquer the Lombards.* When one of the King's dukes came to the city of Metz, which was on the way, the soldiers plundered, slew. They so mistreated the inhabitants that it might have been thought the duke was leading an army against a foreign enemy rather than against his own country.[9]

'[Again, let us not forget the ladies], the wives of Chilperic and Sigebert, two brothers, descendants of Clovis. Sigebert won the hand of the beautiful Brunehilde, daughter of Athanagild, King of the Visigoths [in Spain]. Chilperic married Galeswintha, Brunehilde's sister. At the instigation of his mistress Fredegonda, Chilperic assassinated Galeswintha and placed Fredegonda upon the throne. In 575, Sigebert, Brunehilde's husband, was felled by assassins sent by Fredegonda. Fredegonda also sent an assassin to kill Brunehilde. He returned to report he had failed. Fredegonda amputated his hands and feet. Later Chilperic was assassinated and Brunehilde was widely believed to have arranged it.

'So much for the secular power. The religious authorities were not much better. Becoming a bishop often meant being able to amass a fortune. Gregory of Tours tells us that a conclave of bishops spent their time in feasting and drinking.[10] There was no mention at all of God. No services were observed. When morning came they arose from dinner and covered themselves with soft coverings and, buried in drunken sleep, they would lie till the third hour of the day. And there were women with whom they polluted themselves. And then they would rise and bathe and lie down to eat. In the evening they arose and later they devoted themselves greedily to dinner until the dawn, as we have mentioned above.'

*   *   *

---

* The Lombards were a Germanic tribe who had settled in Italy.

Franks were not the only culprits. The Thuringians attacked the Ostrogoths who attacked the Lombards who attacked the Franks who attacked the Visigoths, the Bavarians, the Saxons and vice-versa: endless wars, led by grand acquisitors to grab someone else's territory. And the behaviour of the bishops mentioned above was also a pattern – not for all bishops but for many who were grand acquisitors too, as we shall see. National school books may describe this predatory behaviour as glorious. But what one side viewed as a glorious victory, the defeated viewed as a treacherous massacre, pillage and rape. Most royal families developed from ancestors who eerily resemble the murderous Mafia bosses of recent history or fiction.

In view of such an unpromising background, not to be conquered militarily by Islam would be in itself a major and surprising European achievement, because the successes of Islam were breathtaking. Eurocentrists have to remember that: the people of Islam have an illustrious military history.

Islam helped unite often warring Arab tribes. 'Islam progressed as far in one century as Christianity in seven.'[11] A compressed chronology will make clear their astonishing successes.

635 The Arab Muslims take Syria.

637 They take Jerusalem and Ctesiphon.

641 They control Iraq, take Persia and Egypt.

691 They take Armenia.

698 They take Tunisia, then Algeria, then Morocco.

711 They begin their conquest of Spain.

732 They try to take France but are defeated near Tours.

809 They take Corsica and Sardinia.

837 They conquer Sicily.

846 They nearly take Rome but are finally driven out of
Italy by 884.

The Pope pays the Arabs to leave Rome alone.

All these conquests were made by Arab Muslims. The Turks
came later. How did the Arabs do it and why? We have no
documents, no letters or memoirs telling us what those Arabs
felt about their faith and their own motives. Professor Frederic
Donner concludes that, yes, at least some members of the
Islamic elite may have been motivated by a desire to conquer
so as to propagate their faith, but many members of that elite
were merchants who understood the importance of controlling trade routes and the wealth-producing capacity of urban
centres. They knew about the power of money. They motivated the almost impossibly independent nomadic tribesmen
in their armies with loot: with grants of land in conquered
territories – provided the tribesmen agreed to settle there – and
with fortunes given to the leaders of the tribes who brought
their tribesmen along to the Islamic army. For example: 'Janr
Ben Abdullah of the Bajlla tribe agreed to put his sizable
following at the service of the Islamic state, but only in return
for a promise of extra booty over and above the normal
share.'[12]

Was there a lot of booty? Was there ever! For example,
when the Arabs invaded Spain, Tarik, their leader

> . . . took pearls, armour, gold, silver, vases and a quantity
> of spoils, the like of which one had not seen. He wrote to
> his superior, Musa Ibn Nossevr, informing him of the
> conquest of Andalus [the Arab name for Spain], and of
> the spoils which he had found. Musa came to Cordova.
> Tarik delivered to him all the plunder. Musa collected a
> sum which exceeded all description.[13]

Roderic, the Visigoth King of Spain, would not surrender peacefully to the Arab army. Therefore he had to be fought and defeated. Here is how Tarik urged his soldiers on before the decisive battle:

> Oh my warriors, you have nowhere to run. Behind you is the sea, before you, the enemy. He has an innumerable army. You have nothing but your swords as your only chance for life – such chance as you can snatch from the hands of your enemy. Attack this monarch who has left his strongly fortified city to meet you. Here is a grand opportunity to defeat him.
>
> You have heard that in this country there are a large number of ravishingly beautiful Greek maidens;* their graceful forms are draped in sumptuous gowns on which gleam pearls, coral, and purest gold, and they live in the palaces of royal kings. The spoils will belong to you.[14]

In other words, fight, win, pillage, rape!

However, those who – unlike Roderic – were prepared to surrender without a fight were safe. For instance, the Arabs defeated Byzantine forces in Egypt and reached Memphis – now Cairo. The inhabitants of the city offered to surrender. The Arab commander Amr ibn Al-Asi, followed the rules of Muhammad and gave the inhabitants of Memphis a written guarantee that they would not be plundered nor would they be killed.

The same commander, when he took Alexandria, met Benjamin, the Coptic patriarch, treated him with honour

---

* In theory, Spain in the eighth century was still part of the Roman (Byzantine) Empire which had its capital in Constantinople. The language of the Byzantine Empire was Greek. To the Arabs of that time, the enemy was Greek. In all probability, the maidens in question were Visigoths, i.e. Germanic. Did they speak Greek? We do not know.

and told him he could enjoy his full authority and run his churches as he wished. The inhabitants had to pay a tax of so much per person. That was better than death, pillage, rape and religious persecution – the Byzantine Empire classed Coptic Christians as heretics.[15]

The conditions the Arab Muslims granted to those who surrendered made good sense. Rather than enemy cadavers, better to have subjects who are alive, work, and pay taxes. The Arab ruling elite, being of merchant stock, apparently understood that cities are the key producers of wealth.

Assuredly, the Arab conquerors were grand acquisitors. But, for their time, and compared with the Christian governments they fought, the Arab Muslims were much more tolerant. Jews and Christians were not molested if they paid a tax and did not proselytize for their religion.

The Arab kingdom of Cordova, founded shortly after Tarik's arrival in Spain, lasted almost eight centuries. It was the centre of the most advanced civilization in Europe. It transmitted to western Europe what the Ancient Greeks had done in philosophy and the sciences. Arab intellectuals in Cordova made important contributions to mathematics. They also produced exquisite architecture, before being expelled from Spain at the end of the fifteenth century by King Ferdinand and Queen Isabella of Spain.

Inevitably, the Arabs divided into sects, into rival dynasties. The Byzantine Empire occasionally produced talented rulers who pushed the Arab conquerors back. The Persians and the Crusaders also fought the Arabs. These wars weakened all concerned and opened the door for the Turks, who were being pushed westwards out of Turkestan, their Asian homeland, by the Tatars or Mongols: all these people, Turks, Tatars, Mongols, belonged to the Altaic language group, had converted to Islam and, of course, were not Semites like the Arabs.

The first Turks to arrive on the eastern frontiers of Byzantium, in the eleventh century, were called Seljuks, after one of their military leaders. On 19 August 1071, the Seljuks utterly destroyed the Byzantine army at Manzikert, by Lake Van, which is near the current frontier between Turkey and Iran. The Seljuks captured the Byzantine Emperor Romanus IV in that battle but they released him unharmed. Upon his return to Constantinople, Romanus was blinded by the Byzantines and exiled to the island of Prote in the Sea of Marmara, where he died. The victory of the Turks at Manzikert opened for them the Byzantine Empire's heartland, Asia Minor, which became the base of the Turkish state for the next thousand years.[16]

In the thirteenth century, another wave of Turks, called the Ottomans, after another military leader, also converts to Islam, progressively captured everything conquered earlier by the Seljuks and by the Arabs. The Ottomans pushed into the Balkans. On 15 June 1389, at the battle of Kosovo Polje (Field of the Blackbirds), the Ottoman Sultan Murad I destroyed the Serbian army.

Western European forces, led by the King of Hungary organized a Crusade to push the Ottomans out of the Balkans. On 25 September 1396, the Crusaders were utterly annihilated at the battle of Nikopolis (now Nikopol in Bulgaria). The Ottomans decapitated several thousand Crusaders, in retaliation: earlier, these Crusaders had decapitated Muslim prisoners. The Turks took Constantinople itself in 1453. The whole of the Balkans was under Turkish domination for nearly five centuries.

The Ottoman Turks had moved west, north and south until they owned Asia Minor, Arabia, Iraq, Iran, Syria, Palestine, the North African coast, the Crimea and the Balkans.

Repeatedly, the Turks tried to take more of Europe than the Balkans. They could not take the Ukraine and Russia because those territories were occupied by the Golden Horde: Mongols converted to Islam. Two major battles decisively turned the Ottomans back in their drive to take what is now western Europe: the naval battle at Lepanto in 1571 and the land battle before Vienna in 1683.

The stage for the battle of Lepanto was set by Pope Pius V, who wished to prevent the Turks coming any closer to the Papal States. He managed, in 1571, to create an anti-Ottoman alliance known as the Holy League. It consisted of the Papal States, Spain, Venice and Genoa. It was principally a seaborne alliance and the man chosen to lead its armada was Don Juan of Austria, a bastard son of Charles V, King of Spain and Emperor of the Holy Roman Empire.*

On one of Don Juan's ships was a Spanish volunteer by the name of Miguel de Cervantes. He would suffer a disabling wound to his hand at Lepanto. That put an end to his military career. Instead he wrote one of the greatest novels of all time – *Don Quixote*.

Don Juan of Austria's fleet had 300 ships, great and small, including six galleasses; these were broader in the beam than regular galleys and with a deeper draught. Thus they had enough stability to carry cannon. On their prow they had a walled platform mounted with swivel guns – a precursor of the armoured turrets on modern naval ships. A total of 80,000 men manned the galleys of the Holy League: 50,000 rowers and 30,000 soldiers. Except for the cannon and muskets, naval tactics had not changed much since the Battle of Actium

---

* The Holy Roman Empire was created by Charlemagne, king of the Franks, in the ninth century, to mark western Europe's independence from the eastern Roman Empire.

in 31 BC where Octavian defeated Cleopatra's lover Mark Antony.

Don Juan ordered his men not to fire until they were close enough to be splashed by Muslim blood. The two fleets fought fiercely, ship to ship. Don Juan's galley attacked the Turkish flagship commanded by Ali Pasha. The Christians boarded the Turkish ship; were repulsed. Then the Turks swarmed over the Christian ship. Back and forth it went for hours. The decks were slippery with blood and guts. The screams of the wounded drowned out the orders. Finally, at their third try, the Spaniards prevailed. They beheaded the Turkish admiral, Ali Pasha, and held his head aloft on the point of a lance. The Ottoman battle flag was pulled down – that had never happened before.

Four hours later, the battle was over, the smoke had cleared. Don Juan had lost 8,000 dead, 16,000 wounded and seventeen ships. The Turks had lost 25,000 dead; fifteen of their ships had been sunk and 177 captured.[17]

But the Turks were not finished. Defeated decisively at sea, they did not stop their attacks by land from the Balkans until they were beaten as they laid siege to Vienna. The Viennese fought bravely. Their food supplies and their munitions ran low. Jan Sobieski, King of Poland, came to the rescue, on 12 September 1683, two months after the siege had begun.

Sobieski had 30,000 Polish troops plus German and Austrian contingents. He was outnumbered by the Turks. But he surprised them. The King and his Polish hussars charged towards the headquarters of Kara Mustafa, the Turkish general, who panicked and fled. Leaderless, the Turkish army suffered heavy losses. Sobieski's victory put an end to Ottoman invasions of western Europe.[18]

The Balkans remained under the Turks for five centuries. Even now, free of the Turks, in parts, for 170 years, the people of the Balkans yearn to be Europeans: deep in their hearts they feel they are not yet; that they are still under what Edward Gibbon called the dead hand of Islam. All Balkan Christian history books describe the five centuries of Turkish domination as a time of horror.* There was the blood tax, of course, a periodic levy of handsome male children for conversion to Islam and service in the Janissaries, the elite bodyguard of the Turkish sultan. But the picture was not entirely negative. Once completed, the Turkish conquest included the Balkans in a *Pax Ottomanica*, an Ottoman peace that was a marked contrast to the preceding centuries of war and conflict.

Most Balkan historians reject the concept of a benevolent *Pax Ottomanica*. Balkan historians say that western Europeans have no concept of how awful it was to live under the Muslim Turkish masters. However, it was also awful to live under Christian masters in those days. For example, the thirteenth-century Christian Vikings engaged in a lucrative trade, selling Christian Slavs as slaves to the Muslim world.[19] And there is nothing, probably, that the Muslims did to the Bulgarians which compares with what they suffered at the hands of the Byzantine Emperor Basil II. The Bulgarians, admittedly, attacked the Byzantine Empire often. They defeated Byzantine armies. They besieged Constantinople. Basil II 'in a ruthless thirty years' war, destroyed the Bulgarian power. After his victory in 1014, he blinded 15,000 prisoners, leaving one eye in every hundredth man to lead the tragic host back to Samuel, the Bulgarian tsar.'[20] Thereafter, Basil II

---

* This is not necessarily true of Bosnian and Albanian history books. The Bosnians were Christian Orthodox Serbs who converted to Islam and acquired equal rights with the conquerors. The same was the case for the Albanians.

proudly wore the title of 'Basil the Bulgar Slayer'. He was a Christian. So were the Bulgarians.

Today, school children are taught in Greece to admire Basil the Bulgar Slayer. Presumably it is a natural tendency for little boys to boast: 'My dad can beat your dad any time, with one hand tied behind his back.' They don't seem to outgrow this tendency.

9

THE CRUSADES

(1095–1204)

The Christian Crusades to take the Holy Land back from the Muslims began in the eleventh century.

The Christians had split in 1054, between the Catholics under the pope, and the Greek Orthodox under the patriarch of Constantinople. This event is still known as the Great Schism. This schism happened primarily because the popes had added to the Creed* the term '*filioque*'. This Latin word meant that the Holy Ghost emanated not only from God the Father but 'also from the Son', Jesus. Secondly, the Greek Orthodox clergy would not accept the papal innovation that priests should not marry. There was also a third, trivial reason: the Greeks would not accept the pope's edict that priests should not wear beards. One should never underestimate the influence of trivial reasons.

In Europe, as we saw in Chapter 8, the German tribes had carved out kingdoms, all Christian, festooned with bishoprics and abbeys. Pope Urban II decided in 1095 that it was time to take Jerusalem back from the 'infidels', the Muslims that is,

---

* The Creed is the universal Christian statement of faith: 'We believe in one God, the Father, the Almighty, maker of heaven and earth . . .'

who had captured the city in 638. Urban II proclaimed a holy war (a *jihad* as Muslims would say), to put Jerusalem back in Christian hands. This was the First Crusade.

There were other motives for this expedition: Europe had too much population for its pre-industrial economy. There were many younger sons of nobles with no inheritance and no chance to make a fortune. Venice had a serious interest in challenging Muslim commercial dominance of the eastern Mediterranean. Last but not least, the Byzantine Emperor Alexius had asked for western European help against the Muslims, who were eating up his territory. If he got the help, he might agree – in gratitude – to reunite the Greek Orthodox Church with the Catholic Church.

Eloquent preachers wandered around Europe proselytizing for the Crusade: 'If you participate all your sins will be forgiven.' Eventually, hundreds of clerics – bishops, abbots and priests, plus 4,000 knights, their horses and equerries were assembled, along with 25,000 infantry. Many more joined but dropped out after a burst of initial enthusiasm. In no way was it a formal mobilization in the modern sense. Individual leaders gathered a cluster of volunteers – the more important the leader the bigger the cluster. The official grand leader was the fifty-seven-year-old Raymond, Count of Toulouse, Marquis of Provence. But the popular hero was the young, blond, brilliantly handsome Godefroi de Bouillon, Duke of Lorraine, a Frank.

While still in their homes, the clusters of Christian Crusaders began slaughtering Jews, in the part of Europe now known as the Rhineland. After all, why not start killing infidels at home before going abroad to kill more? Here are excerpts of how an eyewitness, Albert of Aix, describes the events.

The Crusaders attacked the Jews and slaughtered them without mercy. It was the beginning of their Crusade, the Crusaders said; their duty was to kill the enemies of the Christian faith. The carnage began in Cologne. The Crusaders fell upon the Jews there, destroyed the houses and synagogues and divided among themselves a very large amount of money. Not one Jew survived. Then the Crusaders made their way to the city of Mainz where the Bishop had hidden the Jews in his palace. That did not stop the Crusaders. They attacked the Bishop's palace and killed about 700 Jews, including the women. With their swords, the Crusaders pierced tender children of whatever age and sex. And the Crusaders took all the treasure the Jews had entrusted to the Bishop.

Albert of Aix concludes: 'May the hearts of the faithful be free from the thought that the Lord Jesus wished the Sepulchre of His most sacred body to be visited by these brutish and insensate animals.'[1]

Certainly, no one could attribute the atrocities of the Crusaders to the teachings of Jesus. His teaching forbids such behaviour; but His teachings, obviously, could not counter the preaching by the Church that 'the Jews killed Christ', and the lust to kill and plunder of Rhineland Christian brutes.

A Crusader army of some 1,500 cavalry and 12,000 foot soldiers led by Godefroi de Bouillon, took Jerusalem on 7 June 1099. All Muslim and Jewish men, women and children – every single one – were slaughtered, in the very name of Jesus, on the very same land where, centuries before, He had preached that we should love not only our neighbours but also our enemies. Here are selected quotes from the account of another eyewitness, Raymond d'Aguiliers.

Some of our men – and this was more merciful – cut off the heads of their enemies; others shot them with arrows; others tortured them longer by casting them into the flames. Piles of heads, hands, and feet littered the streets of the city. In the Temple of Solomon, men rode in blood up to their knees and bridle reins.[2]

A western kingdom of Jerusalem was established. Huge fortresses were erected by western barons in what are now Israel, Lebanon and Syria.

A Second Crusade was organized some fifty years later (1146–8), to bolster Christian positions established by the First Crusade in the Middle East. It was a total western disaster. On 2 October 1187, the great Muslim general, Saladin (1138–93), a Kurd, accepted the surrender of Jerusalem. He agreed to let the inhabitants leave if they paid a ransom. They paid, and no civilians were slaughtered.

Some few years later, a Third Crusade (1189–92) failed to recapture Jerusalem. The English King, Richard the Lionheart, took Acre, a coastal city now in northern Israel. Despite an agreement he had signed with Saladin to spare civilians, Richard slaughtered all Acre Muslims, their wives and children.

Jerusalem remained in Muslim hands. This was unacceptable to Pope Innocent III. The moment he mounted the Vatican throne in 1198, Innocent III proclaimed that a Fourth Crusade was needed to liberate the Holy City.[3] And he began taxing his churches to finance the holy war. The Pope issued a 'plenary indulgence', which means a pardon of all sins, for whoever would serve one year in Palestine on the Crusade.

The call to the Crusade was preached by Fulk de Neuilly, a priest. Richard the Lionheart, who had had his fill of crusading, said to Fulk de Neuilly: 'You advise me to dismiss my three daughters – pride, avarice and incontinence. I bequeath them to the most deserving – my pride to the Knights Templar,* my avarice to the monks of Cîteaux,† my incontinence to the prelates."[4]

Most of the fighting men were Franks. Previous Crusades had had terrible supply problems reaching the Middle East by land, especially through Asia Minor. So they decided to go there by sea. They sent delegates to negotiate the use of Venetian ships. The ruler of Venice, the Doge Enrico Dandolo, drove a hard bargain. He was a successful, wily politician and merchant. He said he would sign a treaty to provide fifty war galleys plus transport for 4,500 knights, their horses, 9,000 equerries, 20,000 foot soldiers, supplies for nine months. In exchange Venice would receive 85,000 marks in silver, a huge sum in those days, and half of whatever lands and booty the Crusaders seized.[5] The six envoys of the Crusaders agreed. This treaty was written on fine parchment, affirmed with great oaths, stamped with the imprint of signet rings on sealing wax. It was sent to Pope Innocent III who blessed it.

However, when the time came for the expedition to be launched from Venice, the Crusaders only had 51,000 marks of silver to give Venice, not the 85,000 they had agreed to. Ah well, said Dandolo, nearly blind and allegedly ninety-four years old, he would be generous. He would forget about the 34,000 marks the Crusaders still owed Venice, until some rich conquest enabled them to pay up. Till then he would be satisfied if they helped him capture Zara, a Hungarian port on the Dalmatian coast of the Adriatic, and a commercial rival of Venice.[6]

---

* The Templars were a religious order of knights who fought in the Crusades.

† This refers to the Cistertian community of monks, founded as Cîteaux, and branch of the Benedictines. They were vowed to poverty and silence.

The Abbot of Vaux, of the order of the Cistercians, objected that the Crusaders were there to liberate Jerusalem not to sack Christian cities. The good abbot was there as the eyes and ears of the pope. The Cistercian order was the richest order, and therefore most influential in Christendom, at the time. Doge Dandolo threw a fit. You promised, he said to the counts and barons, that you would help me take Zara. If you do not, then forget about using my ships. They would take Zara, said the counts and barons, pleading with Dandolo, tears streaking down their cheeks, honest they would.[7]

So the fleet set out from Venice, the banners of each nobleman flying; the counts, barons and knights, splendid in their multicoloured tunics, twirling their moustaches and ogling the girls waving them goodbye with silk scarves.

They reached Zara on 10 November. They attacked the walls with siege engines. Five days later, the city agreed to terms: 'pillage us but don't kill anybody, okay?' Okay.[8] And so Zara was taken, robbed blind, raped, but its people were not slaughtered.

It was late in the year, Doge Dandolo then said. Not a good time for sailing. Let's winter here. We can get all the supplies we need here. The countryside is rich. Let's divide the spoils. Venice got half the city, including the port. The Franks took the rest.[9]

While waiting at Zara, for spring, the Crusaders sent a delegation to beg for the pope's absolution. Pope Innocent III was furious. His Crusade had attacked and sacked a Christian city! He threatened to excommunicate them all. He relented, however, gave the absolution, but demanded the restoration of the booty. They thanked him for the absolution, and kept the booty.[10] The Venetians, by the way, refused to confess their guilt, or accept the pope's pardon, 'or allow a priest to meddle in their business dealings.'[11]

And to where would the fleet sail at Easter? The original plan had been that it should go to Egypt and move on to Palestine and Jerusalem from there. But the Venetians had a flourishing commerce with Egypt, exporting timber, iron and arms, importing slaves. 'They had made a secret treaty with Egypt, guaranteeing that country against invasion.'[12] Why not take Constantinople instead, where there was so much more booty to capture? The scrupulous Abbot of Vaux, who had objected to the taking of Zara, objected again. They couldn't attack a Christian city again! But plenty of other senior clerics took the other side. Of course the Crusade should take Constantinople.[13] 'Better to go where we have a sufficient excuse for obtaining money and provisions by conquest.'[14]

And there was a reason more respectable than booty to take Constantinople: to overthrow a wicked usurper, Alexius, who had captured his brother Isaac, the Emperor of Byzantium, blinded him and thrown him in a dungeon. The blinded Isaac had a young son, also called Alexius. The youngster managed to escape and go to his sister who had married Philip, the King of Germany.[15] King Philip sent envoys who said to the Crusaders:

> If you restore young Alexius to his rightful inheritance, he will place the whole Byzantine Church under the authority of the pope; he will give you 200,000 marks of silver, and food for your army; and he will personally lead 10,000 of his own troops to free the Holy Land with you.[16]

The fleet reached its target. The Crusaders drooled at the sight of the rich churches and palaces.[17] They attacked and caused Alexius the usurper to flee. Old Emperor Isaac was freed, and his boy Alexius was crowned Emperor.[18] The Crusaders then demanded the 200,000 marks of silver he had promised them. But there were only 100,000 marks in the imperial treasury. The citizens of Constantinople did not want to pay more, nor subordinate their church to the pope.[19]

Then the Catholic bishops preached to the Crusaders that capturing the Byzantine Empire was the righteous thing to do because the 'Greeks are traitors, worse than Jews.' By the authority of God and in the name of the pope, the bishops promised to absolve all who attacked the Greeks in Constantinople.[20]

Inside Constantinople, while waiting for the attack, a rival Byzantine prince, Murtzuphlus, strangled the boy emperor and took over. He fought, was defeated and eventually abandoned Constantinople, which fell to the Crusaders on 12 April 1204.[21]

Villehardouin does not dwell on the horrors of the sacking but other eyewitnesses do. Here are extracts from the Byzantine Senator Nicetas Choniates.[22]

Holy icons were trodden underfoot. The relics of the holy martyrs were thrown into unclean places. In the great church of Saint Sophia, the sacred altar, formed of all kinds of precious materials was broken into bits and distributed among the soldiers. Mules and saddled horses were brought into the church to carry away the sacred vases and utensils of unsurpassable art and grace and rare material, and the fine silver, and many other ornaments of Saint Sophia. The Crusaders brought in a naked whore into Saint Sophia. She sat in the patriarch's seat, singing an obscene song and dancing frequently. Honourable matrons and maidens and nuns were raped.

There is another eyewitness account, not by a Byzantine but by a westerner, a friar called Gunther de Pairis, who left us memoirs describing his abbot's thefts during the sacking of Constantinople. Here are extracts.[23]

While the victors were rapidly plundering the city, which was theirs by right of conquest, Abbot Martin began thinking about his own share of the booty. He did not want to be the only one left empty-handed. So he took with him one of his two chaplains [Gunther de Pairis] and went to the Pantokrator church. The Crusaders had broken into this church and were busy stealing gold, silver and precious stones. Abbot Martin thought it was unbecoming for him to commit sacrilege except in a holy cause. So he decided to steal holy relics only. He found them by threatening to kill an old Greek priest. Abbot Martin scooped up the cases of the holy relics and stuffed them in his cassock and in the cassock of his chaplain.

These relics, by the way, were encased in magnificent gold containers encrusted with precious stones – for instance, a finger of St Nicholas. Many can be seen these days in St Mark's, in Venice, where they have been for 800 years. Such objects fetched huge sums on the open market: a rich man owning a piece of the corpse of a saint felt, in those days, that he had a key to paradise.

Here is what Pope Innocent III wrote to a cardinal who participated in the sack of Constantinople.

To Peter, Cardinal Priest of the Title of St Marcellus Legate of the Apostolic See in Jerusalem. We were not a little astonished and disturbed to hear that you went to Constantinople. We have just discovered from your letters that you have absolved all the Crusaders. You did not have the authority to give such absolution, nor should you have given it. How are the Greeks to be brought back into ecclesiastical union and to a devotion for the Catholic Church when they see in the Latins only an example of perdition and the works of darkness; so that they now, and with reason, detest the Latins more than dogs?

The Crusaders were supposed to be serving Jesus Christ, not their own ends. Their swords, which they were supposed to use against the pagans, are now dripping with Christian blood. They have spared neither age nor sex. They have committed adultery and fornication. They have raped matrons and virgins, even nuns. Not satisfied with breaking open the Imperial Treasury and plundering the goods of princes and lesser men, they also laid their hands on the treasures and possessions of the churches. They have even ripped silver plates from the altars and have hacked them to pieces among themselves. They violated the holy places and have carried off crosses and relics. Given 12 July 1204.[24]

There we have it: the Crusaders, with their pillaging warrior lords, rapacious priests, extortionist money men, grand acquisitors all; and hordes of lesser acquisitors, there for the stealing of a bauble and the raping of a nun. They sacked a Christian city. A cardinal gave absolution to the 'brutish and insensate animals'[25] that were the Crusaders. The Fourth Crusade was a medieval throwback to the primitive, tribal duo of grand acquisitors: the witch doctor and the brute. It was all masterminded by a more modern type of grand acquisitor, the financier, the moneyman, the Doge and Merchant of Venice, Enrico Dandolo.

Christian Crusaders tore apart a Christian society, the Byzantine Empire that was menaced by 'infidel' Muslims. The barons, counts, marquesses and dukes divided the Byzantine Empire among themselves into little kingdoms that had no chance against the Muslim forces surging over what is now Iraq, Turkey, Palestine, the Lebanon, the Balkans, Syria.

The Crusaders took Constantinople in 1204 but they only managed to keep it till 1261, when the Greeks reconquered it. However, the great Byzantine Empire, already weakened before 1204, was shredded by the Fourth Crusade, and for the next 200 years the Byzantine Empire had to give way, inch by bloody inch, to the Muslim tide.

Constantinople fell, finally, in 1453, to the Turks who behaved better than the Christian invaders of 1204. The Turkish conqueror, Mehmed II ordered the sacking stopped on the first day his troops entered the city, an unheard-of act of mercy. To encourage the return of Greeks and Genoese who had fled the city, he gave them back their houses and provided them with guarantees of safety. He restored the Greek Orthodox patriarchate on 6 January 1454; established a Jewish grand rabbi and an Armenian patriarch in the city. He tried successfully to make people of all faiths feel safe in Constantinople. Meanwhile, most of the time, the Muslims had allowed Christians to visit the Holy Land unmolested, keep their churches there, worship; allowed an annual fair on Mount Calvary; allowed the foundation of the order of the Knights of St John.[26]

In the period of the Crusades, the Catholic Church was based on an elite of cardinals who picked their successors. They had enormous power because one part of the Church's teaching had caught on: the fear of eternal damnation for sinners. To escape eternal burning in Hell, men of the day, however powerful, begged for absolution, the pardon that only the Church could accord, they thought. This gave huge power to the religious elite.

This Catholic religious elite could organize a Crusade that sapped the foundations of the Christian Byzantine Empire.

The Vatican could also make a western emperor bend. In February 1076, Pope Gregory VII had excommunicated Henry, a German king, Emperor of the Western Holy Roman Empire. The pope pronounced against Henry the grand malediction of the Church. He released Henry's subjects from their oaths of obedience to him. The German aristocracy told Henry that if he did not obtain absolution from the pope, they would elect a new emperor. Here, in Pope Gregory's own words, is what happened next at the pope's Canossa residence, high in the Apennines, in January 1077.

> Henry came in person to Canossa. He presented himself at the gate of the castle, barefoot and clad only in wretched woollen garments, beseeching us with tears to grant him absolution and forgiveness. This he continued to do for three days. At length we removed the excommunication from him and received him again into the bosom of the Church.[27]

It is important to remember what Catholic bishops told the Franks and Venetians: attack Constantinople; 'this war is a righteous one because the Greeks are traitors, worse than Jews.' Moreover, the bishops said that, by the authority of God and in the name of the pope, they would absolve all who attacked the Greeks.[28] According to the bishops, it was all right with the Christian God to attack another ethnicity, even a Christian ethnicity. In Constantinople, the Catholic bishops sanctified the ethnic hatred of strangers, especially those who speak an unfamiliar tongue.

Parenthetically, one should not conclude that brutality and ethnic hatred were a monopoly belonging to the Catholic Church or to the Franks and Venetians who took Constantinople. The Greek Orthodox Byzantines were no better. Their treatment of Christian sects other than the one approved by the Byzantine emperor and the patriarch of Constantinople, was appalling. Constantine V (741–75) attacked the Christian Iconolaters, who worshipped icons. He tortured Iconolaters, tore out their tongues, eyes and noses, beheaded their prelates.[29]

Through the sanguinary zeal of Inquisitors appointed by a Byzantine empress, another Theodora (981–1056), 100,000 members of the Christian Paulician sect* 'were extirpated by the sword, the gibbet or the flames.'[30] One result of such atrocities was that the persecuted Christian minorities allied themselves with the Muslims. Here is what Gibbon says.

> Carbeas, a valiant Paulician, whose father had been impaled by the Byzantine Inquisitors, swore allegiance to the Muslim Caliph. The dissolute Byzantine Emperor Michael was compelled to march in person against the Paulicians; he was defeated. In alliance with his faithful Muslims, Chrysocheir, Carbeas' successor, a Christian, pillaged Christian cities, Nicomedia, Ancyra and Ephesus. The Cathedral of Ephesus was turned into a stable for mules and horses. A new Byzantine Emperor, Basil I, was reduced to sue for peace, to offer a ransom for the captives and to request that Chrysocheir would spare his fellow Christians. Chrysocheir replied: 'Let the Emperor abdicate.' In response, Basil led his army into the land of heresy which he wasted with fire and sword.[31]

---

* The Paulicians especially valued the Gospel of Luke and the Pauline Epistles. They rejected the sacraments but nevertheless considered baptism of the greatest importance. They were iconoclasts and rejected extreme asceticism.

10

CONQUERING
LATIN AMERICA

(16th century)

In Europe things did not change very much with the passage of centuries. There was the Hundred Years War between England and France.[1] I think of it as a drug war. The drug of choice, then, was wine. The best wine came from Aquitaine (the Bordeaux region) and from Burgundy. The English and French kings fought one another furiously to control these choice wine-growing regions – a lot of commercial profit was at stake.

The war lasted intermittently for more than 100 years – from 1337 to 1453. The pretext was inheritance. The royal families of the two countries had intermarried. So who had the right to inherit what? Dying kings occasionally left wills, but as the saying goes, where there's a will, there are relatives. By 1422, the English and their Burgundian allies controlled Aquitaine and all of France north of the river Loire. Joan of Arc became involved, buoying up the spirits of the French. She was captured by the Burgundians, who sold her to the English, who burned her at the stake for heresy, the pretext of choice for burning people in those days. Eventually the Burgundians switched sides, and by 1453 the French had taken back all their land from the English except for Calais, which Queen Mary eventually lost. All the above is well documented and no one disputes what happened. The only difference is in how national school books treat these events. In French books the heroes are French, the villains English, and vice-versa. But it was all about who controlled the largest turf, with more lands to exploit and more subjects to tax.

The enemy did not have to be from another country. No sooner had the English stopped fighting the French in the Hundred Years War than they began fighting one another in the so-called Wars of the Roses. The noble house of York which used a white rose as an emblem fought the noble house of Lancaster which used a red one. Both houses claimed the throne because they were both descended from Edward III who reigned from 1327 to 1377 and led England against France in the Hundred Years War. His descendants fought one another from 1455 to 1485. Richard Plantagenet, Duke of York, claimed the throne. But he was defeated and killed by the Lancastrians at Wakefield. His son was proclaimed King Edward IV, and slaughtered the Lancastrians mercilessly at the battle of Towton, the bloodiest engagement of the war. He had ups and downs. The great nobles betrayed and counter-betrayed. But Edward IV died king, in his bed. However, his brother who succeeded him, Richard III, was not so lucky: the Lancastrians under Henry Tudor defeated and killed Richard III at Bosworth field on 22 August 1485. Henry Tudor became Henry VII. His son was Henry VIII, he who beheaded his wives.

Richard III suffered the fate of all the defeated. His character was totally blackened. History is written by the victors and the playwrights who work for them. Shakespeare paints Richard III as a monster. He is now being rehabilitated by busy doctoral candidates.

That concluded the Wars of the Roses, but there were so many such wars. In the 210 years from 1469 to 1679 there was hardly a year without a war. There were wars fought by, against, among and with Austria, Bohemia, Denmark, England, France, various German states, Hungary, Ireland, Italy, Moldavia, the Netherlands, Norway, the Ottoman Empire, Poland, Portugal, Russia, Scotland, Spain, Sweden, Venice. There were years in those two centuries when several different wars were going on at the same time.

The Appendix on p. 229, A Sobering Chronology of War, provides a list of dates, the sort of list that poisons the life of school children. Readers do not have to memorize it. Let them contemplate the monstrous enormity of it. Think of the pillage, raping and slaughter suffered to get the grand acquisitors more turf.

The list contains wars of religion, which we shall examine in Chapter 11. The rise of Protestantism in its two initial forms, Lutheranism and Calvinism, contributed to the rise of the bourgeoisie, of city merchants and artisans who, as in the days of Solon, began to sow the seeds for a revival of democracy.*

This burgeoning of a bourgeoisie that would eventually claim power is one of the two seminal developments that took place as Europe passed from the fifteenth century to the sixteenth. The other was the discovery of the Americas.

Without discontinuing their mutual slaughter for turf on their own continent, the European grand acquisitors almost immediately sought new killing fields in this new continent. The most spectacular leaders of these invasions were the Spanish conquistadores, Hernan Cortés and Francisco Pizarro. They were of the stuff that the mythical ancient Greek heroes were made of: Jason who stole the Golden Fleece; Ulysses who tricked the Trojans into letting him take their city;

---

* Catholic merchants and artisans also played a role in the eventual revival of Solonian democracy that had been dormant for centuries. But they were influenced by and they influenced their Protestant colleagues.

Theseus whose killing of the Minotaur symbolizes the seizing of the Minoan empire by the Greeks.

Chronologically, in our story of the Americas, Cortés comes first.

Cortés (1485–1547)

As an adolescent, Cortés was known to be quarrelsome and a successfully avid womanizer. In 1504, at nineteen, he left Spain and sailed for Hispaniola,* where he became a farmer, was active in municipal affairs and impressed everyone with his aristocratic bearing and manners.[2]

He caught syphilis but was lucky – he was one of those in whom the disease becomes latent: it's there but not progressing to the awful third stage, which affects the nervous system and kills.

In 1511, at the age of twenty-six and recovered, he sailed with Diego Velázquez from Hispaniola to conquer Cuba. There, Cortés acquired a substantial estate and Indian slaves: the slaves were local aborigines, not Indians, of course, but the name has stuck. Cortés built the first house in Santiago, the new capital of the island; he was elected mayor there twice. He continued to impress everyone with his aristocratic bearing but also with his administrative efficiency. Which may be why, in 1518, Governor Velázquez of Cuba appointed him captain general of an expedition to conquer the mainland of Mexico.

In no time at all, Córtes found eleven ships, sixteen horses and 508 Spaniards willing to serve under his banner. He was much admired by the Spanish community in Cuba. Some were even saying things would be better if he ruled rather than

---

* The island of Hispaniola which today contains Haiti and the Dominican Republic had already been colonized by the Spaniards.

Velázquez. This was reported to Velázquez, who became furiously jealous and anxious lest he be overthrown by Cortés. Cortés heard that Velázquez was trying to replace him as leader of the expedition; so, before Velázquez had completed the arrangements for firing him, Cortés sailed.

On the mainland of Mexico, Cortés put his soldiers through rigorous training and imposed strict discipline. He told them that there was no retreat. To prove it, he burned his ships, save one. Win, conquer or perish.

When he had to, Cortés fought the Indians; but he won them over when he could, exploiting their dislike for the Aztecs, the dominant local tribe, who had subjugated them and forced them to pay tribute. So many of the Indians joined Cortés, in particular the Tlaxcaltecs. He was given presents, including twenty women. One of these, Malinche, he took as his mistress. We can assume that she learned Spanish very quickly because she became his interpreter. As we shall see, she played a critical role in the conquest. She also gave Cortés a son, Martin.

The Aztec emperor, Montezuma, was not happy that Cortés had landed on the Yucatan peninsula. So Montezuma sent messengers begging Cortés to go away. But the emperor also sent fabulously rich gifts – a huge mistake. Seeing the gold, silver and jewels, Cortés insisted he would visit Montezuma in Tenochtitlán, the Aztec capital, now called Mexico City.

Montezuma could have kept the Spanish forces out of his capital. But Montezuma was very religious. He believed in the legend of his faith that the god Quetzalcoatl would come some day to rule the earth. This god was depicted as having a beard, light skin, red hair and green eyes. From all reports, Cortés also had a beard, light skin, red hair and green eyes. In Montezuma's mind, Cortés resembled and therefore was Quetzalcoatl. So Montezuma made the pivotal mistake that would seal his and Mexico's fate: he let Cortés enter Tenochtitlán.

When, on 8 November 1519, Cortés, his Spaniards and an allied contingent of 1,000 Tlaxcaltec warriors entered Tenochtitlán, he was received like a god. We do not know when Cortés realized that he was believed to be the god Quetzalcoatl. Did the Indians he first met on the Yucatan peninsula believe him to be a divinity? Or was it only the ultra-religious Montezuma who so believed? And was it Malinche who explained the Quetzalcoatl angle to her Spanish lover and master? At any rate, Cortés decided to make Montezuma his captive and rule Mexico through him. Malinche, at Cortés' bidding, played mind games with Montezuma, our sources say, and turned him into a willing tool of Cortés.

One would like to know more about this young Indian girl. Did she, too, believe Cortés was the god Quetzalcoatl? Did she simply love Cortés? Was she merely serving the man to whom she had been given as a slave and who had raised her social status? We do not know.

What were the mind games Malinche played with Montezuma? Did she accentuate his belief that Cortés was Quetzalcoatl? And how? We can only let our imagination run wild. Whatever she did, it worked.

By then, Velázquez, the Spanish governor of Cuba, could not contain his jealousy of Cortés and sent two expeditions to depose him. Cortés annihilated the first, defeated the second; its troops joined him. However, when he sallied forth to fight his fellow Spaniards, he left a garrison of just eighty people to hold Tenochtitlán. This garrison panicked when it saw thousands of Aztecs converging on Montezuma's palace. The Spaniards slaughtered 3,400 Aztec notables who had only come there for a religious ceremony. Outraged, the inhabitants of the capital attacked the Spanish garrison (the Aztecs were no cowards). The Spaniards barricaded themselves in the palace and sent out Montezuma to pacify his people.

Here the Aztec emperor had a second chance. He could have told his people he would lead them to avenge the outrageous killing of 3,400 noble Aztecs. But no. Montezuma had sworn allegiance to the king of Spain; he had meekly converted to Christianity and allowed sacred Aztec statues to be replaced in his temples by Catholic holy images. The Aztecs had lost all respect for Montezuma, and when they saw him coming out of the palace, they stoned him. He died two weeks later. Of his wounds? Of a broken heart? Humiliation?

Cortés came back to the Aztec capital, but had to retreat with heavy losses. Within a week, however, he defeated the Aztecs at the battle of Otumba. Eventually he took back Tenochtitlán, street by bloody street, and became the uncontested ruler of the Aztec empire.

The success of Cortés only served to increase the jealousy of Velázquez who plotted with his friends in Madrid against Cortés. They said he had become a powerful monarch and would renounce his allegiance to Spain and proclaim himself an independent king.

Cortés defended himself by writing letters to the king of Spain. Texts of five of those still exist. Here are excerpts from the first one:

This great city of Tenochtitlán contains a large number of grand temples housing the images of idols which I precipitated from their pedestals, and cast them down the steps of the temple. In the place of these I put images of Our Lady and the Saints, which excited not a little feeling in Montezuma who said that if the idols were ill-treated, these would be angry and the people would perish with famine. I answered, through the interpreters, that he was deceived in expecting any favours from idols. That he must learn there is but one God, the universal Lord of all, who had created the heavens and earth, and all things else, and had made him and us. That God was without beginning and immortal, and they were bound to adore and believe Him, and no other creature or thing. Montezuma replied, his attendants assenting to what he said, that if I would instruct them in these matters, and make them understand the true faith, they would follow my directions. I forbade them sacrificing human beings to their idols as they had been accustomed to do; because, besides being abhorrent in the sight of God, your sacred Majesty had prohibited it by law. I ordered to put to death whoever should take the life of another. In regard to the domestic appointments of Montezuma, every object – plant, bird, animal – found in his dominions is imitated in gold, silver, precious stones and feathers; the gold and silver being wrought so naturally as not to be surpassed by any smith in the world.

The key points of this and the other letters were (1) the incredible wealth of the Aztecs; and (2) that Cortés was converting them to Christianity. He thus appealed to the religiosity and avarice of King Charles. Along with his letters, Cortés sent the Spanish monarch vast amounts of gold, silver and precious stones. Enchanted by the flow of treasure from Mexico, the king of Spain made Cortés a marquess and ordered the royal courtiers to leave him in peace.

They pretended they would, but didn't. The people on the immediate staff of a king don't like those who bypass them and get direct access to the boss. So they gnawed at Cortés, instituting enquiries to question his conduct, bringing him back from Mexico to defend himself in court; which got him into debt. The courtiers and some of his subordinates harassed him relentlessly. Sick and poor, he died in Spain.

Pizarro (c. 1475–1541)

Francisco Pizarro was the bastard son of a poor girl who was seduced by Captain Gonzalo Pizarro. The little boy lived with his mother's parents and herded swine. He never learned to read or write. As soon as he could, he entered the military life and fought in Italy. In 1502, at the age of twenty-seven, he sailed for Hispaniola. In 1513, at thirty-eight, he served with the rank of captain in the expedition led by Vasco Núñez de Balboa, the European discoverer of the Pacific. Pizarro, people said, was silent, unambitious, totally reliable in a tight spot. Then he settled down and for four years from 1519 was mayor and magistrate of the newly founded town of Panama. He amassed a modest fortune.

But Pizarro was not a man for the settled life. At forty-eight, he set off again with two partners Diego de Almagro and Hernando de Luque, a priest. Others joined. They sailed on the Pacific, south of Panama; suffered in storms; lost men. But in 1528 they encountered a raft laden with precious metals from Peru. Pizarro sent to Panama asking for reinforcements. The Spanish governor there refused and ordered Pizarro back to avoid further losses. On an island off the coast of Ecuador, Pizarro drew a line on the sand with his sword. Let those who want wealth and glory cross it, he said. Thirteen did. He returned to Panama, sailed to Spain to ask the king for a commission to conquer what appeared to be a very rich land.

King Charles gave Pizarro a decoration, granted him a coat of arms – made him a noble in other words. He also appointed him governor and captain general of the province of New Castile, the official name given to a territory stretching some

1,000 kilometres south of Panama along the Pacific coast.

With four of his brothers, Pizarro returned to Panama. In January 1531, when he was a leathery fifty-six years old, he set sail for Peru with 180 men, some artillery and thirty-seven horses. Four months later, he had communicated with Atahualpa, the Sapa Inca (which meant the emperor of the Incas). Atahualpa discussed the matter with his council. Should they attack these strangers, councillors asked, and destroy them immediately? Why bother, said Atahualpa. What could 180 men do? So the Sapa Inca gave permission for Pizarro to visit the city of Cajamarca.

Pizarro arrived on 15 November 1531, entered the city, set up his artillery and sent his brother Hernando to request an interview with the emperor. The Sapa Inca was camped with his huge army near the city. The next day, Atahualpa, borne on a litter, entered the great square of Cajamarca with an escort of between 3,000 and 4,000 men. Outside there was an army that Pizarro's brother said numbered 40,000 (or 80,000 according to other Spaniards who were scared out of their wits). Here is how Francisco de Xeres, Pizarro's secretary, describes the fateful scene:

> Pizarro sent Vicente de Valverde, a priest, to exhort the Inca to accept Christianity and King Charles as his master. Atahualpa took the Bible proffered by the priest and flung it to the ground. Then he said, through the interpreter, that he knew how badly the Spaniards had behaved, ill-treating Inca chiefs and stealing cloth from the king's storehouses. Friar Vicente replied that the Christians had not done any of those bad things; some Indians who accompanied them were the culprits. The cloth would be restored. Atahualpa said he would not budge until all the cloth was returned to him.

Pizarro then attacked and he himself dragged Atahualpa down from his litter and made him prisoner.* The other Spaniards, among them thirty-seven on horseback, slaughtered Atahualpa's escort.

So there sat 40,000–80,000 Inca soldiers pondering the event. Atahualpa was not just their emperor; he was also an incarnation of the Sun God. His subjects were supposed to obey him totally. If the Incas attacked, they would certainly overwhelm Pizarro's force despite its terrifying horses and cannon. But what if these strangers killed the Sapa Inca?

The thought crossed Atahualpa's mind too. He promised to fill with gold the room in which he was held prisoner; reportedly the room measured 18 by 20 feet (approximately 5.4 × 6 m) and was 8 feet (2.4 m) high. His troops heard of this: their god-emperor did not want them to fight; he wanted them to collect his ransom.

The ransom arrived – the roomful of gold plus a large bonus of silver and precious stones. Was Atahualpa freed? Of course not. The Spaniards accused Atahualpa of plotting to overthrow them and condemned him to be burned to death. He was told he would be spared if he became a Christian, which he did. Pizarro reduced the sentence from burning to strangulation. Atahualpa was garotted in front of his people on 29 August 1533.

Astonishingly, the Inca armies surrounding Cajamarca retreated, and Pizarro progressed toward Cuzco, the royal capital, which he occupied without a struggle in November 1533. Pizarro ruled Peru through Manco Capa, a half-brother of Atahualpa whom the Spaniards established as the Sapa Inca. Pizarro sent much gold to the king of Spain with his

---

* On his visit to Spain Pizarro had met Cortés, who no doubt described the capture of Montezuma and the advantage of holding an Indian emperor prisoner.

brother Fernando, who was made a knight of Santiago. Francisco Pizarro was made a marquess.

Almagro, one of Pizarro's original partners, felt he was not getting a fair share of the spoils even though he was given what today is Chile. He rebelled, took Cuzco, the Inca capital, temporarily, was eventually arrested and executed by Pizarro. Almagro's relatives and some of his followers attacked Pizarro's palace in Lima on 26 June 1541. The old conquistador fought fiercely, but died of sword wounds. At the last, with his own blood, he drew a cross on the floor, kissed it and died, shouting 'Jesus'.

How to explain these two conquests? How to explain Montezuma's failure to keep the Spaniards out of the Aztec capital, from where they sallied to take the whole of Mexico? Montezuma could indeed have kept the Spaniards out. He ruled over a territory almost equal to modern Mexico; he had much wealth from trade and from the tribute conquered nations paid him. He was respected and admired by his people: among other things he had built a double aqueduct to bring drinking water to his capital. Moreover, Montezuma had tens of thousands of soldiers and was not an inconsiderable military leader. As commander-in-chief he had won forty-three battles. With a population of over 300,000, the Aztec capital was larger than any city in Europe at the time and had extensive and intricate fortifications.

Again, how to explain the conquest by Pizarro's 180 Spaniards of the Incas' Peruvian empire? Surely the Incas could have overwhelmed the Spaniards. After all, there were millions of Incas.* The Incas were remarkable engineers; superb

---

* These population figures – all population figures about Latin America in the sixteenth century – are open to doubt. There certainly was no Inca census. We know from the text of Pizarro's secretary that the Spanish estimates of how many Inca soldiers they were *seeing* before Cajamarca, varied between 40,000 and 80,000.

goldsmiths. They used the cold temperatures of their mountain peaks to 'freeze dry' food for storage. They had a system of decimal counting using strings instead of written symbols. They did not know the wheel; they had no writing; but they had a system of official communications which resembled a relay race: a messenger was given an oral message, ran a given distance and spoke the message to another messenger waiting there and so on – from one end of the empire to the other.

In his excellent book *Guns, Germs and Steel*,[3] Jared Diamond tried to answer the question of why so few Spaniards managed to conquer Mexico and Peru, defeating millions of people. The words of Diamond's title are his answer – guns, germs and steel – plus the horses. How valid is this answer?

The Spaniards had very few guns. Both the Aztecs and the Incas had such an overwhelming superiority in numbers that they could have mounted human wave attacks at the guns from all sides and subdued the gun crews. Admittedly the Spaniards had steel helmets, steel breastplates and steel swords, yet ancient Greek peltasts, soldiers with no armour at all, equipped only with sling shots and bows and arrows, often defeated the heavily armoured and highly trained Spartan infantry: the peltasts stayed out of the Spartans' range and rained stones and arrows on them. In any case, human waves of Indians attacking from all sides would have overwhelmed the tiny Spanish contingents. Years later, armoured Spaniards with steel swords, cannon and horses, had a much harder time fighting the Argentinian Indians, who resisted fiercely even though they were no better armed than the Aztecs or the Incas.

Diamond also says that the Spaniards brought with them germs to which the Indians had no immunity. Yes, but the devastating epidemics of smallpox and measles had not yet done their work when Cortés and Pizarro attacked in Mexico and Peru.

No, the explanation for the astonishing success of a handful of Spaniards in Mexico and Peru is that they were led by Cortés and Pizarro, two militarily talented and wildly daring Spanish grand acquisitors, who beat the Aztec and Inca grand acquisitors: for both Montezuma and Atahualpa were grand acquisitors: slaughtering, conquering, subjugating and exploiting neighbouring nations.

Of course, in a clash between grand acquisitors, superiority in weapons may decide who wins – other things being equal. But for Cortés and Pizarro, other things were not equal. They won against truly overwhelming odds by seizing and holding the leaders of their opponents.

The Aztecs and the Incas, unfortunately for them, thought that Montezuma and Atahualpa were gods. And these two Indian rulers, as prisoners, did their captors' bidding and paralysed their people. This lasted long enough for the conquest. After that, the epidemics did their worst.

How many Indians died of these epidemics? Undoubtedly, very many. Diamond says that 'by 1618, Mexico's initial population of about 20 million had plummeted to about 1.6 million.' By 'initial', Diamond means before the first epidemic started in 1520.[4] I do not doubt that a large percentage of Mexico's native population died; but how do we know it had been 20 million to start with? Or that Peru had a population of 12 million when first Pizarro arrived?

Yes, the conquest of the Americas devastated the native populations but not only through European diseases. The natives – let us inaccurately call them Indians – were exploited abominably by their conquerors. Indians were assigned to a Spanish settler and they were obliged to pay him a tribute and give him their labour. This practice, called *encomenda*, was just a form of slavery. Another form of slavery was debt peonage: Indians were forced to work for a Spanish landlord for wages or a share of the crop; when their income turned out to be insufficient, the landlord would lend them money on such terms that they could never be free of debt and would, therefore, be his slaves for life.

Large landlords were absolute masters on their estates. They made the 'laws', imposed them, executed 'offenders', fornicated with their female subjects at will and unsurprisingly received absolution for their sins from the priests who were on the landowners' payrolls.

The Spanish crown, in theory, was interested in preserving the natives so that they could pay tribute. It sold colonial public service jobs to the highest bidders. The officials in these colonial government jobs did nothing to regulate the behaviour of the Spanish settlers. The settlers bribed the officials, so these would not interfere with the ruthless exploitation of the natives.

Corruption was, therefore, a congenital disease of the Spanish and Portuguese rule in the Americas. And violence. Large landowners developed their own armies and were veritable warlords. Spain's and Portugal's colonies in the Americas fought for and won their independence in the nineteenth century. 'Liberator' generals became rulers, *caudillos*, who put down the private armies, replacing them with a national army of their own. It was rule by violence. And corruption continued to flourish, of course. Government jobs were still sold by the caudillo to the highest bidders, who recouped what their jobs had cost them by extorting money from the people.

Caudillo rule lasted a long time, till quite recently. Think of Batista, Noriega, Trujillo, Perón, Pinochet, Duvalier, Stroessner. They held elections and won hugely because bullets trump ballots and also because caudillos always controlled the media and the army. Caudillos were replaced eventually by *juntas*;

these were committees of officers representing all branches of the armed forces; they held the real power even though there generally was a figurehead. Bolivia was ruled by military juntas well into the 1980s. Argentina was last ruled by a military junta from 1976 to 1983; Uruguay from 1973 to 1985. And so on. Nearly everywhere in Latin America, the corruption continued unabated. In 1985, a civilian not supported by the military, José Sarney, was inaugurated president of Brazil; but there too a military junta had ruled for the previous twenty-one years.

There was a racial element in all this. To start with, following the conquest, there were never enough white women. So the white settlers fathered children (*mestizos*) by Indian women, and (*mulattos*) by black slave women. Among these, some with light skin came to 'pass', especially if they had inherited from a loving white father. The lighter the skin, the higher you could go. Colour was all important, in the armed forces too. It is an unspoken policy but a very real one. This is similar to the Platonic assumption that there is an elite with all the rights and a mass of inferior people with only obligations: not a good foundation for democracy. At least, much of the Latin American Church no longer sees itself as the servant of whoever rules the country. More and more priests are turning to liberation theology, which is concerned for the subjects rather than the masters or the Vatican, which still insists that the women who live in unspeakable slums should not use contraceptives. Will liberation theology help democracy make lasting inroads? It is too early to tell.

11

THE CONCEPTION
AND BIRTH-PANGS
OF PROTESTANTISM

(1517–1610)

Luther, Calvin and Henri IV of France

Protestantism shook Europe to its foundations, shook its kings, shook its popes. Its great champion was a German Augustinian monk called Martin Luther (1483–1546), but there were precursors to Luther.

The Englishman John Wycliffe, also spelled Wyclif (1330–84), translated the Bible into English so all the people could read what God said rather than accept what the Church claimed God said.[1] The Scriptures, Wycliffe preached, were the only source of Christian doctrine. He also wanted the Church to give up its wealth to the poor, which did not make him popular with the Archbishop of Canterbury, who banned all his writings.

Jan Hus (1372–1415) lived in what is now called the Czech Republic. He was influenced by Wycliffe and rebelled against the economic oppression of the people by the powerful and by the senior clergy. He also condemned the indulgences that were being sold to finance the fight of popes against anti-popes: at one time there were three popes simultaneously – each calling the other two anti-popes. Hus was tricked into attending a Council of the Church at Konstanz, Germany. 'Let's just talk this over,' the prelates told him. They burned him at the stake for heresy.[2]

But the real founders of Protestantism are Martin Luther (1483–1546) and John Calvin (1509–64). What they wrought led to social development different in some parts of Europe from others; different development too in North America under Protestantism from that in Latin America under Catholicism. Which brings us to Julius II, the warrior pope, and to the building of St Peter's basilica, which Julius II financed by turning loose religious scam artists who sold indulgences like snake oil. These indulgences were pieces of paper you could buy from the Church that forgave your sins and guaranteed you would not spend eternity in Hell. People could also buy an indulgence that shortened the time a dead relative stayed in purgatory before entering paradise. This stuck in the craw of Martin Luther and led to his rebellion against the Church and launched the Protestant movement and a new round of religious wars.

Julius II was born Giuliano della Rovere, in 1443. He grew up poor; but he was very lucky: in 1471 his uncle Francesco della Rovere became pope under the name Sixtus IV and made the twenty-eight-year-old Giuliano, son of his only brother, a cardinal; giving him, moreover, six bishoprics in France, three in Italy plus a slew of wealthy abbeys and other rich sources of income. This was a breathtaking act of nepotism, a word which means favouring your *nepos*, Latin for nephew.*

---

* The illegitimate son of a pope was also called his '*nepos*' and given lucrative privileges.

condemned some people to eternal damnation before they were even born, whereas others, the elect, God favoured in this life and in the next, no matter what they did on earth. Calvin was consoled by the thought that the elect would be spared by God – he thought of himself, presumably, as being one of the elect. Luther and Calvin both rejected the celibacy of Catholic priests. They had many differences of opinion but this is not a book on theology.[4] It is about the political effect Luther and Calvin had.[5]

It has been said of Catholic and Byzantine theologians that they had long disputations on the number of angels who fit on the head of a pin. Similar things can be said about Protestants and any statement about them will cause disputations. It is enough to say that the Lutherans held that the Scriptures contained all that was necessary for salvation, which came by faith alone. Baptism was necessary and also the sacrament of the Lord's Supper, though they rejected the doctrine of transubstantiation: that the bread actually changes into Christ's flesh during Holy Communion. They developed – with bishops – into an establishment Church that is joining forces now with the quintessential establishment Church, the Episcopalians or Anglicans.

The Protestant theological line that goes back to Calvin emphasizes personal salvation and, in fact, conversion to the faith. Consequently many of them consider they are the elect of God chosen to revolutionize society. The effect of early Lutheranism and Calvinism did revolutionize society. The theological descendants of Calvin are now called by various names – Reformed, or Presbyterians, Born Again, Puritans, Fundamentalist Christians, Baptists, Anabaptists. To simplify matters – no offence meant – they will all be called Calvinists hereafter. They will also be included in the more comprehensive term 'Protestants'. To be perfectly clear, hereafter, for the purposes of this text, all Calvinists are also Protestants; but not all Protestants are Calvinists.

Before Protestantism, the clergy interpreted the will of God. St Peter, the first bishop, allegedly chosen by Jesus, appointed bishops by the laying on of hands. An elite emerged among the Catholic bishops called cardinals, who exercised the right to elect a pope. Thereafter the popes picked the cardinals as well as the bishops, who picked their subordinates. Therefore, before Protestantism, the interpretation of the word of God came to the ordinary Christian down a hierarchy established by St Peter. This clerical hierarchy, strong in its alleged monopoly of God's teaching, associated itself with the temporal power by anointing kings. These kings then claimed that they reigned 'by the grace of God'.

Into this cosy arrangement, the Protestants erupted, casting doubt on the legitimacy of the Church's claim to speak for God; casting doubt, therefore, on the divine derivation of the anointment of kings; which put in doubt the allegedly divine right of kings to rule.

Any man with a Bible in his hand, the Protestants said, was the equal of any prelate in understanding God. Luther translated the Bible from Latin to German.* Soon, other translations of the Bible appeared in various languages so the common literate man could read the good book. The multitudes might now be as able as any prelate to understand the will of God. Gutenberg's invention of movable type made the Old Testament and the New Testament easily available.† And the desire and obligation of Protestants to read the Bible led to the spread of literacy – a social revolution.

---

* Luther imitated the syntax of Tacitus who, like many Latin authors, tended to put the verbs at the end of very long sentences; this influenced German writing. An academic joke says that a German professor wrote a book in six volumes, with all the verbs in the sixth.
† Gutenberg died in 1468.

Moreover, the doctrinal descendants of Calvin gave power to their congregations. The pastor had to heed the parishioners' votes on how their places of worship were run – an important step towards a revival of Solon's democratic institutions.

Calvinists 'knew' they were right and that they had the right to impose their lifestyle on whichever their nation was. And they were awfully earnest in everything, especially their views of morality – they knew they were predestined to do just that.

Couldn't a king argue that he was predestined to be a king? The Calvinists' counter-argument would be that if they overthrew a king it would be because they were predestined to overthrow a king. Which is what the Calvinists did in Britain: they beheaded Charles I and named their leader, Cromwell, lord protector of the realm.

Many of these stiff-necked Calvinists, earnest religious moralists all, took their attitudes and lifestyle along with them when they founded colonies in America. They were admirable in many ways. Just as, through the centuries, there have been admirable Catholics or Orthodox or Muslims etc. But the Calvinists carried within them the seeds of the rotten apples that they, like other religious groups, would inevitably produce. The excessively literal interpretation of the Scriptures by large numbers of Calvinists led to the hanging of women in Salem, Massachusetts, in 1692, on the grounds that they were witches and, in 1925, to the tragicomedy of Dayton, Tennessee, where a young schoolmaster was tried for daring to teach the theory of evolution.

To avoid being sued for citing contemporary religious frauds, it is safer to mention a fictional Calvinist, Elmer Gantry, the protagonist of the novel bearing his name. Sinclair Lewis, the author of this book, did not miss his target, the greedy acquisitors who disgraced and still disgrace their Calvinist faith for money. But these bad apples cannot wipe out the contributions of Calvinism mentioned above, contributions to the development of democratic institutions and literacy; which led the Catholic Church to clean up its act where Protestantism was strong.[6]

Many Calvinists stayed in Europe, where they were persecuted by those whose authority they challenged: the prelates and the kings. In France, these Calvinists were called Huguenots and they were fought by the Catholics for thirty-six years. There were wars of religion all over Europe but 'wars of religion' is largely a misnomer. Everyone, of course, claimed the religious, moral high ground. But, more often than not, the claims had nothing moral about them: they were just grabs for more ground, literally, and for more people to be taxed by the grand acquisitors. To gain territory in Lorraine, the Catholic French King Henri II supported the Protestants. Protestant German princes fought against French Protestants. The very Catholic King of Spain, Philip II, sided, on occasion, with the Protestant Henri of Navarre. Catholics also fought one another in these so-called wars of religion. Protestant mercenaries on one side fought Protestant mercenaries on the other side. And the same was true of Catholic mercenaries.

The most attractive personage in those times of troubles is Henri IV of France, a brilliant, roguish, eloquent, raunchy guy, whom the religious right of his day hated. Henri (1553–1610), a member of the Bourbon family, was born Prince of Navarre, a small Protestant kingdom in the foothills of the Pyrenées, the mountains between France and Spain. His contemporaries referred to him as 'Navarre' until he became king of France. From a tender age, he fought successfully in the field of battle at the head of Protestant contingents against Catholic armies.

A peace treaty was signed between France's two religious camps in 1570. In June 1572, on his mother's death, Prince Henri became king of Navarre. To seal the peace agreement, Navarre married Marguerite (Margot), sister of Charles IX, the Valois king of France. The marriage took place on 18 August 1572. Most of the French Protestant nobility were invited. This was a good opportunity, the Catholic leaders thought, to decapitate the Protestant movement by killing its leaders. Just six days after the wedding that was supposed to symbolize the reconciliation of the two religious factions, before dawn on 24 August, the feast day of St Bartholomew, the massacre of Protestants began, with the approval of the queen mother, the ultra-Catholic Catherine de' Medici.

Navarre's Protestant attendants at the Louvre were massacred before his eyes. He, a prisoner in the French king's palace, was not sure, that terrible night, whether he would escape slaughter. He was only spared because he had just married the French king's sister. Navarre's beloved mentor, the Protestant admiral Gaspard de Coligny, Seigneur de Chatillon, was slain, despite the great services he had rendered the king of France.[7]

The Duc de Guise, head of the Catholic 'Holy League', was in full command of the massacre. He told his troops that they would face no danger and would collect much booty: for the small acquisitors serving as mercenaries, booty was important. To avoid killing one another, they wore a white arm band and a white cross on their hats. And they were told to start slaughtering when the palace bells rang.

Coligny had heard the noise. He put on his dressing gown. He did not think he was in danger because he was the king's devoted servant. But then he heard a gunshot in his courtyard. He told his retinue to flee through the attic and the roofs. He said his prayers. The slaughterers entered and Coligny fell under repeated sword thrusts.

They threw his body out of the window so the Duc de Guise could have it identified. They cut off Coligny's head and sent it to Rome. They castrated the body, dragged it through the streets and hung it by the feet from a gibbet.

Protestant men were butchered. The women were butchered too, after they were raped. The orgy of killing spread to the provinces, to Protestant cities such as Bordeaux, Bourges, Lyon, Orleans and Rouen. The victims were industrious people, often well-off bourgeoisie, fine targets for envy and pillage. The horror lasted for weeks. The Catholics claimed that only 2,000 were killed. The Duc de Sully, a Protestant, later the chief public servant of France, put the toll at 70,000.

The Catholic king of Spain celebrated the killings. Pope Gregory XIII, to whom the head of Coligny had been sent, held a thanksgiving mass and struck a commemorative medal to mark the elimination of so many heretics.

Navarre remained a prisoner, to all intents and purposes, at the palace of his brother-in-law Charles IX, who died and was succeeded by his brother, Henri III. Navarre, who had converted to Catholicism to save his skin while at the royal palace in Paris, escaped in 1576. He renounced his conversion and reverted to Protestantism. As king of Navarre he signed a peace treaty the next year to put an end to the fighting between the king of France and the Protestant forces, which were faring badly.

Then, François, Duc D'Anjou, brother of Henri III, of France died in 1584. Henri III, a homosexual, was childless. The royal Valois line was ending. Navarre suddenly became heir presumptive to the throne of France – he had the best genealogical claim. But the grandees who ran the Catholic forces of France, the 'Holy League', would not accept Henri of Navarre as heir to the throne. The pope excommunicated him and declared him devoid of any right to inherit the crown. And the Holy League chose the daughter of Philip II of Spain as the next ruler of France.

Henri III realized that, the way things were going, his realm would become a vassal of Spain. He allied himself with Navarre, then had the Duc de Guise, head of the Holy League, assassinated, in December 1588. On 1 August 1589, stabbed by a Holy League assassin, Henri III, on his deathbed, proclaimed Navarre his successor.

For nine long years, Navarre now Henri IV, king of France, fought the Holy League for his kingdom. He won many important battles against Catholic armies that outnumbered him. But to get Paris itself he had finally to reconvert, becoming a Catholic again in 1593. 'Paris is well worth a mass,' he said, famously. Many didn't quite believe in his conversion; but many of his opponents were tired of the war. So they accepted him and he entered Paris triumphantly. The pope removed the excommunication he had earlier proclaimed and even annulled the marriage of Henri IV and his wife, Marguerite de Valois, known as la Reine Margot, of whom more anon.

Henri IV still had to fight Spain and the Holy League; after he defeated them decisively in 1597, a peace treaty was signed in 1598. In the same year, Henri IV, in his Edict of Nantes, stated that the Catholic Church was the state Church but also gave the Protestants religious freedom and the right to hold public office. The thirty-six years of brutal war were over and Henri IV could give his attention to working his economic miracle.[8]

Henri IV knew how to pick good men. The most important of these was Maximilien de Béthune whom he made Duc de Sully. He also allied himself with the bourgeoisie which he correctly saw as a determinant economic factor.

Henri IV signed international treaties to increase commerce.

He improved the French armed forces with an officer cadet school, higher pay, better fortifications and artillery. He drained marshes, dug canals, built roads, established a silk industry, manufactures of cloth, glassware, tapestries. He wiped out a huge national debt and left a reserve of 18 million livres when he died in Paris on 14 May 1610, assassinated by a fanatical Roman Catholic named François Ravaillac.

Henri IV, Henri le Grand as the French call him, was one of those statesmen blessed with moderation and acute intelligence. There wasn't a bigoted bone in his body. The distinguished British historian Norman Davies calls Henri IV cynical.[9] Is that because Henri of Navarre went from Protestant to Catholic to Protestant to Catholic? The French respond that Henri of Navarre was a pragmatist who did what he had to do to end bloodshed and bring prosperity. He said: 'Those who follow their consciences are of my religion, and I am of the religion of those who are brave and good.' Except for his scandalous personal behaviour, he would have met with the approval of Confucius. Solon would have liked him, royal adulteries notwithstanding. Henri of Navarre – Henri IV – had seen horrors, treachery, envy, intolerance, hatred. His life was often threatened. He was made an outcast by the pope. But Henri IV, unlike Agrippina, did not decide to survive by adopting the feral morals of his opponents. He did not seek revenge. He forgave. He was a good man. But, as we'd say today, he couldn't keep his pants zipped.

Admittedly, it must have been difficult for Henri IV to feel uxorious towards his wife Margot. After all, her brother and her mother began slaughtering his friends and attendants before his eyes while the festivities were still going on for his wedding with Margot. Then the king of France kept Navarre a virtual prisoner for four years.

However, considering his subsequent lifelong addiction to

adultery, Henri of Navarre would have probably slept around even if his own guests at his wedding had not been slaughtered. His wife slept around too. Retaliation has been suggested. Her hot Italian blood has been blamed – her mother, Catherine de' Medici, was Italian. Her brother banished her from the royal court because of her 'nymphomania'.* She was also intelligent, cultured, a talented writer and spunky enough to lead troops against both her brother and her husband Henri.

The marriage of Henri IV and his Reine Margot was annulled by Pope Clement VIII after twenty-seven years so that Henri IV could marry another Medici, woman, Marie. The Medicis were very rich bankers and Henri IV needed a fat dowry to pay off his personal debts.

Why write of Margot in a brief history of the world? Because she and her husband were so well matched. Henri IV, the most successful Protestant leader in a Catholic country, broke all the rules of strict, 'respectable' conduct that he had been taught by his very Calvinist mother. He changed and rechanged religion. He behaved disreputably as a husband, but never acted as if he had the right to tell others what to believe. He was eloquent, brave, sexually dissolute and full of fun. He married against his will and against her will the daughter of his Catholic enemies. He heartily cuckolded her for twenty-seven years; and she cuckolded him, no less heartily, for twenty-seven years, despite her very strict Catholic upbringing. He was the most beloved king of France. And she also became, with the years, beloved of the people, beloved by Navarre's son and heir Louis XIII who heaped honours upon

---

* Dr Alfred Kinsey, author of *Sexual Behaviour in the Human Female* (1953), is reported to have said that nymphomania simply means 'she is having more sex than I am having.'

her. She threw prodigious parties. She wrote pretty verse. Her death surprised everyone: she had seemed so indestructible. France grieved. It is poetic justice that in a time of religious fanaticism and suffocating hypocritical moralism among many leaders of both sides, Henri and Margot, two very important people, were such lovable reprobates.

12

WHERE THE SUN THAT NEVER SET, DID SET

(1783–1865)

The Artisans of Freedom

After the death of Henri IV the wars went on. First there was the Thirty Years War, 1618–48. It was all about who controlled which part of the heart of Europe. It was also between Catholic forces and Protestant forces. Roman Catholics and Protestants each sought allies in their fight for dominance. The Catholics had the support of Austria's very Catholic ruler. Protestants counted on the Protestant king of Sweden, and on the Protestant people of the Netherlands who had kicked out their Spanish masters after an eighty-year war. The various armies used mercenaries.

The war was carried out by what became known as the *wolf strategy*: because the mercenaries could not collect their pay, they pillaged cities, towns, villages and farms. Catholic Spain lost the Netherlands and was no longer *numero uno* in Europe. Catholic Austria was diminished. Protestant Sweden lost control of the Baltic. Catholic France became the dominant power in Europe.[1]

The War of the Spanish Succession, 1701–14, was the same

sort of thing. Carlos II, the last Austrian king of Spain, who ruled Austro-Hungary as well, died childless. So who was going to inherit what? The Spaniards, the French, the Dutch, the Italians, the English got involved. There were partition agreements that pleased some but not others. And there was a thirteen-year war. Eventually the grandson of France's Louis XIV became King Philip V of Spain and the Habsburg Arch-duke Charles became king of Austria and Hungary.

Another turf war was over, and the turf of Europe was looking distinctly worn. The grand acquisitors began to look further afield.

The Aryan linguistic group, that is Europeans and their descendants in the Americas, set out on a course that over the next 200 years would make them the greatest predators in history.

The Spaniards and the Portuguese did not only colonize the Americas. They took large territories in Africa and Asia. The Dutch established themselves in the Americas, South Africa and what is now Indonesia. The French took sections of North America, chunks of Africa, Madagascar, Laos, Cambodia, Vietnam, Tahiti. Kicking out the French, the British took all North America east of the Appalachians and north of Mexico; most of the islands in the Caribbean and the South Pacific; Australia, New Zealand; eventually much of Africa, India (which then included Pakistan and Bangladesh), Sri Lanka, Malaysia, Burma (now Myanmar), Nepal, Sikkim, Bhutan. The Germans took colonies in Africa and the Pacific Islands. The Belgians took the Congo; they also took Rwanda and Burundi from the Germans after the First World War. The Italians took Libya, Eritrea, Somalia and Abyssinia. Russia took Siberia, the Caucasus and large Muslim territories to the south such as Turkestan, Kazakstan, Tajikistan and Uzbekistan. The US expanded westward into Indian lands, south into Spanish-speaking territories; they also took the Philippines, Puerto Rico and some Pacific islands.

After the First World War, Germany lost all its colonies to victors. The Ottoman Empire lost the Middle East. In 1939, before the Second World War, Europeans and their American offspring owned 90.5 per cent of Africa; 98.9 per cent of Polynesia; 56.5 per cent of Asia; 100 per cent of Australia.[2]

After the Second World War, some natives regained their countries: either they threw out the colonizers, or the, colonizers simply went home because what they spent holding on to a colony gave much better returns if invested at home in new industries.[3]

It might seem cavalier to go through the colonization period in just 300 words. No disrespect is meant for those who were subjected to colonialism: for them it was a traumatic part of their history. Mostly, they would like it not to have happened – if they survived it. By and large, being colonized was awful. The natives were often treated as slaves; always as inferior humans. They worked long hours, underground in mines, in the fields under any kind of weather; often separated from their families; hardly ever paid a living wage; constantly humiliated, whipped, raped, lynched. In some places, such as British India, they rose to be judges and senior administrators, but always as second-class citizens. Some studied in Britain but if they came back with a British bride, they were said to have acquired a LL.D – not a doctorate in law but a 'landlady's daughter'. And the Brits were not the worst of colonizers.

The British liked to say that the sun never set on their colonial empire – so extensive was it. The fact that it was so extensive for so long is one of the reasons why English has become the leading second language in the world. In India with a population of 1 billion people, there are twelve major languages. The common means of communication for these distinct language groups is English.

To work in the new global sectors of the modern economy, you speak your mother tongue but you must also speak English. Thus, the former British Empire has given us our major international communications link. But this empire on which the sun never set also gave us the place where that sun *did* set first – the thirteen colonies that became the English-speaking United States of America, now the leading actor on the world stage.

There are phases in the making of the US as we know it. The most important was the very first: independence from Britain. It was a rebellion against an aristocratic system of government which took its subjects for granted – not only in Great Britain proper but also in the thirteen colonies. There, large numbers of people of British descent could not elect representatives to the Parliament in London. Yet London decreed what the law was in its American colonies.

Many colonists were Calvinists. They had fled persecution at the hands of the Catholics; suffered discrimination at the hands of the Church of England, the established Church of the British Empire. Just as the Calvinist burghers in Holland had long fought the right of the Catholic king of Spain to govern them, so the British Calvinists had overthrown an English king, Charles I, and beheaded him in 1649. They had then ruled Britain until 1660, but they had divided into so many quarrelling sects that the restoration of the monarchy became inevitable: Charles II ascended the throne of his beheaded father.

Calvinists were not in awe of traditional power figures such as the king of England, who was also the head of the established Church of England. After all, Calvinists thought themselves equal if not superior to any archbishop in saying what the Bible stated was the word of God.

The Catholics who emigrated to the thirteen colonies were often of the reformed kind, unlike the Catholics who went to Latin America from Spain and Portugal. One of Britain's thirteen colonies in North America, Maryland, where there was a considerable Catholic population, passed a law guaranteeing freedom of religion, an unthinkable event in colonial, Catholic Latin America.

London taxed the thirteen colonies and forbade them to expand west of the Appalachian mountains. To enforce these measures, the British sent soldiers whose upkeep came partially out of the pockets of the colonists. Fighting started in 1775. In 1776, on 4 July, the thirteen colonies declared themselves independent. Their representatives voted for the *Articles of Confederation* by which the new nation would be governed. This was one of the momentous occasions in world history. Regardless of who or what the 'Fathers' of the Confederation were, they set forth good changes that still affect us and they did so in words in which most civilized, freedom-loving people see themselves.

Yet, respected American historians, after meticulous research, have been telling us increasingly that those storied founding fathers had feet of clay.* Which fathers have not? Still we must briefly examine their flaws, if only to prove that flawed men are capable of greatness: if that had not been so, humans would still be hiding in caves, dodging sabre-toothed tigers.

Thus, Francis Jennings, an eminent historian, tells us that founding father John Hancock was the biggest smuggler in Boston; Henry Laurens, the biggest slave trader; George

---

* The term 'founding fathers' is not applied only to those who signed the *Declaration of Independence* or the *Articles of Confederation*. George Washington signed neither document but is surely a founding father.

Washington and Ben Franklin had participated in land grabs of dubious legality or morality. And so on.[4] But to them we owe the *Declaration of Independence*. Excerpts follow.

We hold these truths to be self-evident, that all men are created equal, that they are endowed by their Creator with certain unalienable rights, that among these are life, liberty, and the pursuit of happiness. That whenever any form of government becomes destructive of these ends, it is the right of the people to alter or to abolish it, and to institute new government. We, therefore, the Representatives of the United States of America, in General Congress assembled, do, *in the name, and by the authority, of the good people of these colonies*, solemnly publish and declare: that these United Colonies are, and of right ought to be, free and independent States; that they are absolved from all allegiance to the British Crown and that, as free and independent States, they have full power to levy war, conclude peace, contract alliances, establish commerce, and to do all other acts and things which independent States may of right do.

Possibly the most memorable, most quoted words of this document are: '*We hold these truths to be self-evident, that all men are created equal, that they are endowed by their Creator with certain unalienable rights, that among these are life, liberty, and the pursuit of happiness.*' But the most important, the most potent, the most revolutionary of the above words are: '*We, the Representatives of the United States of America, in the name, and by the authority, of the good people of these colonies . . .*' This is the foundation of Solonian democracy, revived in North America, 2,370 years after Solon proclaimed it in ancient Athens: government acts in the name of the people and by the authority of the people. Which means that government, to have authority and legitimacy, must have been elected by the people. The *hereditary* right of kings is disowned. The *divine* right of kings anointed by the Church is disowned. Any authority but that conferred by the people, is disowned.* The people have the right to overthrow a government and establish another.† But such action should not be taken lightly and should be justified: 'A decent respect to the opinions of mankind requires [that the people] should declare the causes which impel them to the separation,' says the *Declaration of Independence*. And Thomas Jefferson's document – for he largely wrote it – gives a long list of reasons for overthrowing the authority of King George III. Here are excerpts.

He has forbidden his governors to pass laws of immediate and pressing importance. He has dissolved representative houses repeatedly and refused to cause others to be elected. He has refused to pass laws encouraging immigration. He has made judges dependent on his will alone, for the tenure of their offices, and the amount and payment of their salaries. He has kept among us, in times of peace, standing armies, without the consent of our legislatures. He has affected to render the military independent of and superior to the civil power, giving his assent to their Acts of pretended legislation. He has cut off our trade with all parts of the world; imposed taxes on us without our consent; deprived us in many cases of

---

* Such concepts, in some form or other, in part or in whole, had been discussed by Hobbes, Hume, Locke, Voltaire, Jean-Jacques Rousseau, Montesquieu. But the concepts had not been used. The thirteen colonies actually used them to challenge the most powerful government on earth.
† Readers will remember that Confucius said rulers fell when they lost the 'mandate of heaven', when they lost the support of their subjects.

the benefits of trial by jury. He has plundered our seas, ravaged our coasts, burnt our towns and destroyed the lives of our people. A Prince, who is such a tyrant, is unfit to be the ruler of a free people.*

Of course, it took more than words. It took blood – for eight years. Finally, in 1783, the US was formally recognized by the Treaty of Paris. The war had been so long in part because the *Articles of Confederation*, the first constitution of the USA, did not allow for a functional, elected central authority. After doing the job for which he had been selected – to win the war against the British – George Washington refused offers to become king or ruler for life of his new country.† He returned instead to his plantation. He became so trusted that he was later given the task of presiding over the drafting of his country's Solonian political structures: the Constitution of the United States, and was elected the first president.

Under the new Constitution, the two Chambers of Congress, the Senate and the House of Representatives, and the Supreme Court, had authority superseding that of the thirteen

---

* The grievances may have been exaggerated, but then this was war; and it has been said that truth is the first casualty of war.

† Washington was urged by some to assume a king's power but he turned it down, accepting, thereby, the principle that power belonged to the people and that the people could revoke power. This may be his greatest contribution to history. By Washington's time, others had accepted the revocability of power, for instance, the members of Britain's House of Commons. But the British prime ministers were generally members of the hereditary House of Lords and the king still retained, if only theoretically, irrevocable power. The ordinary subject of the British crown lived under the oppressive inequality of a stifling class system. Switzerland also practised a form of democracy, with revocability of power, before democracy was established in the United States.

States. The judges of the Supreme Court were appointed by the elected president and confirmed by the Senate.* As in Solonian Athens, only male citizens had the vote – women and slaves did not. It took a very long time for all citizens, regardless of race and gender to have the vote.

The Indians? Mostly they were exterminated, or decimated by disease, or pushed out of their lands into 'reservations', tracts of land unfit for cultivation or grazing.† Their ill-treatment was not surprising. The *Declaration of Independence* had said they were merciless savages: 'The inhabitants of our frontiers, the merciless Indian savages, whose known rule of warfare is an undistinguished destruction of all ages, sexes and conditions . . .' What else could the good colonists do but defend their women and children by inflicting 'undistinguished destruction of all ages, sexes and conditions' on the Indian 'savages'. The Indians, of course, were also defending their lands, their women and their children.

Meanwhile, in the United States that potent seed, democracy, had been planted: the *people* were the source of all authority. Democracy was often distorted. Its privileges were often restricted to a class or a racial group. But democracy was there, latent, a sort of immune system eating away at political disease. People whites only, of course – could dream of going to America where they would be free of oppression; free of exploitation by rich, often hereditary, landowners; free to seize for themselves, from the Indians, acreage of a size beyond their wildest dreams.

So they came from Europe by the boatload. Those who came to the Americas were the more adventurous. They faced

---

* Senators were not directly elected, at first: they were chosen by the States.
† Ironically, in some few cases, reservations turned out to be rich in oil and gas.

a vast land with huge resources that offered them the chance to become wealthy by making, perhaps inventing, things that others needed. The US did not have a monopoly of inventors or scientists or craftsmen or industrialists, but it seemed to attract the more enterprising among them. It was a heady brew of a country, a free society with huge numbers of slaves. Would it stay united long enough to continue as a democratic beacon?

The US did not have a monopoly of slaves – the sugar planters in the Caribbean had the most: 65 per cent of all the slaves shipped from Africa. Profits were huge. You could make 50 per cent profit on your investment each year, running a sugar plantation in Barbados. In the southern USA, about 40 per cent of the population was made up of black slaves, working tobacco and cotton plantations. In South Carolina, nearly two thirds of the population were slaves; in Mississippi, 55 per cent. The economy of the southern United States was a slave economy and a very profitable one, with a higher per capita income among whites than the North.[5]

Slavery was soon under moral attack. Quaker and Wesleyan Protestants launched campaigns everywhere against slavery itself; and against the way slaves were seized by raiders or sold by their tribal chiefs to traders who chained them, packed tighter than sardines, in filthy ships whose smell could be detected miles away at sea. The horrors of slavery were publicized. Shamed, European countries began abolishing slavery. In 1807, Britain banned the slave trade and used its fleet to enforce the ban. In 1834, the British Parliament abolished slavery throughout its dominions.

Some northern states in the US also began abolishing slavery, and the moral pressure by the abolitionists in the United States intensified year after year. The North and the South were growing differently. The North was becoming industrialized.

White southern men saw in the North an ugly obstacle standing in the path of romantic destiny, the visible sign that there were cold and designing folk who would not let the lovely, white-pillared, half-imaginary past perpetuate itself.[6]

Besides the North and the South, there was a third part of the US, territories still awaiting statehood – in particular Kansas. When it became a state, would it have slavery or not? The South said yes. The North said no.

Some thought a compromise might be found, but there were fanatics on both sides: abolitionists, like old John Brown, who killed pro-slavery people; pro-slavery champions who retaliated. One of the latter, Preston Brooks, a congressman from South Carolina, savagely caned the abolitionist Senator Charles Sumner, who was sitting alone in the Senate Chamber.[7] Talk of secession was in the air.

South Carolina remembered how the Caribbean's sugar planters were ruined when Britain abolished slavery. So, fearing the growing political power of the anti-slavery movement in the northern states, South Carolina seceded. Other southern states followed.

President Abraham Lincoln would not accept secession, and so there was war. Half a million men lost their lives. The South had the more imaginative generals. The North had industry, more people, and two generals, Ulysses S. Grant and William Tecumseh Sherman, who were not imaginative but were persistent and efficiently ruthless.

Lincoln signed a proclamation emancipating the slaves. He said that the emancipation had given the North 180,000 black soldiers; they may have sealed the South's fate. Tragically, Lincoln was assassinated in 1865, the year of the northern victory. His policy of reconciliation with the South died with him.

After the war, northern profiteers sucked the South dry. Old evils flourished. Universal male suffrage had become law, but the southern states made sure the right to vote was not exercised by blacks. One hundred years after the end of the civil war, white people trying to help blacks to vote were shot dead in the South.

Racism, an ancient moral leprosy, remains the world over, not only among whites. The Chinese and other yellow people feel racist towards whites, blacks and browns.* There are, everywhere, small-minded people who feel inferior; they need – and create – an 'underclass' to which they can feel superior. This is one reason why blacks in the USA are still treated as second-class citizens. But they have made progress.

Calvinist black religious leaders, notably the late Martin Luther King, have been in the forefront of the black fight for civil rights: especially for the right to vote, for the end of school segregation and for equal treatment at the hands of the justice system. Many whites have supported the blacks out of democratic convictions and out of Christian ethics. We have a case here of a society which used the thoughts of Solon and of Jesus to protect *some* of its white members from oppression by grand acquisitors but which excluded a whole group, the blacks, from fully belonging to society. Were the blacks not created equal?

They were treated as not equal, for a long time. But this is changing. In Selma, Alabama, in 1965, I watched blacks attacked and beaten while marching for the right to vote. Recently, Selma elected its first black mayor, an impressively educated, successful man. The power of the vote has begun working for the blacks too.

---

* I know. I was a prisoner in Korea and the butt of Korean and Chinese racist jokes.

The USA still has a long way to go before it sheds racism. Till then, when American statesmen speak against oppressive governments elsewhere in the world, they will always be told to stop oppressing blacks and Indians before criticizing other regimes. But by adopting Solon's rules of government and occasional Christian compassion (towards whites initially, others later), the US placed its mark on world history and showed the way.

Much more will be said of the US later in this book. But in the next chapter we must first deal with the effect elsewhere of those famous words in the *Declaration of Independence*: '. . . in the name, and by the authority of the people . . .'

13

THE FRENCH
REVOLUTION AND
ITS AFTERMATH

(1789–1821)

There are no perfect outcomes of human endeavour. But the concept that rulers act 'in the name and by the authority of the people,' had been put into execution and it had worked; it was now out there in the world. And it was infectious.

The French Revolution used the concept almost immediately in its *Declaration of the Rights of Man*, giving credit to the Americans.* Wars of liberation broke out not long afterwards in the Balkans. As they had before, the Irish challenged the right of London to rule them – but more on the Emerald Isle later. American independence was a whirlwind of liberty that blew all over Europe. But there were other causes for the French Revolution: too many aristocratic, feudal landowners were oppressive, arrogant and grossly inefficient at feeding the growing French population; as in Athens before Solon, the non-aristocrats, the bourgeoisie, resented being excluded from

---

* The Count de Mirabeau, a nobleman, member of the French revolutionary assembly, is the one who gave credit to the Americans.

exercising political power; the French thinker Montesquieu, who had (among others) influenced the framers of the American constitution, was much read by the restive among the French bourgeoisie; and the king of France actually gave help to the rebelling American colonists who had declared that all men are created equal and should be governed by those they elect.

Did the king and his advisers have a strategy session at which they said such things as: 'England kicked us out of North America; wouldn't it be nice to have England kicked out of North America?' Very probably, but did no one around King Louis XVI wonder what would be the consequences of helping replace the rule of a hereditary monarch in North America by an elected republican regime? Would not the same thing happen in other countries? It did. The politically ambitious bourgeoisie in France said: 'We helped make the Americans free. Why not make ourselves free?'

In 1788, the very year the American Constitution was ratified, there were risings in major French cities. The king and his ministers talked of improving things but nothing happened because the nobles rejected reform. The 1788 harvest was bad. Food became even scarcer. Allegedly, Marie Antoinette, wife of Louis XVI, said, 'If they have no bread, let them eat cake.'* On 14 July 1789, the populace of Paris seized the Bastille, the fortress where the kings traditionally incarcerated their enemies. There were only seven prisoners left there. They did not quite understand what was happening and why they were being cheered. A symbol of tyranny had fallen.

---

* The evidence is shaky that she said these words, but it was widely believed that she did.

Talleyrand (1754–1838)

The Estates General were summoned by King Louis XVI to deal with the crisis. This assembly traditionally represented the nobles, the clergy and the '*tiers état*', the third estate, i.e. those who were neither nobles nor clergy.* The revolutionaries transformed the Estates General into a National Constituent Assembly. Here we find a talented rogue, the Bishop of Autun, Charles Maurice, Comte de Talleyrand-Périgord, who was eventually made Prince de Bénévent, by Napoleon. Born in Paris in 1754, Talleyrand had a club foot and could not, therefore, follow his noble family's military tradition. He entered a seminary to join the priesthood but was expelled for taking up with the first of his innumerable mistresses and concubines. Being well connected, young Talleyrand was nevertheless named abbot of the prestigious Abbey of Saint Denis in Reims.

In the National Constituent Assembly, to everyone's astonishment, Talleyrand, principal spokesman for the very conservative clergy, renowned defender of Church rights, proposed a constitution that would provide representative government: repeal the tithe;† nationalize and sell French Church property to pay off the national debt. The Assembly also abolished feudalism. It declared, as the Americans had done, that citizens had the right to liberty, equality, and the right to resist oppression.‡ The administration of the French provinces was rationalized. Judges, who had come to be

---

* Newspapermen came to be known as the 'fourth estate'. This is an allusion to the political influence they exercise even though they do not represent any group of the population.
† A tax paid to the Church. It amounted to 10 per cent of a person's income.
‡ These rights did not apply to slaves in French colonies.

considered pliable instruments of the king's regime, would, thereafter, be elected by the people. Talleyrand played a determinant role in getting all these measures approved: he always knew, before anyone else, which way the wind was blowing.

The majority in the Assembly tried to create a constitutional monarchy in which the king would reign and elected representatives of the people would govern, as is the case now in Britain, Scandinavia, Spain, Belgium, Holland. But King Louis XVI did not understand that change had become inevitable. He became the symbol of resistance to the changes the National Constituent Assembly wanted. So he and his wife were eventually beheaded on the guillotine.* On the day they died, their son became Louis XVII. The boy king died of tuberculosis, aged ten, in prison.†

Originally, the other European dynasties had not reacted. But that changed when the French Assembly proclaimed a new principle of international law: 'People everywhere have the right of self-determination.' Subject nationalities seeking freedom from foreign masters, in what are now Holland, Belgium,

---

* The guillotine had been invented by Joseph-Ignace Guillotin, a physician who wanted executions to be as painless as possible. It is true that being guillotined was less painful than being drawn and quartered or even hanged; better also than being beheaded by an axeman who often had to strike several times before severing the head.

† Was the little boy the son of Louis XVI? We are in the area of pure gossip here. Louis had had to have lectures from his physician on what to do to his bride in bed. The gossip said that she consoled herself with a vigorous Swedish valet. We find 'vigorous Swedish valets' in gossip about other royal persons. A Swedish valet was supposed to be the biological father of Prince Albert, husband of Queen Victoria. That is why, Lord Melbourne, Prime Minister of Great Britain, agreed to arrange the marriage between Queen Victoria and Prince Albert. Lord Melbourne bred horses and knew the importance of fresh blood: Queen Victoria was said by some to have a withered left arm.

Ireland and Italy, among others, applauded what the French had done and were persecuted in consequence. Revolutionary France declared war on its neighbours to help neighbouring revolutionaries.

The various royal dynasties were alarmed. That the French had beheaded their king was bad enough. But did they now want to overthrow all dynasties? So Austria and Prussia sent their armies into France and made for Paris. There was an explosion of ethnic patriotism in France and thousands volunteered. They marched into battle singing what became the most bloodthirsty national anthem in the world, *The Marsellaise*:

> *Entendez-vous, dans les campagnes,*
> *Mugir ces féroces soldats?*
> *Ils viennent jusque dans nos bras*
> *Égorger nos fils, et nos compagnes.*
> *Aux armes, citoyens!*
> *Formez vos bataillons!*
> *Marchons, marchons!*
> *Qu'un sang impur abreuve nos sillons.*

(Do you hear those ferocious soldiers bellowing in the fields? They come to snatch from our embrace and slaughter our sons and our brides. Citizens, to arms! Form your battalions! March! March! Let the invaders' impure blood quench the thirst of our furrows).*

Notice the words 'impure blood'.

Royal dynasties all over Europe had subjects of many ethnicities, often living side by side, at peace if not in friend-

---

* This is a free rather than literal translation.

ship. The French now marched to a hymn of ethnic hatred. The multi-ethnic structure of European kingdoms was threatened. The French defeated the invading Prussians who formed a coalition with Austria and Britain to continue the war.

The external threat to France was serious. The National Constituent Assembly gave power to 'Le Comité du Salut Public', the Committee of Public Salvation, which recruited a huge army of 1 million men. To equip and supply them, the Comité raised taxes steeply and imposed price controls: there were risings in protest. These were drowned in blood. Hundreds of thousands were arrested. Tens of thousands were guillotined, many without being charged or tried. This became known in history as The Terror.

The French army won. It had talented leaders – for instance Murat, Soult and Ney, all three from the working class. All three would rise to the rank of marshal under Napoleon: a stunning demonstration to non-aristocrats everywhere that they could be better than the nobles. After the victory over the invaders, the Comité du Salut Public and its regime of terror was no longer needed. The most sanguinary members of the Comité – Robespierre, Saint-Just and Couthon – were arrested and guillotined the next day, 27 July 1794. There have been attempts to present Robespierre and Saint-Just as champions of the people, forced by circumstances to use any means in saving the Republic. They did save the Republic, temporarily. But whatever their intellectual qualities, they were mass murderers, whichever way one looks at it. Saint-Just was the bloodiest. He said: 'We must not only punish traitors, but all people who are not enthusiastic. There are only two kinds of citizens: the good and the bad. The Republic owes its protection to the good. It owes only death to the bad.' Hitler and Stalin thought that way too.

A new constitution gave France a House of Representatives,

a Senate and a five-man presidency called the Directoire – note the similarities with the USA. The bourgeoisie had clearly come to power, as in the United States.

Napoleon (1769–1821)

A royalist uprising in Paris was torn to shreds by the artillery of a twenty-six-year-old general, Napoleon Bonaparte; he had already proved himself to be a brilliant commander in the field, beating armies outnumbering his poorly equipped troops. After he was wounded in battle, he wore scarlet trousers so that, should he be wounded again, his soldiers wouldn't see he was bleeding: they thought of him as magical and invincible. And they loved him. They nicknamed him '*le petit tondu*' because he wore his hair cut very short. '*Petit*' means small or short but '*le petit*' means 'the kid'. So the nickname meant 'the close-cropped kid'. For his time, Napoleon was not short, measuring five foot six inches. But because of that nickname, short and excessively bossy men are said to suffer from a 'Napoleon complex'.

Born in Corsica on 15 August 1769, he had been studying in France since the age of nine. He had become a young officer under the king, but had thrown in his lot with the Revolution. Republican France went on conquering European states, giving its institutions to these 'sister republics'. Country after country signed peace treaties, except Britain. Napoleon proposed to weaken the English by taking Egypt and cutting off Britain's shortest route to its holdings in India. He took Egypt in July 1798. But in August, the British Admiral, Horatio Nelson, destroyed the French fleet at the battle of the Nile, in Egypt's Aboukir bay. Some say that, in this period, history threw up its greatest general, Napoleon, and its greatest admiral, Nelson, fighting on opposite sides. To this day, in battles far from home, the victories at sea are the decisive ones. Aboukir was such a battle.*

Back in Europe, in Napoleon's absence, a new coalition of Britain, Russia, Austria and Turkey was winning against the French army. Napoleon evaded Nelson's fleet, got back to France and overthrew the Directoire in the night of 9/10 November 1799. He made himself sole ruler of France under the title of First Consul. This is where the French Revolution veers away from the path of the American Revolution. Washington believed in democracy and did not want to become a dictator. Napoleon believed that he was a man more brilliant than all others, and that, therefore, he and not the ordinary people should rule – a conclusion in keeping with Plato.

Napoleon proclaimed the end of the Revolution. Talleyrand negotiated with Austria and England and there were no hostilities for the first time since 1793.† Paris was no longer the vortex of a tornado. After the butchery of the Terror, there was a huge release of tensions and of morals. Rich, young, bourgeois fops dressed extravagantly and took to saying about everything, 'C'est incroyable', which they pronounced 'incoyable' – incwedible. The females of that species wore long, loose dresses with their breasts on the half shell, so to speak.

One notorious lady and a leading society belle was Josephine Tascher de la Pagerie, Vicomtesse de Beauharnais, who was born in Martinique.‡ She was able to catch the fancy of

---

* Contemporary US power far from home depends on naval task forces centred around aircraft carriers.

† Talleyrand was a great foreign minister. He used to tell his junior subordinates 'Surtout Messieurs, pas trop de zèle' – not too much zeal. Upon being promoted, one subordinate knelt before Talleyrand and said: 'Monsieur le Prince, you are the first to have been so kind to me. I have been so unlucky.' Talleyrand fired the man on the spot saying, 'I don't want unlucky people on my staff.'

‡ Her husband had been guillotined during the terror. She had two children by him.

Napoleon before he went to Egypt. She married him but did not return his passion. When he was away in Egypt she flirted outrageously (possibly had an affair) with another army officer. Napoleon forgave her at the request of her children – his step-children – to whom he was truly attached. From the frontlines on which he won his great battles, he wrote her passionate letters to which she did not respond.

As first consul, Napoleon proclaimed a new constitution on Christmas Day 1799. It had no ringing proclamation of the rights of man, or of liberty and equality. The newly rich of the Revolution were guaranteed that they would not have to give back properties that had belonged to the aristocrats (who were banished from France 'for ever') or properties taken during the Revolution from the Church. Talleyrand lined his pockets in the process of selling confiscated Church property.

With his new constitution, Napoleon, the first consul, had a monopoly of power: he chose the members of the legislative assemblies; the public servants; the judges (whose independence he nevertheless assured by appointing them for life). Prefects named by him ran the '*départements*', the administrative provinces of France. He created the Bank of France and stabilized the currency. He improved the education system.

One of Napoleon's most important legacies is the Civil Code that bears his name and was enacted in 1804. This set of laws guaranteed individual liberty, freedom of conscience, equality before the law, the separation of Church and State: except that Napoleon named the bishops and obtained the approval of this practice from Pope Pius VII. The pontiff had no choice but to say yes, with French troops breathing down his neck. The Napoleonic Code was a bourgeois charter, protecting property rights, defining rights of inheritance, the rights of employers (but not of workers). Civil divorce, introduced by the Revolution, was retained in the Napoleonic Code. In today's terms, the Code did not do much for women's rights.* Generally, the Code brought order and logic to what had been an untidy thicket of legislation and customs, ancient feudal rights, Canon Law and Germanic precedents set by lay tribunals of north-eastern France.† The influence of the Napoleonic Code can still be seen in the legislation of many European and Latin American countries and of Quebec, a Canadian province. It still is the fundamental legislation of Louisiana, which was a French possession until US President Thomas Jefferson purchased it from Napoleon in 1803.

Napoleon gave much attention to his army. Military service became obligatory (but a conscripted young man with money could buy himself a replacement). Every member of the armed forces had an equal chance for promotion. Two military academies were established, one, Saint Cyr, to train infantry officers, another, La Polytechnique, for engineers and artillery. They are still functioning.

He was a military genius, ranking with Alexander of Greece, Hannibal of Carthage, the Kurd Saladin and the Mongol Genghis Khan. Napoleon won battle after battle and came to control the coast of the European continent from the west of Italy, around Spain and all the way to Holland. He shut all those ports to British merchant ships. So Great Britain declared war on France in the spring of 1803. And Napoleon began preparations to conquer Britain.

While his invasion fleet was being built, Napoleon had himself crowned emperor on 2 December 1804. By then he had shown that he had all the grand acquisitor instincts of the

---

* An apocryphal story concerns conjugal rights: Napoleon was told that an ecclesiastical Spanish court had ruled in the thirteenth century that a man had the right to demand his conjugal rights twenty-seven times every twenty-four hours. Napoleon allegedly said that if Spaniards could do it twenty-seven times, so could the French.

† Most of the French were descendants of the Germanic Franks.

existing dynastic families: grabbing territory from other dynasts; placing his brothers and brothers-in-law as kings of various states. He revived the orders of nobility and rewarded his faithful servants by making them barons, counts, viscounts, marquesses, dukes and even princes. His mother Letizia, watching all her glittering relatives and remembering the straitened circumstances in which she had lived before her son's accession to power, kept saying in her Corsican accent, '*Pourvou qué ça doure*' (if only this could last).

Napoleon's plan to invade Britain failed. On 21 October 1805, a Franco–Spanish fleet that was to ferry troops to Britain was caught and destroyed by Nelson off Spain's Cape Trafalgar. Nelson had insisted on wearing full dress uniform while standing on the quarterdeck of his flagship, the *Victory*. His subordinates protested that his glistening medals and sashes would make him a target. It did. A French marine took aim and hit Nelson. 'I am hit in the spine,' the dying Admiral said. He had saved Britain which was thereafter the uncontested mistress of the sea. The admiral's body was brought back to London, preserved in a barrel of rum. A legend dear to Britain's Navy has it that the sailors drank the rum on the way to England.*

London kept organizing coalitions against Napoleon. He kept beating them on land. He took Vienna on 13 November

---

* Nelson had abandoned his respectable wife and taken up with Lady Emma Hamilton, a common whore before she married Lord Hamilton, the British representative in Naples. Nelson had left a letter asking England to look after his 'dear' Emma, should he die in battle. England did not look after her. The great admiral's scandalous love affair with a married woman did not affect his personal popularity or his position. If the rules about such things that now prevail in the US Navy had been applied in Britain, Nelson would have been removed from his command and Britain might not have won the battle of Trafalgar. If similar rules had been applied to Generals Eisenhower and Patton, they too would have been removed from their commands in the Second World War.

1805. Nineteen days later, though seriously outnumbered and far from his base of supplies, he defeated the combined armies of Austria and Russia at Austerlitz (now Slavkov u Brna in the Czech Republic). This battle is considered the best example of his tactical genius.[1]

Peace could still be negotiated. Talleyrand knew things would turn out badly if the fighting continued – France would become exhausted. He told Napoleon so. They disagreed. Napoleon declared that Talleyrand was just a silk stocking filled with shit ('*de la merde dans un bas de soie*'). This was reported to Talleyrand who remarked: 'Such a pity that so great a man should be so ill-mannered.' Talleyrand left the government in 1807.[2]

Napoleon was not inclined to make peace. He wanted the British to sue for peace. Instead, they attacked, landing on the Portuguese coast in 1809, invading Spain; there, under Arthur Wellesley (later Duke of Wellington), they began beating Napoleon's troops.

Still, Napoleon was riding high. Josephine had not given him an heir so he had their marriage annulled by the pope. (Napoleon housed Josephine in a luxurious residence, Malmaison, where she lived lavishly. He paid all her debts.) Napoleon then married the daughter of the Austrian emperor, Princess Marie Louise, in 1810. A son was born in 1811 and given the title of King of Rome.

Meanwhile, because things were not going well for the French in Spain, Talleyrand had secret talks with Tsar Alexander I of Russia, urging him to oppose Napoleon. Was this pique on Talleyrand's part? His admirers say that he was building contacts which would help France when Napoleon's luck ran out. The Tsar soon showed signs that he was not inclined to accept Napoleon's dominance of Europe and participate in the blockade of England. Which led Napoleon to make his greatest mistake: in 1812, he invaded Russia with nearly half a million men – significantly, not all of them French. The Russians, under Kutuzov, whom Napoleon had beaten at Austerlitz, fell back, burning everything, leaving no supplies for the French army. Napoleon took Moscow but the Russians had burned most of the city.

Napoleon had to retreat in a savage Russian winter. His non-French contingents abandoned him. In December 1812, the Prussians who had served under him, turned on him. Most of his allies abandoned him. There even was a coup d'état in Paris. Napoleon put it down and raised a new army – he had brought back only 10,000 men from Russia. He won more battles. But France was exhausted and sick of war.

In late 1813, a European coalition defeated Napoleon's army. Still, Napoleon fought on. With units of young raw troops, he still won incredible victories. None of these were decisive, however. Finally, Paris capitulated to the foreign armies. Louis XVIII, brother of Louis XVI, returned. Napoleon abdicated on 6 April 1814. He was exiled to the island of Elba in the Mediterranean. He was only forty-five.

The Bourbons came back with all the aristocrats exiled by the Revolution. They tried to set the clock back. Though tired of Napoleon's continuous wars, the French people were not prepared to renounce what they had gained during the Revolution and Napoleon's rule. They certainly were not prepared to give up lands they had acquired and which the returning aristocrats and church-men wanted back.

Napoleon decided to exploit this discontent. He landed in France on 1 April 1815. Large numbers of his ex-soldiers rallied to him. He marched into Belgium, defeated the Prussians on 16 June 1815. Two days later he met Wellington at Waterloo. Napoleon was beaten: one of his generals,

Grouchy, who was to intervene in the battle, did not arrive on time; instead, the Prussians arrived to help Wellington.

This time Napoleon was exiled to the small island of St Helena in the middle of the Atlantic and died there in 1821, at the age of fifty-two. What did he die of? This is still a matter of contention. One theory, that he died of stomach cancer, is now under attack on the grounds that people who die of stomach cancer are not fat; Napoleon was pretty fat when he died. Another theory is that he was poisoned with arsenic by one of his French attendants. There are traces of arsenic in a lock of his hair. The debate will go on.

France was lucky in that the man who defeated Napoleon, Arthur Wellesley, Duke of Wellington, was civilized. He would not allow his allies to impose too harsh a peace on France; he wanted occupying forces withdrawn from France after three years, if France paid war reparations. Talleyrand was hugely skilled in negotiating terms for his defeated country, as the foreign minister of the restored Bourbons. His one failure was that he let Prussia have considerable territory on the west bank of the Rhine. This was traditionally French. The Rhine river was the natural frontier between the French and the Germans. After Talleyrand's concession, French river traffic to the North Sea had to go through German soil and could be blocked. The dispute over who should have that strip of riverside land was an important factor in three subsequent wars between the French and Germans, in 1870, 1914 and 1939.

Talleyrand deserves an epilogue here. He was a financially corrupt, lascivious priest. He betrayed King Louis XVI, betrayed his Church, betrayed Napoleon, who had made him a prince. Was he a rat bailing out of successive sinking ships? Yes. But his major betrayals came when the salvation of

France required it. Talleyrand tried to save Louis XVI by urging him to become a constitutional monarch. He tried to save France and Napoleon by urging him to sign an honourable peace when this was still possible. With his powerful intellect, Talleyrand dominated the Congress of Vienna (1814–15). There the map of post-Napoleonic Europe was drawn and Talleyrand limited the damages to France. He had many other diplomatic successes before his death at the age of eighty-four, in 1838. All well-read diplomats celebrate his skill.

What should we think of Napoleon himself? He was a grand acquisitor. But more than power and possessions, he seemed to love the process of acquiring them: war. He loved the excitement of the battles at which he was so good. A lot of men lost their lives in consequence – half a million in France alone. Many others lost limbs. When shown once a long list of casualties Napoleon said: 'Paris, in one night, will produce enough replacements.'

Napoleon was not a Hitler or a Stalin. He did not slaughter civilian populations; did not treat non-French people as inferior. He was not 'anti' any ethnicity. He freed the Jews from their ghettoes and gave them the same rights as other Frenchmen. And Napoleon changed Europe.

Though he proclaimed the end of the Revolution and was not a democrat like Washington, Napoleon spread throughout Europe his Civil Code, which guaranteed individual liberty, freedom of conscience, equality before the law, and the separation of Church and State. French troops brought to many European countries the ideal of the American revolution – that people had the right to be governed by their elected representatives. This ideal was not immediately triumphant. It was applied and then abolished, in places. But it did not die. It eventually revived, as we shall see.

Napoleon remains France's greatest mythological character. Even French authors who have deplored one or another aspect of his career revere him. Frenchmen often feel they have fallen short of the standards he set. Deep in their gut, even the most democratic Frenchmen can't help feeling the world would have been better if he had not been defeated, if the French language, and not English, had become the world's dominant tongue.

14

PROMETHEUS AND THE PAX BRITANNICA

(19th century)

The nineteenth century brought two extremely important developments: (1) the birth (or the conception) of the scientific and technical wealth that surround us today; (2) a further step, in Europe, of the Solonian democratic revival which started in the US.

Prometheus, a Titan, stole fire from the gods and gave it to humans. It's an ancient Greek myth symbolic of those primitive thinkers who stopped being terrified of fire and worked out how to use it – the first giant step. Like Prometheus, the nineteenth century bore the beginnings of powers that had only been envisaged for gods.

- the speed to propel ourselves further and faster on earth and above it;
- the gift to have our voice span the globe instantaneously;
- the force of lightning, tamed and at our disposal through any wall socket;
- the talent to cure like Asclepius, ancient Greek god of medicine;

- the craft of Hephaestus to forge magical weapons and tools;
- the intellectual reach of Athena, who could make the human brain think the unthinkably complex;
- Zeus-like power to destroy enemies, and the world itself, with a nuclear thunderbolt.

What did we create with our ingenuity in the nineteenth century? Here is a partial list: steam engines, internal combustion engines; the telephone, the telegraph, wireless communications;* music in a box at home – the gramophone; theatre on a reel projected on to a screen; atomic science for good or bad; steel that girds continents with railways, spans water with the graceful arcs of bridges; the machine-gun; the first steps of modern medicine; leaps in chemistry, including the explosives of Sweden's Alfred Nobel, who hoped that they were terrifying enough to end war. (While experimenting, Nobel – he of the prize – blew up his whole factory. When he continued his experiments, he became the prototype of the mad scientist. But he made huge amounts of money.)

The nineteenth century saw the mechanization of production that we call the Industrial Revolution. Peasants filled city hovels to work in the new factories. Hand weavers lost their livelihood and rebelled, smashing machines; in Britain they were called the Luddites. The government hunted them down, hanged some and deported others.

The nineteenth century was dangerous, unsettling, revolutionary. The seeds of the American Revolution were blown across Europe by the winds of the French Revolution and its Napoleonic deviation. Democratic Solonian thought sprouted all over the continent; some of its sprouts were intellectually deformed by anarchism and communism. The established

---

* Marconi first operated a wireless telegraph transmission in 1896.

acquisitors, grand or paltry, fought it every inch of the way. When their acquisitiveness was restricted in their own countries by democracy's hesitant first steps, they exploited other countries. The nineteenth century's political plot-line in Europe is as follows:

- The nobles try to hold on to power, refusing to share it with those below.
- The upper bourgeoisie takes power from the nobles, establishes an elected assembly and refuses to let those below vote.
- The lower bourgeoisie takes power from the upper bourgeoisie and refuses to let those below vote.
- The workers try to share power with the lower bourgeoisie, not always successfully.*
- People who speak the same language but live – divided – as subjects of different foreign rulers, fight for unity and independence.†

Nowhere is the above plot-line better illustrated than in France. Its bourgeois revolution overthrew the monarchy and the nobles, but was sent into hibernation by Napoleon, who fell in 1815. The monarchy and the émigrés nobles came back and did not share power with the upper bourgeoisie; which overthrew them in 1831 but did not give the vote to the lower bourgeoisie; which took power from the upper bourgeoisie in 1848 but did not give the vote to the workers. That's when the nightmares of the propertied classes began: the exploited

---

* Eventually, in twentieth-century Russia and China, the workers will trust the bourgeois founders of the Communist Party; these make the popular vote meaningless and launch Stalinist tyranny.
† This linguistic unification grew (but not everywhere) into nationalistic excesses such as Nazism, Fascism and the genocides of the Second World War.

workers' cause was taken up by fiery intellectuals who called themselves Anarchists and Communists.

The French Anarchist Pierre Joseph Proudhon was not so threatening as he sounded. But he did say in 1840 that 'private property is a crime,' a phrase that can be seen as the watershed along which the bourgeois democrats and the workers split for decades.* Proudhon was also against centralized government, further frightening the bourgeoisie, which peopled the centralized government bureaucracies. Then came Karl Marx and Friedrich Engels, who wrote *The Communist Manifesto* in 1847.† The whole of history was class struggle, Marx and Engels said. But there would soon be a dictatorship of the proletariat and the exploiting classes would vanish. 'Workers of the world unite,' *The Communist Manifesto* said. 'You have nothing to lose but your chains.'‡

These threats from the left were one reason why Napoleon's nephew was elected president of France in 1848 as defender of the bourgeois republic. He made himself emperor in 1852, with the title of Napoleon III, and put the bourgeois revolution once more into hibernation. However, in 1870 he stupidly allowed himself to be drawn into a war with the Prussians, was defeated and fell. The French bourgeoisie, upper and lower, established a republic but did not give the vote to the workers who had fought heroically against the Prussians.

So the workers rose in 1871 and established a rival government called the Commune, which wanted things returned to where they had been in 1793, the time of Robespierre's

---

* Jesus did say that it was easier for a camel to go through the eye of a needle than for a rich man to enter the Kingdsm of God. (*Matthew* 19: 24).
† First published in German in 1848.
‡ Marx's criticism of the rich echoes Isaiah and Jesus.

Terror.* These revolutionaries, who called themselves the Communards, erected barricades, looted, burned public buildings – among them the royal palace of the Tuileries. The army, led by bourgeois officers, slaughtered 20,000 Communards, arrested another 40,000 or so and deported 7,000 to penal colonies beyond the seas.

Meanwhile, the legendary Otto von Bismarck, prime minister of Prussia had taken up the cause of German unification and pan-German patriotism. He thought that doctrines such as anarchism and socialism and communism were spawns of the devil. As a landowning aristocrat, he was incensed by condemnations of private property. He didn't even like the Liberal bourgeoisie in the lower house of the Prussian Parliament; nor did they like him. But the Liberals passionately wanted all German-speaking people unified into one state.† So they gave their support to Bismarck in Parliament.

Bismarck fought three quick wars,‡ the last against France. He formed alliances with other German states for these wars. He turned these alliances into one German empire. Only Austria remained outside the Prussian-led unified German state.§ The Prussian king became emperor and Bismarck prime minister and foreign minister. Nevertheless, after the defeat of France by the German army in 1871 and the Communard revolution in Paris, leftist movements in Germany grew. Bismarck said that German Socialists and

---

* See Chapter 13.

† There were thirty-nine separate German states and statelets after the Congress of Vienna redrew the map of Europe following Napoleon's defeat.

‡ Against Denmark, Austria and France.

§ In the Franco-Prussian war (1870–1) the victorious Germans took from the French Alsace-Lorraine, an area rich in coal and iron deposits. The French never forgave this. We shall revisit the issue when dealing with the First World War. Alsace-Lorraine had large German-speaking populations in 1870.

Anarchists should be exterminated like rats. But the 'rats' were acquiring a growing number of followers.

Bismarck tried to woo the workers to the cause of the establishment: he gave them accident insurance, old age insurance and even an early form of free medical care – in this he was far ahead of his time. Yet with every election the left grew. Bismarck used repression, but that did not work either (he repressed the Catholics, among others). Having lost the confidence of a new emperor,* Otto Eduard Leopold Bismarck, who started as the son of a mere squire with small land-holdings, resigned in 1890, aged seventy-five, hugely rich and dripping with titles: Prince von Bismarck, Duke von Lauenburg, Count von Bismarck-Schönhausen. He then worked on self-serving memoirs which laid the foundation for the enthusiastic United German patriotism which would serve Hitler so well.†

The seeds of the French Revolution did not only try to sprout in Germany. Democratic and nationalistic movements manifested themselves elsewhere. Italians fought and threw out their Austrian masters. Belgium, the Netherlands and Denmark democratized their institutions without fighting. Austria's emperor showed flexibility and avoided a bloody revolution by his German-speaking subjects. Hungary, an Austrian possession, was almost made an equal partner with Austria. However, other subjects of Austria such as the Bosnian Serbs disliked being ruled from Vienna and this became the fuse that eventually started the First World War.

In the Balkans, Christian subjects of the Turks began wars of independence. Greece won its freedom first in 1829. Serbia,

---

* Kaiser Wilhelm II who reigned over Germany during the First World War.
† Patriotism is the last refuge of the scoundrel, said Samuel Johnson, (*James Boswell, Life of Samuel Johnson LLD.*)

Bulgaria, Romania followed. In all these conflicts, Austria, Britain, France, Germany and Russia pulled strings and occasionally came close to blows among themselves. The Crimean War (1853–6) pitted Russia against Britain, France and Turkey. Russia wanted to exercise a protectorate over Christian populations in the Turkish part of the Balkans. Britain and France opposed any move of Russia towards the Mediterranean.

Lastly, let us deal with Britain, which had beaten Napoleon and become the undisputed superpower of the time. The 100 years between Napoleon's defeat and the First World War were called the *Pax Britannica*, the British Peace: not that there were no wars in those hundred years, but none on the scale that Napoleon had imposed upon Europe.

The Industrial Revolution had begun in Britain in the latter decades of the eighteenth century. Britain had not been fought over as had the other European countries. Its infrastructure was intact. It had a vast network of canals, fine ports, an abundance of coal and iron ore. Britain's economy grew at a fast pace. So did its population and the workforce of its factories. The nobles were marrying their sons to the daughters of common men who had amassed huge fortunes exploiting colonies or erecting factories.* The new money built fabulous residences and refurbished old castles where luxury reigned. New-money débutantes, twinkling with diamonds, were presented at Court. The new and old rich Britons danced, feasted, chased foxes. They became models for the rich elsewhere.

---

* Those of colonial wealth were called nabobs. The industrial millionaires eventually came to be called robber barons, especially in the US. Daughters of American millionaires married titled Britons: Jennie Jerome, mother of Winston Churchill, was one of those.

In the source of all this new money, in the factories and in the mines, life was brutish. The air was hardly breathable, work accidents were horrendous, hours were long and the people had no power to improve things. Some organized themselves into unions or staged public protests. This alarmed the establishment.

In 1819, food prices were rising. Craft workers were being replaced by machines. There was an industrial depression; even workers in the new steam-driven factories were being laid off. On 14 August, 60,000 people gathered in Manchester's St Peter's Fields to protest against the misery of their lives. They also wanted parliamentary reform that would give all male citizens the vote. These demonstrators had no weapons. There were women and children among them. They were loud but peaceful. Nonetheless, the moneyed people were terrified. What if this was the prelude to a French-style revolution? So the magistrates sent in the Yeomanry, the 15th Hussars and the Cheshire Volunteers, who galloped into the crowd slashing at the poor with swords. How many were wounded? How many were killed? The accepted figures were 500 injured, eleven killed. The peaceful demonstrators thought there were more victims; the authorities fewer. It was called the 'Peterloo' massacre (a combination of St Peter's Fields and Waterloo). It took British workers generations to forget those slashing swords.*

The owners of old money based on land ownership were brutal too. In Scotland, tenants were violently thrown off the land to make room for sheep pastures. Those who remained had to pay much higher rents and no longer had the right to

---

* British dockyard workers repairing my destroyer in the Second World War spoke to me of the Peterloo massacre as characteristic, still, of how management believed labour should be treated.

graze their own sheep on what had been common land. The United States and Canada benefitted – the more enterprising of the displaced Scots crossed the Atlantic. In the US, after the Civil War, these immigrants found a land that was expanding at the expense of its aboriginal inhabitants; they also found a vigorous nation industrializing at a furious pace, producing more and more jobs.

A casual reading of British history might give the impression that democracy came earlier to Britain – that it was there already even before the fall of Napoleon or even before the American War of Independence.* Not so. In 1815 there was a parliament with an elected House of Commons and a hereditary House of Lords. But the House of Commons was not dominant as it is now. Moreover, it was controlled by the landed gentry through constituencies they actually owned. These were called pocket boroughs because they were, figuratively, in the pocket of the local lord. Some of these constituencies had no more than a few dozen inhabitants, all in the pay of the manor house; they voted as they were told. There were nearly 150 of those pocket boroughs in a parliament of 658 seats. Moreover, the distribution of seats favoured the landed gentry. Burgeoning industrial towns had no members of Parliament. In 1815, the county of Cornwall with an estimated population of 400,000, had forty-four members; London, with more than 1 million inhabitants, had four.

After Wellington struck down Napoleon at Waterloo in 1815, it took seventy years to get Britain's parliamentary system reformed so that workers, both urban and agricultural, achieved the right to vote. Eventually, legislation decreed that each constituency had to have at least 50,000 voters; that all

---

* One often hears Americans say that their political institutions originated in Britain. That is not an indisputable fact.

male citizens should have the right to vote, even if they were Catholics. With the democratic vote, the lives of the average Briton began to improve, but slowly, too slowly. No wonder that it was a group which called itself the British Communist Party that commissioned Engels and Marx to write *The Communist Manifesto*.

In nineteenth-century Britain, the new rich, merchants and manufacturers, were as arrogant, grasping and unforgiving as the old, and they had as much influence over government as the nobles had had.

For example, the very rich shareholders of Britain's East India Company* persuaded the government in London to make war on China. The purpose of the war? To force the government of China to accept unlimited sales of opium by the East India Company to the Chinese people. There were two such wars, 1839–42 and 1859–60. In the second, Britain had the help of France. These conflicts have come down in infamy as the Opium Wars. To this day, Communist and anti-Communist Chinese consider they were irreparably humiliated in the Opium Wars, launched by Europeans who cared only for money.

Between those wars (1857–8), the East India Company caused the Indian Mutiny. The company's private army had British officers. Its Indian soldiers were called *sepoys*. They were given new rifles that required them to bite off the end of a lubricated cartridge. This cartridge was covered with a mixture of cow and pig grease. The cow part of the mixture was sacred to the Hindu soldiers; the pig part ritually polluting for Muslims. The sepoys refused to use the new cartridge. They were flogged, tortured, thrown into cellars without bread or

---

* The East India Company, a commercial enterprise, administered India for their British shareholders.

water, deprived of pay – which threatened their families with starvation. Enraged, they mutinied, killed many of the British officers, captured several cities, including Delhi. British forces retook the cities. Large numbers of captured sepoys were tied to the front of cannons and these cannons were then fired. The one good thing about this mutiny was that the administration of India was taken away from the East India Company. The British government ruled, thereafter, through a viceroy.

Were the Americans better to foreign nations? US Commodore Matthew Perry forced Japan to open itself to foreign trade. The Japanese submitted – having seen how easily the technically better armed Britons had defeated the Chinese in the two Opium Wars. Being who they are, the Japanese proceeded with efficient speed to industrialize their economy and their armed forces. In the Russo–Japanese war of 1904–5, the Japanese won, destroyed Russia's Far Eastern fleet and took Korea. This was the first time in centuries that an Asian nation had triumphed over a great European power. But to this day, the Japanese consider what Commodore Perry did was a humiliation.

The Opium Wars, the Indian Mutiny, Commodore Perry's pressure on Japan were extreme instances of European contempt for non-Europeans with remarkable civilizations.

Did the Christian churches protest? Not enough. They thought foreign conquests were excellent opportunities for converting the heathen. Besides, the church people were caught up in nationalistic patriotism: in this, Bismarck's Germany was not alone. Britons indulged in this sentiment and were, as French intellectuals put it, '*patriotards*', which means obnoxious, ignorant and narrow-minded patriots.* Set to Elgar's marvellous music, the verses of Arthur Christopher

---

* France had its full quota of *patriotards* too. Everyone did.

Benson (1862–1925), son of the Archbishop of Canterbury, express Britain's brazen patriotism best:

> Land of hope and Glory, mother of the free,
> How shall we extol thee, who are born of thee?
> Wider still and wider, shall thy bounds be set;
> God who made thee mighty, make thee mightier yet.

In the nineteenth century, large numbers of Britons did seem to believe their imperial spread was all ordained by the deity. The colonies yielded huge fortunes to men whom we would now call billionaires. They mattered, and still matter more than other people. Laws and taxes have often been tailored to the needs of billionaires. They have great influence on how western countries are run, the sort of influence a duke with a large private army had in earlier days. In fact we have a case of a billionaire king who has given billionaires a bad name, King Leopold II of Belgium.

At the end of the nineteenth century, Leopold conquered the Congo, declared it his personal property and turned it into a horror. The natives were forced to harvest ivory and, later, rubber. Their families were held hostage while the men went into the forest to bring back the sap of the rubber tree. If they did not fulfil the quota, their hands were cut off by King Leopold's mercenaries who said in their defence that they only cut off the workers' hands after they killed them. It was a sort of accounting practice. They were issued bullets which they were not supposed to waste. For each bullet they used, they were supposed to bring back a hand.[1]

European grand acquisitors (and their North American counterparts), were almost as brutal towards their own poor as they were towards people they colonized in other continents. This was publicized in inquiries of the British

Parliament. An eight-year-old boy working in a factory had to be there at five in the morning. If he was late he was 'beaten severely'. He finished work at nine p.m. If the children in the factory slowed down from fatigue, they were strapped. The place was 'perpetually' filled with the crying of the beaten children.[2]

There were 'bonded' children in those factories: a mother sold the services of Peter Smart, her little son, to the factory for six years. He received a total of about £100 in today's currency. In theory, the child did not work on Sundays, so he worked a total of 1,872 days for five pence a day. His mother had to sell his services because she had smaller children and needed the money. The bonded children were locked up at night. Some managed to run away but they were caught and severely whipped.

Things were even worse in the mines. Isabella Reed, twelve years old, carried coal through the tunnels from the coalface to mine pit. She carried 125 pounds on her back. She made twenty-five to thirty trips a day. The distance of her trips could be 500 yards each. Another child towed carts full of coal a mile or more. They beat her if she was 'not quick enough'. The men at the coal face were all naked and they 'took liberties with me', she testified.* Her day started at five in the morning and finished sixteen hours later, six days a week, sometimes seven. These children did not go to school, of course.

The grand acquisitors who owned the mines saw nothing wrong in all this. One of them, Thomas Wilson Esq., testified before a parliamentary committee in London and said that the government had no business interfering with the way he

---

* Such torments have produced striking literature, for example the French novel *Germinal* by Emil Zola.

treated his workers.* Nothing could be worse than government attempts to regulate business: that would be the 'greatest injury and injustice'. He 'most decidedly' objected to the proposition that 'coal-owners, as employers of children, are bound to attend to their education.'

Reformers criticized the behaviour of mine and factory owners. They did not like being criticized. Had not Calvin said that the rich were rich because God had predestined them to be rich? They were particularly shocked at being criticized by a Calvinist peer of the realm, the Earl of Shaftesbury.† Wouldn't someone defend the rich?

Herbert Spencer did. He became the hero and prophet of entrepreneurs.‡ It was Spencer, not Darwin, who first used the phrase 'the survival of the fittest.' For the good of the race, Spencer said, the 'inferior' must disappear, leaving the world to the 'superior'. Consequently, the children of the inferior must not be given a free education. The children of the superior who can afford to pay should be educated at good schools. It is the law of nature that the strong should 'shoulder aside' the weak and leave them to starve if they can't feed themselves. Those who are stronger, more ingenious and harder working have an exclusive right to the fruits of their labour. It is immoral to tax them. Therefore governments should limit themselves to 'the primitive duty' of protecting the person and property.

That was the gospel according the Saint Spencer. And how the grand acquisitors loved it. Not only, by their interpretation of St Paul, were they predestined by God to be who they were,[4]

---

* In the USA things were somewhat better because workers could escape life in factories and the mines and go to claim land being taken away from the Indians.
† Known as Lord Ashley before he succeeded to the title.
‡ Herbert Spencer (1820–1903) was a sociologist.

but Darwin's evolution would not have happened, had there not been creatures who crushed the weaker of their species. In the same spirit, in 1893, John D. Rockefeller sent a telegram approving of Pinkerton Agents gunning down strikers.[5] And the railway barons of Canada gave the most dangerous work to imported Chinese indentured workers.

Apart from trades unions,* the most important developments in the relations between British capital and labour were the actions of nineteenth-century reformers like the Calvinist Earl of Shaftesbury. As elected members of Parliament he, and his supporters managed to pass legislation that made life less horrible for the employees of the grand acquisitors and gave those employees, and all male citizens, Solon's powerful weapon: the vote.

There is more to the Pax Britannica. It was the British Empire and the British Navy that put an end to the slave ships. It was not inexpensive to do. Britain abolished slavery in its lands and its possessions, starting the greatest liberation movement in history.

A British public service developed, progressively – the most honest in the world for its time. And the miracle of the world's most populous democracy, India: it is an Indian creation, surely, but, equally, a British creation. That in the midst of the most regressive and oppressive social system in the world, brahminism, British-style democracy grew, is an enormous achievement for all those young district commissioners who studied at Oxford or Cambridge and went, in their

---

* To defend themselves, the workers formed trades unions. These, too, developed their own breed of grand acquisitors, who lived high on their members' contributions and dabbled in crime in the twentieth century. There have been admirable Labour leaders too, notably the American Walter Reuther (1907–70); and admirable employers: the Cadbury family in England is a shining example.

twenties, with a sense of justice and incorruptibility, to run millions of people in India. It was an unimaginable success for the British-trained Indian judges and barristers; for British-trained Indian politicians and an Indian officers' corps that obeyed the constitution. No other former colonial master can boast such an achievement.

Nor should one forget the three, originally white, offspring of Britain: Australia, Canada and New Zealand. There, the British parliamentary and judicial institutions were success-fully adapted to new territories that are now evolved, cultured democracies, that have fought against tyrannies in two world wars. They prosper. They deal, mostly in peace with becoming multi-ethnic and multi-racial, as they try to redress the wrongs their aboriginal populations suffered.

The British system would itself evolve, becoming a model for constitutional monarchies everywhere. The powers of the House of Lords would be reduced peacefully. Eventually, before the Second World War, Edward VIII, a king with dangerous ideas, abdicated. And all this happen in a country that had developed remarkable quality would newspapers, the *Observer,* the *Guardian, The Times, The Scotsman.* The traditions of such newspapers became ideals for the rest of the world to copy; and these traditions served as a basis for the BBC, a state-financed broadcasting network that was not a servant of the government.

15

THREE WORLD WARS: TWO HOT, ONE COLD

(20th century)

The twentieth century in one sentence: There were two world wars; a cold war; many smaller wars; one great depression; two monster regimes and their fall – nazism and communism; decolonization; mass carnage; warplanes; atomic weapons; rockets in space; satellites that see everything; the transistor, computers and robotic tools; antibiotics; the beginnings of gene therapy, but also AIDS, drug addiction and drug-resistant bacteria or viruses; the car; the aeroplane; the internet – more people meeting more people than ever before; a tidal wave of American films, television and music seen by traditionalists in much of the world as a deadly threat to their cultures; and transnational capitalists who escape the rule of nation states.

We saw that Japan beat Russia in 1905. A small revolution followed in Russia. It was drowned in blood by the Tsar's troops. He accepted the creation of a parliament, the Duma; but the imperial functionaries and the nobles retained undiminished power: a harbinger of horrors to come.

In the Balkans, in 1912, Bulgaria, Greece, Montenegro and Serbia attacked the Turks and pushed them out of Macedonia.

In 1913 Serbia and Greece fought Bulgaria over the partition-
ing of Macedonia.*

We saw that in the nineteenth century, various ethnic groups
began freeing themselves from foreign kings. The Balkan wars
were a continuation of the process and were the prelude to the
First World War. The Austro-Hungarian Empire still ruled
Slavs. Next door, the independent Slav Serbian kingdom (which
had won freedom from the Turks in the nineteenth century)
wanted to take Slav territories from Austria and Hungary and
unite them into one Slav state. In 1914 when the heir to
the Austro-Hungarian throne visited Sarajevo in Bosnia-
Herzegovina, he was assassinated by a Serb. To cut a long
diplomatic story short, Austria declared war on Serbia. Russia
sided with Serbia. Germany, Bulgaria and Turkey sided with
Austria. France sided with the Serbs. So did Britain, when
German troops crossed the Belgian frontier to attack France.†

The Austro-Hungarian monarchy had the old, grand-
acquisitorial reason for going to war: it did not want to lose
its many Slav possessions.‡ The Germans came into the war to
make sure the Russians didn't trounce the Austrians, thus
bringing Slav power to the centre of Europe. The Turks and
the Bulgarians had lost territory in the Balkan wars and
wanted it back. The French militarists wanted to avenge their

---

* In 1912, under the Turks, Macedonia had the same boundaries as in the
fourth century BC, extending over parts of the following twentieth-century
states: Bulgaria, Greece, Yugoslavia and Albania. It was peopled by
Greeks Albanians, as well as the Bulgarians and Slavs who had arrived
on the scene in the seventh century AD.

† The Germans had a plan to defeat France and then concentrate on the war
with Russia.

‡ Among these Austro-Hungarian Slav possessions were Bohemia, Moravia, Galicia, Bukowina, Ruthenia, Slovakia, Transylvania, Bosnia-Herzegovina, Slovenia, Croatia, Dalmatia: these accounted for more than half
the Austro-Hungarian Empire's territory.

defeat of 1870 and retake Alsace-Lorraine from the Germans. Britain came into the war because it had signed an international guarantee of Belgium's neutrality. Britain did not want Germany controlling Belgium just across the Straits of Dover.

The 1914–18 World War had some brilliant military moments. The German general Ludendorff beat the Russians. The British, with a minor deployment of forces, got the Arabs to rise against Turkey. The Turks, under Colonel Mustafa Kemal, proved better tacticians than the western allies in Gallipoli, the peninsula that forms the western shore of the Dardanelles, the strait that leads from the Aegean towards the Black Sea. The Austrians routed the Italians at Caporetto. There also were horrors. The Christian Armenians in the Caucasus regions of the Muslim Ottoman Empire favoured the Christian Russian Empire and were slaughtered by the Turks, the rulers of the Ottoman Empire. How many were slaughtered? The numbers are in dispute, varying between 500,000 and 1.5 million.*

In retrospect, the rest of that war was mindless. On either side of the line that separated the German troops from the Anglo-French, the combatants built continuous trenches stretching from the Belgian coast on the North Sea to the Swiss border. These two lines of trenches were separated by what was called no-man's-land. One night, the Anglo-French troops would rain a gargantuan artillery barrage on the German trenches; it was ineffectual because the German machine-guns were too well dug-in. After the barrage, the Anglo-French soldiers would come out of their trenches and rush across no-man's-land at their enemies. German machine-guns mowed them down. The survivors went back to their trenches. Some

---

* My father's uncle, Dr Nicholas Vassiliades, living in Constantinople (now Istanbul) and conscripted as a colonel in the Turkish army's medical corps, saw the massacre in Armenia. From the records of the Turkish army's medical corps, he placed the slaughtered at more than 1 million.

nights later, the Germans acted just as stupidly and were slaughtered by Anglo-French machine-guns. Thousands and thousands died in each of those attacks. Second lieutenants lived, on average, only a few days after reaching the front: these were the young officers who had to lead the charges across no-man's-land into the hail of machine-gun bullets.

Counting casualties on both sides, 8,427,015 servicemen were killed or died of their wounds in the First World War.[1] (Battle of Verdun, 700,000 casualties; Battle of the Somme, 1.2 million casualties.) It was a case of a superb defensive weapon, the heavy machine-gun, to which an adequate antidote, the tank, had not yet been sufficiently developed. The necessary engineering knowledge had been available for years and some tanks were built, but they were too slow and their range too short. The prevailing military thinking was that tanks were simply support for infantry. Only in the Second World War would the tank become an independent striking weapon, mechanized cavalry that could cut a defensive line, ride over wide trenches, break through and catch the enemy from behind.

On the eastern front, the mauled Russian troops mutinied against their inept Tsarist generals. The Communists took power after a while and signed an armistice with the Germans. In the west, uncertain of winning on land, the Germans tried to starve Britain by proclaiming unlimited submarine warfare. American ships were sunk; this brought the US into the war in April 1917. The Germans, exhausted and facing the prospect of ever-fresh American troops, signed an armistice at 11 a.m. on the eleventh day of the eleventh month of 1918.

The war was a tactical and strategic disgrace. The generals on both sides had known the power of the machine-gun. It had been used in earlier wars. Yet they stuck with the outdated Waterloo tactic of the infantry charge. The British troops rightly called their commander, Field Marshal Douglas Haig, 'butcher Haig'.* He had said that the side would win which had one soldier left standing while the other side had none.

After the war had ended, the victorious western powers attacked Russia to overthrow Lenin's Communist government. They were beaten by the Russian peasants and soldiers who were defending their land against foreigners and had been promised by Lenin, the Communist chief, that they would each receive their very own part of the nobility's vast landed estates. That promise was never kept.†

The Greek army invaded Turkey but was thrown into the sea, along with hundreds of thousands of former Greek subjects of the Ottoman Empire. The Turks were left with only Asia Minor and stripped of all their possessions – Armenia, Iraq, Syria, Lebanon, Jordan, Palestine, the Arabian peninsula. The Ottoman Empire became the Turkish Republic. The Austro-Hungarian Empire was dismembered. Austria and Hungary – separated – lost their Slav territories. Thus, Bohemia, Moravia and Slovakia became the independent state of Czechoslovakia; Slovenia, Croatia, Bosnia-Herzegovina and Dalmatia became parts of the Serbian kingdom renamed Yugoslavia.‡ Germany was restricted in what weapons and warships it could have, lost territory, all its colonies in Africa and the Pacific; it had to pay crippling compensation, which put it in economic misery. The conditions imposed on the losers showed terrible statesmanship – one must not lead defeated enemies to believe that they can redress things only

---

* After the war, Haig was made an earl and was given 500,000 gold sovereigns for his services.

† Communism gained power because it was a reaction against the abominable treatment of the poor peasants and poor urban workers by the rich. In a sense, communism was a Christian heresy – without Jesus' compassion. The line of thought is clear from Isaiah, through Jesus to communism. The non-rich of humanity have often considered the rich as evil.

‡ Which included Montenegro and the Slav-speaking part of Macedonia.

through another war. That helped bring Hitler to power fourteen years later.

There were tensions among the victorious allies, especially between Britain and the US. Which power would dominate world shipping, world trade? Would US companies have access to the huge oil reserves in the Middle East territories Britain had seized from the Turks? For a while, accommodations were negotiated among the victors even after the isolationist Warren G. Harding was elected president of the US in 1920 and additional isolationists entered Congress. There was prosperity in the US. The economy was humming and there was a wave of irrepressible faith in the stock market. Everybody, or so it seemed, obtained bank loans without collateral and bought stocks. Fortunes were made as prices rose.

By 1929 at least 40 per cent of stock market values were based on nothing more than wishful thinking. Worried, the Federal Reserve Board – the US central bank – tried to cool off the market by raising interest rates to make borrowing more costly for investors. Was it because the Federal Reserve Board was worried that investors became worried? No one knows, or can know for sure. At any rate, on the 18 October 1929, 'Black Thursday', the market began a catastrophic slide. It was as if all those people who had believed unanimously that the market was bound to keep going up, believed no less unanimously that it was bound to keep going down.* Three years later, in 1932, stock prices had dropped to 20 per cent of what they had been in 1929. Having made loans, they could not recoup from ruined investors; 11,000 US banks became insolvent and closed. Great numbers of ordinary people lost all their money and consumed less and less. Consequently,

---

* For an elegant description of what happened, see John Kenneth Galbraith, *The Great Crash, 1929*, Boston: Houghton Mifflin, 1955.

production shrank. Manufacturing output in 1932 was 54 per cent of what it had been in 1929. One quarter of US workers lost their jobs.

Every government banned imports to protect its own production and to reduce its unemployment. By 1932, international trade had fallen to half what it had been in 1929. Workers in export sectors lost their jobs. The USA not only stopped importing from Europe; it did not invest there any more. The Europeans (including the British), who had contracted huge debts in the US to fight the First World War, were no longer earning dollars to pay what they owed. The Germans were burdened with war reparations. The so-called free market was just unable to turn things around.*

Franklin Delano Roosevelt was elected president of the US in 1932 and launched larger public works projects to boost the economy.† Unemployment fell from 25 per cent to 15 per cent – though not enough. This state of affairs lasted until Adolf Hitler started the Second World War in 1939.

Hitler, as the elected leader of the largest party, became Chancellor of Germany in January 1933. He had come to power because Germany's democratic politicians could do nothing to relieve the country's misery. In March he was

---

* Frederick Von Hayek, high priest of right wing economics, said that if the Federal Reserve had not intervened the depression would not have happened.

† Roosevelt's predecessor, Herbert Hoover, had already started on this path. Public works to restart the economy was the recipe of Keynes, the great economist. However, Joseph son of Jacob, was the first to suggest this recipe. The Pharaoh dreamt that seven thin cows had eaten seven fat cows. His advisers could not interpret the dream. (A modern Pharaoh would have said, 'Don't we have a good Jewish economist anywhere?') They brought him Joseph who, in modern terms, said: 'Pharaoh, Sir, the economy sees seven years of boom and seven years of depression. During the boom, tax, create a surplus, and when the depression comes, spend the surplus to boost the economy' (*Genesis*, 41: 1–37).

voted full power by the German Parliament. In a very short time he abolished democracy. Germany, thereafter, was run by Hitler and a small group of acolytes – a parody of Plato's Republic. With huge public works and international barter deals, Hitler's finance minister, Hjalmar Schacht, ended the depression in Germany by 1936, the best economic performance anywhere. The rest is common knowledge. Hitler was a grand acquisitor seeking more land. His people, he said, needed *lebensraum*, room to live in. Hitler repudiated the peace treaty that had followed the First World War, stopped paying reparations, re-armed and scared Britain and France into appeasing him, vainly. He swallowed Austria and Czechoslovakia. Then he signed a deal with Russia whereby both attacked Poland and each took half of it. Thereupon, Britain and France declared war on Germany on 1 September 1939.

There followed a period of so-called phoney war when nothing much was happening. Then, in April and May 1940, with unprecedented speed, German forces took Holland, Belgium, Denmark, Norway and France. A clutch of brilliant German generals had learned the lessons of the First World War: they nullified their opponents' old-fashioned defences by cutting through or around them with tanks, and they paralysed Anglo-French military transportation with dive-bombers.

Winston Churchill became prime minister of Great Britain. His spirit and oratory kept the British fighting through desperate times. The heroic Royal Air Force, outnumbered, but guided by radar, gradually beat back a German bombing campaign that was to have been a prelude to an invasion of Britain. President Roosevelt declared that America would be the arsenal of democracy, but by persevering in lonely adversity on land, air and sea, it was the British who saved the free world.

Mussolini, Italy's dictator, brought his country into the war on the side of Germany and attacked Greece through Albania in October 1940. The Italians were ignominiously beaten back; as they were, also, when they tried to attack Egypt from Cyrenaica, now Libya, which the Italians had taken from the Turks in 1911. Outnumbered eight to one but with more tanks than their opponents, the British had spectacular successes and captured 135,000 Italian troops out of 300,000.

In 1941, Germany overran Yugoslavia and Greece and attacked the Soviet Union. It was Hitler's, like Napoleon's, worst mistake.

Meanwhile Japan, who had invaded China in 1937, had become an ally of Germany, and took French Indochina in the summer of 1941. President Roosevelt froze all Japanese assets in the US and embargoed all shipments of oil and war materiel to Japan. So the Japanese committed *their* worst mistake: they attacked and heavily damaged the US fleet at Pearl Harbor, on 7 December 1941. They woke the American giant. The year 1941 was a hinge of fate.

Germany and Japan had successes. The Japanese controlled most of south-east Asia. The Germans almost reached Moscow and the Soviet oil fields, but were stopped. That the USSR eventually repulsed Germany's attack is almost unbelievable, given what a mess Joseph Stalin, the Soviet dictator, had made of his country. He was – no mistake about it – a grand acquisitor who killed countless innocent people in peacetime to keep the territory he had.*

Stalin grabbed more territory after the war. In the grip of a flawed ideology, communism, he collectivized and bureau-

---

* For example, the Georgians, in the Caucasus, who tried to become independent after the First World War. Thousands of Georgians were executed, although Stalin himself was Georgian, not Russian.

cratized Soviet agriculture, which thereafter could hardly feed the people – there were huge famines. He nationalized every other economic activity. His central planning totally ignored the laws of supply and demand. Russians used to joke that centralized planning achieved the miracle whereby a Soviet store had nothing the people wanted and everything they did not want. Stalin starved or butchered millions, suspecting them of disloyalty. Before the Second World War, he even killed his most successful military commanders, men who had distinguished themselves against the Germans in the First World War.

But the Russian people responded magnificently to the German attack, not only on the field of battle, not only by throwing up talented new military commanders, but also by producing sophisticated weapons. Russian tanks became the most serviceable in the world, with greater range, speed, firepower, armour and fewer breakdowns than any other tank. The surrender of a German army at Stalingrad on 31 January 1943 was a clear omen of Hitler's eventual defeat. On 5 July 1943, in the battle of the Kursk Salient – the largest tank battle in history – the Soviet forces crushed the Germans and advanced inexorably towards Berlin.

There were other crucial allied victories. The magnificent success of the American fleet at the battle of Midway and the bloody ejection of the Japanese from what they had captured in the Pacific were great military achievements. With American and Canadian help, the British won the long Atlantic battle against German submarines that would otherwise have starved Britain into submission.

Then there were El Alamein, the allied landings in North Africa, in Italy, the south of France and finally D-Day, 6 June 1944, when American, British and Canadian troops invaded Normandy. They came ashore through mines, across beaches swept by machine-gun fire. The Americans had opted for the toughest beaches with the highest cliffs. Epic battles followed. The Germans were pushed back to their own soil. In May 1945, they surrendered.

Hitler had already committed suicide. He will be remembered as a monster who industrialized death, gassing human beings in so-called bathhouses, cremating them in giant ovens, 6 million of them. This was the Holocaust. On 20 January 1942, the Germans had completed their preparations for a 'final solution', the total extermination of Europe's Jewish people, among them Jews who had fought bravely for Germany in the First World War. Germans also exterminated gypsies, cripples, the retarded, all for the 'purity of the race', a Platonic principle.

From a military point of view, they displayed magnificent fighting qualities, bravery, tactical and strategic skill, endurance. Towards the end, against overwhelming odds, they fought on fiercely. German civilians, under a constant rain of bombs, kept the arms and supplies flowing to the troops. German industrial production at the end of the war was the highest it had ever been – the factories had gone underground. But the honour for which the German officer caste had always cared was irrevocably tarnished by the Holocaust, by machine-gunning survivors of ships sunk by German submarines, and by mass butcheries of captured Polish officers and of the wives and children of resistance fighters (for example, 245 women and 207 children burned alive by the Germans in the French village of Oradour).

A bloody war. There is blame enough for both sides. Allied bomber fleets deliberately dropped incendiaries in a circle around their target which became a blazing funnel, sucking the oxygen out of a German city and asphyxiating civilians in their shelters. The Russians, on German soil, robbed and raped as the Germans had done on Russian soil. Even after the war, starving German girls had to sell their bodies for tins of food to victorious western allied soldiers.

More than 14 million European servicemen on both sides were killed or died of their wounds; 27 million European civilians were killed.[2] The US forces lost 295,000 service men.

Japan surrendered in August 1945 after Hiroshima and Nagasaki were flattened by American atomic bombs. President Truman reasoned that if he didn't use these bombs, 1 million American servicemen would lose their lives capturing Japan itself. Those who doubt him say that, when the bombs fell, diplomats were negotiating Japan's surrender. But the Japanese were still fighting. Japanese dead in the war totalled 1,506,000 servicemen and 300,000 civilians. Did the destruction caused by the first two atomic bombs make the idea of a nuclear war among great powers unthinkable? We all still hope so.

However, non-nuclear wars and massacres did not stop. Soviet forces butchered Ukrainians suspected of having collaborated with the Germans. These were in addition to the millions exterminated before the Second World War. The total tally of Stalin's victims 'is unlikely to be much below 50 million.'[3] Equipped with Soviet arms, Mao Tse-tung's Communist forces in China fought the 'Nationalist' forces of Chiang Kai-shek, pushing them off the mainland into the island of Taiwan. Starting in 1946, Communist guerrillas tried to drag Greece into the Communist bloc and were only defeated in 1949. The Soviets blockaded West Berlin in 1948 and 1949. The city was saved by a massive US airlift. North Korea, with the backing of the USSR and later China, invaded South Korea in 1950. United Nations forces, headed by the Americans, fought a bitter three-year war to save the capitalist south.

Attempts to assert some degree of independence from the USSR in East Germany (1953), Hungary (1956), Czechoslovakia (1968) and Poland (1956, 1970) were brutally suppressed by the Soviet army.

The Soviet armed forces and arms industry had collected the cream of scientists, technicians and managers. The rest of the economy was a disaster. The political management was corrupt. Company managers falsified the books to pretend they had fulfilled the various five-year plans. Russian workers used to say: 'They don't pay us very much, but we don't work very much either.' Agricultural production was lower than it had been before the First World War. The economy was so dysfunctional, its productivity so low, that eventually it could not sustain the arms race.

Why the mess in Russia? Because it was run at the top by the grand acquisitors of the Politburo. They chose their own successors and those chosen were the younger men who most slavishly flattered their elders before betraying them. They were not statesmen but people skilled at grabbing and holding power. For example, Leonid Brezhnev owed his rise to his patron Nikita Khrushchev, whose boots he licked. In 1964, Khrushchev took Brezhnev as his number two. Three months later Brezhnev overthrew Khrushchev.

Brezhnev ruled the USSR from 1964 to 1982. He had an extravagantly large collection of Rolls-Royce cars. His daughter was covered in diamonds given her by chiefs of Russian state industries to curry favour with her father. The corruption went all the way down to the lowest officials. The judges served not justice but the Communist government. The whole structure belied the original Communist motto: 'From each according to his ability, to each according to his needs.'

Moreover, communism went against human nature, denying citizens the chance to better themselves, to acquire property, to follow the profit motive – a major factor in economic growth.* The importance of profit became most evident in agriculture: those who worked in the huge collective farms were allowed to cultivate small plots for their own use and to sell produce from those plots. It came to pass that the total production of the tiny 'for profit' plots exceeded the total production of the huge state farms. Corruption, inefficiency, denying the human instinct for economic self-improvement, the crushing weight of competing in military production with the US – these are among the reasons for the Soviet collapse.

In the late 1980s, the Soviet leader Mikhail Gorbachev thought he could lead his country, by peaceful stages, from a police state, with stultifying central planning, to some form of Scandinavian socialism. There would be free-enterprise capitalism alongside government social services in health, education and pensions. There would be an elected legislature with power to make laws. Non-Russian components of the USSR would be able to secede gradually and peacefully.

It did not work. It could not. There was no one around who knew anything about democracy – they only knew about tyranny. There was no one who knew anything about free enterprise – they only knew about rogue state enterprise. The non-Russian components of the USSR were not interested in gradual evolution – they wanted independence at once from foreigners, and for the Balts, the Ukrainians, the Kazakh, etc. the Russians were the foreigners.

---

* In repetitive and, therefore, monotonous jobs, such as those in agriculture, commerce and industry, the profit motive is the only motive for productivity. In the arts, literature, the sciences, politics, public administration, teaching, one finds people who do not necessarily work for money. Their motto, allegedly, is 'art for art's sake'. This is not to say they would not like to be better paid for their work. Teachers, doctors, public administrators do sometimes withhold their services to obtain better contracts.

So, former satellites of the Soviet Union broke away, the Berlin wall fell, Soviet Socialist republics became independent. In Russia proper, systems broke down before they could be replaced. There was no – there had never been – commercial law. There was no property law, since everything had belonged to the state. The military, the bureaucracy saw their worlds crumbling. Those who had been talented and lawless black-marketeers became the successful lawless capitalists. Military officers and scientists began selling weapons and secrets abroad to supplement their vanishing incomes. Eventually, a successful secret police officer, Vladimir Putin, manipulated the system and was elected president. As this is written, he is trying to make freedom work. It may take a long time, even though Russians are a talented people with great science, art and literature. As yet, they have no experience of freedom.

Then there is the other – the only – vast state that calls itself Communist: China. In the nineteenth century, China's imperial house was crumbling. In the Opium Wars, it had been impossibly humiliated by western powers. Subsequently, warlords ran rampant. One, Chiang Kai-shek, prevailed for a while and fought the Japanese invaders. But in 1949 Mao Tse-tung and his gang of ruthless autocrats pushed Chiang off the mainland.

In 1950, Mao's troops stopped the US-led UN forces from taking North Korea, fighting them to a standstill where the Korean conflict had begun – at the 38th parallel. It was a considerable Chinese achievement, since the US and its allies had complete control of air and sea. In 1962, during the Cuban missile crisis* the Chinese attacked India. However, the missile crisis was quickly resolved and US president John

---

* See next chapter.

Kennedy promised help to India. Chinese forces then withdrew. They had been poised to take the fertile lowlands of Assam in north-east India, which also have important oil fields.

Repeatedly, Mao launched impossible reforms and killed massively to apply them. He dispossessed even small land-owners; put intellectuals into agricultural hard-labour camps; forced small villages to produce steel in tiny blast furnaces (it wasn't really steel). His biggest ventures, the Great Leap Forward and the Cultural Revolution, resulted in famine and in the death of millions: the lowest estimate is 23 million, the highest 35 million. He killed more of his own people than any other leader in history, with the possible exception of Stalin. Mao once said, publicly, that he was not really worried about the consequences of a nuclear war: 'Half the earth's people might die but there would still be half left.'[4] He lived in extreme luxury, surrounded himself with pretty assistants with whom he fornicated, sometimes with three at a time. No one quite knew what destructive thing he would do next. Finally he died. Some weird successors were finally replaced by Deng Xiaoping who reduced the stifling uncertainty, allowed some free enterprise and made it possible for foreign capital to operate in China. China's industrious people, many of them talented and brilliant, have produced an economic miracle, the greatest growth rates of any economy. They have avoided starvation even though only 10 per cent of their land is arable.

Those who considered China a Soviet satellite were wrong. Soviet–Chinese relations soured in the 1950s. In 1960, there was an official break in relations. The USSR stopped giving any aid to China; other Iron Curtain countries followed Moscow's lead.* China was ostracized by its former ideological allies.

---

* Iron Curtain = Eastern European. Winston Churchill said in a post-war speech that Communism had made an iron curtain fall across Europe.

China is neither Communist nor Socialist as the terms are defined in Europe. European Socialists are just democrats who hold free elections and surrender power when they lose. (Some Americans mistakenly lump European democratic Socialism with Soviet Communism which never held free elections and never peacefully surrendered power.) China is an autocracy run, as in Plato's Republic, by an all-powerful group who consider themselves above the rest. There is no prospect of democracy in China in the foreseeable future. There is no one in power in China who knows about freedom; students who demand it get shot in Tiananmen Square. Governments of developed countries mute their criticism of China because it is a gigantic market for their goods.

Meanwhile, China's main source of fuel is coal that burns dirty. China cannot afford the expensive scrubbers that would reduce the pollution. There are 1.2 billion Chinese. Can the 'West', in all good conscience, ask them not to burn their coal to save the world's atmosphere? The Chinese say that the problems with the atmosphere were, and still are, created by the rich western countries who have no moral right to argue that China should stop growing so as not to pollute.

Where will China's bursting population spread? Many would smuggle themselves into the US. They may have to leach across a very long border into Russia's Asian lands, or into India. But both India and Russia have nuclear weapons, as does China.

Chinese overpopulation is a ticking bomb.

16

THE GLOBAL VILLAGE

(21st century)

Living in a global village means that, as in primitive villages, we can always hear and see one another, know too much about one another, be affected too much by one another, even if the 'another' lives half a globe away. This new state of affairs grew through the twentieth century with the telephone, telegraph, radio, cinema, television and air travel; grew exponentially after the invention of the transistor in 1947;* which led to ever tinier chips, to tiny portable phones, smart bombs, spy satellites and satellites that instantaneously moved money, spread news, spectacles, propaganda and advertising around the earth.

The US is the principal provider of entertainment with international appeal; purveyor also of news to the whole world (e.g. CNN); master of popular fashion and music; the mother-house of more global companies than any other nation. Not only the Americans themselves but many others around the world see the US either as the only power able to solve problems or as the power that has caused these problems.

---

* The transistor was invented in the Bell laboratories in New York by three American physicists, J. Bardeen, W. Brattain and W. Shockley.

Giant transnational corporations make decisions that nation states used to make. A giant US firm buys a subsidiary in another country. Research and management services are thereafter provided to the subsidiary by the US mother-house. For those services, the non-American subsidiary is charged an amount equal to its profits; these profits, thus, are transferred to the US. Large corporations in rich countries other than the US act the same way – it's normal business practice. Anyway, all really large companies are making themselves global, detached from nation states. To the extent possible, they go where the taxes are lowest, the workers cheapest, the environmental and labour laws weakest; they do this up to the point where chaos (the flip side of unfettered acquisitiveness) makes it unprofitable. That is, they seek out new bargain-basement jurisdictions until the savings are offset by the cost of doing business amid uncertain laws, unfree citizens and corrupt institutions.

Meanwhile, many citizens of western democracies find themselves competing for work with people in the east and south who have little bargaining power and great need. Some wealth is thus shared, although much of it ends up in the hands of grand acquisitors. Lower incomes and lost tax revenue may compel progressive western countries to drop social programmes that previously made them the envy of the less fortunate. So there are protests in rich countries – mostly from the young, denouncing corporate rapacity and globalization and their perpetrator's inherent selfishness.

Nations moving towards democracy, towards 'power for the people', see that foreign corporations in their midst are not subject to the power of the people. 'Is democracy, then, a sham?' they ask.

Within nations, even democratic ones, not all citizens have equal rights, equal opportunity to obtain power and privilege;

there are people who feel they are not heard and that their personal interest is sacrificed to the wishes of transnational corporations which subsidize the election of pliant politicians. Race and ethnicity are causes for inequalities within democracies, more specifically within democracy's superpower, the USA. These problems are slow to resolve in advanced nations but they are quickly broadcast to the whole globe. How will the poor and less advanced nations, trying to democratize themselves, solve their own problems of ancient ethnic and religious hatreds when the rich and powerful seem unable to solve such problems on their homeground?

Ireland

The Irish problem is old. Ireland is a Gaelic island, the Emerald Isle, the greenest place one could ever see. It was invaded and annexed by the non-Gaelic army of Henry II of England in the twelfth century and converted to Catholicism; invaded again in 1649 by Oliver Cromwell, the Calvinist who had beheaded Charles I of England; invaded once again by the Protestant William of Orange who defeated the Irish Catholics at the battle of the Boyne on 1 July 1690. And so on.

Cromwell and William of Orange paid their Protestant soldiers and officers by giving them land taken from the Irish Catholics. The Church of England, the official church founded by Henry VIII, obtained rich properties and built the biggest churches. It was called the Church of Ireland in the Emerald Isle and its sumptuous places of worship were largely empty. Jonathan Swift, Dean of St Patrick's Cathedral, in his first service, was confronted by a congregation of one. He said: 'Dearly beloved Roger, the scripture moveth both you and me.'[1]

As the Protestants took more and more of the land, the Gaelic Irish left, joined foreign armies, settled in Britain and eventually in the US. To those who stayed, the Protestant landlord seldom paid wages; he gave them smallish plots of land on which to build skimpy cottages and grow food, chiefly potatoes, for themselves and their families.

Then the potato famine struck in 1846. A fungus destroyed the plants and the tubers in the ground. Because they were getting no saleable crop from their peasants, the landlords threw them out, and tore down their homes, so no other starving people might squat there.

Charity was dispensed only to those who moved into the institutions called workhouses. In those, men and women were segregated and young children were separated from their families. Diseases thrived in the workhouses and killed terrifying proportions of the inmates. Some kindlier landlords gave land to extend the cemeteries.

The Internet has a wealth of material on the famine by Irish, American, European and English sources.[2] Here is an extract from the article of an English Protestant journalist on an Irish peasant he encountered:

> He was not an old man. He was under forty years of age. His cheeks were sunken, and his skin sallow-coloured, as if death were already with him. I saw the poor man and his poor family. A mother skeleton and baby skeleton; a tall boy skeleton; four female children skeletons, and the tall father skeleton. Their only food was about seven ounces and a half of cornmeal per day for each person. No fuel was used by this family, nor by other working families, except what was required to boil the cornmeal into a stirabout – they had no money to buy more fuel.

Hundreds of thousands died. Two million emigrated, carrying with them the nightmare of the famine, told and retold down the generations. Such horrors are not forgotten. In Ireland itself there was unrest, rebellion. For long, Catholics could not vote or hold public office. In 1881, the English Parliament passed a Land Act guaranteeing tenure and fair rents to tenants, and allowing them to sell their holdings. Protestants and Catholics established majorities in different parts of the island, the Protestants in what is now called Northern Ireland. This did not satisfy the Catholics. In 1921, southern Ireland became independent. Northern Ireland remained a part of Great Britain, with a Protestant majority and a Catholic minority, each with militias and terrorists. The Protestants rigged the electoral map of Northern Ireland to give the Catholics fewer seats than their due.

The Protestants feel they have been in Northern Ireland for centuries enough to have a right to stay, and they do not want to be a minority in a united Ireland. The Catholics want a united Ireland. Can there be an agreed solution or steps towards one?

The Irish problem has recently been handled as well as could be. Major American corporations have built plants and offices in Ireland, both north and south. The European Community has accepted Ireland as a member and subsidized its farmers. Economically, both Northern and Southern Ireland are doing better than ever. The importance of holding land – that old bone of contention – is lessened in consequence. Irish women, Catholic and Protestant, have a stronger voice and have been using it for peace. American presidents and prominent American politicians such as former Senator George J. Mitchell who chaired peace negotiations between Catholics and Protestants in Belfast, have worked hard and with sensitivity to solve the Northern Ireland conflict. British governments, Tory or Labour, have done their utmost to bring peace. But the old fanaticisms remain.

This is a cautionary tale. Protestants and Catholics now live peacefully side by side in the US, in England. But the solution to the Northern Ireland problem is always so near and yet so far. What hope is there, then, for relations between the rich in the west and the poor in the east?

The Balkans

The Serbs are central to understanding the recent wars in the Balkans. Between 1358 and 1521, the Turks conquered the Balkans. Last to fall was Belgrade, the capital of the Serbs. Readers will remember that Muslims gave first-class citizenship to those whom they conquered and who converted to Islam. Some Serbs, now called Bosnians, converted.[3] As they spoke Serbian, they became the policemen, tax collectors, customs officials, local administrators of the Turkish occupiers and lorded it over Serbs who had not converted. The Christian Serbs never really forgave this. Under the Turkish occupation, the Albanians, who also converted to Islam, 'encroached' on territory the Christian Serbs considered theirs.

The Croatians, who were Serbs, converted to Roman Catholicism in the ninth century and thereafter were in the orbit of Hungary and then the Austro-Hungarian Empire. The Catholic Croats were taken after the First World War into the Serb-dominated Yugoslav federation. They had wanted it to be a loose confederation, but the Orthodox Serbs imposed a unitary regime.

Hitler created a Croatian puppet state that included Bosnia and Herzegovina. The leader of this state, Ante Pavelić, had his own terrorist organization, the Ustaše, with Croatian and Bosnian members. He killed hundreds of thousands of Christian Serbs and Jews in an orgy of ethnic cleansing.[4]

What goes around comes around. When Yugoslavia disintegrated in the early 1990s, there was revenge killing, epidemic raping, more murderous ethnic cleansing. Croatians, Bosnians, Serbs and Kosovars* grabbed territory from one another; it was always somebody or other's ancestral land, to which they were sentimentally attached. For example, the Serbs are sentimentally attached to 'the field of the black birds' in Kosovo where, on 15 June, 1389, their army was destroyed by the Turks. Many Serbs believe they actually won the battle; that field, they say, is central to their national identity.

There was NATO intervention and finally, in early 1999, bombing of Serbia by NATO (mostly US) warplanes. Serbia's factories, its transportation and communication systems, many public buildings, its bridges over the Danube were destroyed. The Serbian armed forces, however, escaped almost unscathed, as was evident when they retreated out of Kosovo. The 'destroyed' Serbian tanks were rolling nicely.

The Serbs had been allies of Britain, France and the US in two world wars. Yugoslavia was the first Soviet satellite to defy Moscow after the Second World War. The vast majority of the Serb people had committed no crime, no atrocity against Kosovars, Bosnians or Croats. Yet NATO destroyed the Serb economy.

The west must find something other than aerial bombardment to make dictators like Milosević of Serbia fall. His people did not overthrow him earlier because they shared his rancour and resentment over ancient and modern quarrels with Croats, Bosnians and Albanians. Tribal hatreds persist. It is ironic that early in 2001, NATO asked the Serbian army to

---

* Albanians living in south-west Serbia, seeking independence.

help prevent what could be a bloody conflict between the Macedonian Republic and its Albanian minority.

Latin America

The US considers Latin America its own backyard. The US says it would rather that Latin American governments were democratic republics like the US, but it has supported shady right-wing dictators, corrupted more often than not by rich US companies: Trujillo, Batista and many others.

In the early 1950s, President Arbenz of Guatemala instituted an agrarian reform that would have confiscated vast idle tracts of land and given them to poor peasants. He also wanted companies, including foreign companies, to pay more taxes. The biggest owner of idle land was the American United Fruit Company. The CIA arranged the overthrow of Arbenz in June 1954. The poor of Guatemala got no relief. US investors got juicier concessions.

In 1959, Fidel Castro overthrew the execrable, thieving Batista in Cuba. Castro expropriated properties of US citizens, notably of Mafiosi and eventually established a free education system (something that had existed only on paper), and a free government health service that works remarkably well. Because US citizens' property had been expropriated, the US broke diplomatic and trade relations with Cuba in 1960. Castro signed a pact with the USSR.

The CIA and the Pentagon organized an invasion by Cuban exiles to overthrow Castro. The newly installed President Kennedy was deliberately misled by the CIA and the Pentagon and approved the invasion. It was an organizational disaster for the US and was crushed at the Bay of Pigs by Castro's troops. Castro became more raucous in his anti-US speeches.

On 14 October 1962, a US spy plane spotted Soviet missiles

being assembled on Cuban soil. They were of a kind that could reach major US cities. President Kennedy blockaded Cuba. The Soviets removed their missiles thirteen days later.* Castro had committed a huge mistake. He had put a nuclear knife to the throat of the US giant. The Cuban people have been punished economically by a US embargo ever since. Now that the USSR no longer exists, the US has little to lose in restoring trading links with Cuba, but they have not done so – perhaps because Castro still relishes being verbally offensive towards the Americans.

Vietnam

The Vietnam war had as its central and most charismatic figure a man called Ho Chi Minh.† Ho wanted Vietnamese independence from the French colonizers – from all foreigners essentially; he did not really have any other ideology. He did not come from a culture of individual freedom; nor was there a Vietnamese tradition favouring the rule of law rather than the rule of men. Between the two world wars, Ho was attracted by Lenin's anti-imperialist doctrine.‡ The USSR made a practice of inviting and feasting nationalist leaders from everyone else's colonies. Ho was invited to Moscow. When the Japanese invaded his country in the Second World War, he worked with the US Office of Strategic Services (precursor of the CIA) and fought the Japanese. The Japanese evacuated Vietnam in 1945. Ho proclaimed Vietnam's independence echoing the words of the US Declaration of Independence: 'All men are created equal and have the right to life, liberty and happiness.'

---

* The US made a deal with the Soviets and some months later removed its Jupiter ballistic missiles from northern Turkey.
† His real name was Nguyen Sinh Cung. During the Second World War, he adopted the name Ho Chi Minh which means 'he who enlightens'.
‡ Which Lenin did not apply to the Russian Empire.

The French tried to retake Vietnam and make it their colony again. In 1950, the USA began giving aid to the French, mainly because Washington thought Ho, if he won, would join the Communist bloc. By 1954 the French were beaten and went home. Vietnam was cut in two at the 17th parallel by an agreement that promised elections to decide whether the two halves of the country should be united. The northern half was under Ho, an often brutal ruler, as rulers in Vietnam had always been; the southern half was run by a series of no less brutal governments backed by the US.

Washington did not allow the promised elections to take place. North-Vietnamese guerrillas, the Vietcong, turned south Vietnam into a battleground. Increasing numbers of US troops were thrown into battle. Hiding in jungles, in tunnels, in mountains, sniping, mining, setting primitive traps, the Vietcong proved that native guerrillas supported by the population will win even when faced with all the armament of a modern superpower: carpet bombing, chemical warfare, total domination of sea and air.* The US pulled out after more than 58,000 of its servicemen died, their names now engraved on a sombre wall of black stone in Washington, D.C.

Vietnam lost 1.4 million combatants and countless civilians. The reunited country afterwards fought a short war to keep out the Communist Chinese. In another war, it overthrew the Cambodian monster Pol Pot, whose Communist government had killed 2 million of its own people.

In hindsight, the US was wrong to think that Vietnam would become a close collaborator of either the USSR or China; wrong to fight a war to keep Ho from kicking out his country's

---

* Afghan guerrillas, too, beat a superpower: in 1979 the Soviet Union invaded Afghanistan to support a Communist government there. After ten years of bloodshed, the Soviet troops had to withdraw.

western masters. By fighting Ho Chi Minh, America tarnished its self-proclaimed reputation as a champion of decolonization. Former colonies noticed: for them the US became just another white, western colonizer.

Vietnam now calls itself a Socialist Republic. It is not socialist in the sense that Sweden is socialist, nor is it Communist. Simply, it is a dictatorship. Vietnam fought for independence from foreign rule, not for democratic individual freedoms.*

But why did Vietnam not follow the example of the American colonists and become a western-style democracy after achieving independence? Most of the American colonists were rebelling against their own, against the British, that is. They wanted freedom to be governed locally by their own elected representatives, not by a distant king. The Americans began their life of independence with an English tradition of elected colonial assemblies, with a system of laws and a judiciary to apply them – property law, commercial law, British common law. Even though Britain was not yet a true democracy, it had established in its North American colonies institutions that allowed full democracy to flourish eventually.

That the Vietnamese did not follow in America's footsteps towards democracy in no sense indicates any inferiority. When decolonized Asian people are admitted into a developed country, they beget children who surpass white children academically. If their former countries still live with systems western democrats would find intolerable, it is by accident of history. Somewhere, some thousands of years ago – a short time in terms of human history – they did not take or did not reach the turn in the road that the West has taken.

---

* Americans tend to equate the western Socialism of a country such as Sweden with Communism. Western Socialism is compatible with democracy and accepts to surrender power when it loses an election. Communism is totally incompatible with democracy and never yields power peacefully.

Korea, Singapore and Malaysia, among other ex-colonies in Asia, have modernized and progressed mightily without really adopting western democracy. They have pursued technological and economic improvement as a first priority. Lee Kuan Yew, Singapore's prime minister from 1959 to 1990, was a more or less benevolent autocrat (there are some), not a democrat. Under his rule Singapore became one of the world's richest countries, per capita. Of course, economic progress is not the only criterion for judging a society. How free are the people? Is there justice for all? Can they peacefully overthrow a bad ruler? What is the fate of women? How about corruption? Will they give democracy priority eventually? One hopes so.

Africa

The way a colonial master treated his black subjects in Africa was even worse than the way he treated his Asian subjects. For centuries, black Africans had been hunted by other Africans and by Arab traders to be sold as slaves. They were considered a lower form of life. They lived in tribal societies. African colonies gained their independence after the Second World War and had to jump from tribalism to the twentieth century. They were not trained to run a country by their colonial masters. They had no one with any experience of combining government and individual freedom.

Somalia and Ethiopia, two countries in the horn of Africa, have a dispute over land. The Soviet Union first backed Somalia, then Ethiopia. Somalia disintegrated into a collection of tribal warlords. Drought made things worse. One and a half million Somalis were starving. Food aid couldn't reach them because it was stolen by tribal gangsters. In 1992, the US, Canada and others sent in troops to distribute the food properly. The well-armed, well-organized white soldiers failed. It didn't matter that they were there to help. A few were killed, literally torn to pieces by mobs, in full view of TV cameras. In March 1994, the US withdrew and apparently decided never to risk its troops in such a situation again. European countries seemed to reach the same decision.

In Belgium's former African colonies of Rwanda and Burundi, two tribes, the Hutu and the Tutsi, have engaged in reciprocal massacres since the 1960s. In 1994, the slaughter exceeded all previous savagery. Hundreds of thousands were killed, many of them hacked to pieces by their neighbours. The UN estimates that 2 million people fled the killing and sought refuge in neighbouring Zaïre, now renamed Congo.

One can add the suffering of a whole list of African ex-colonies: the Congo itself, Angola, Uganda, Mozambique, the Sudan, South Africa, Nigeria, the Chad, Sierra Leone and the Central African Republic, which once had as emperor an alleged cannibal – Bokassa – from whom Valéry Giscard d'Estaing, president of France, accepted 'gifts' of diamonds in the 1970s.

Those who see in these cases a pretext for considering black Africans intellectually inferior had better remember the massacres by whites: the Crusades, the elimination of aboriginal inhabitants in the Americas, the Holocaust. They should also remember that Tanzania, on the east coast of Africa, had a remarkably able and honest ruler, Julius Nyerere.

We should also remember the extraordinarily civilized, intelligent, forgiving Nelson Mandela, a black lawyer whom racist, white South Africa imprisoned for twenty-seven years without breaking his spirit nor quenching his mercy. He put an end to white supremacy before retiring. Alas, in his country now, murder is endemic and AIDS is an epidemic, as it is over much of Africa.

The Muslims and the Jews

Palestine, all of it, was ruled after the First World War by the British, who took it from the Turks. European Jews, in increasing numbers, bought land from Muslims and settled there. Armed clashes between Jews and Muslims followed. One can debate whether the British should have allowed this influx of Jews before the Second World War; but the Holocaust proved to the Jews that they could never be sure again of being safe in Europe. They were sold to the Nazis by the French, by Italians, by Poles, Hungarians, Romanians, Spaniards, Croats, Bosnians, Ukrainians. They were persecuted in Russia. They wanted a state of their own. Let us not forget that, early in the Second World War, a ship wandered the seas full of Jews fleeing Hitler. Country after country, including Britain, the US, France and Canada, turned it away. Holland took in those Jews. One day later, the Nazis invaded Holland. The Jews from the ship ended up in Hitler's gas chambers. Jews, in the years after the Holocaust, needed a place of refuge. Where but the land promised to Abraham by God himself?

Muslim Palestinians said, and say: 'Why should we Muslims lose our land to compensate Jews for having been persecuted by European Christians? We Muslims never persecuted the Jews through the centuries. Why must we pay for European sins?'

After the Second World War, Britain no longer wanted the task of keeping Jews and Muslims from fighting one another. In 1947, the United Nations produced a crazy-quilt partition map, splitting Palestine between them. In 1948, the Jews proclaimed the foundation of the state of Israel. All their Muslim neighbours attacked. Far outnumbered, the Israelis won brilliantly. One officer of the defeated Egyptian army, Gamal Abdel Nasser, bitterly blamed his government for letting him and his troops down in the war against the Jews.

Eight years later, Nasser, by then leader of a junta that had overthrown Egypt's obtuse King Farouk, wanted financial aid from the US to build a huge dam across the Nile at Aswan. But he also signed an agreement to buy weapons from Communist Czechoslovakia. The US, disapproving of links with Communist countries, stopped its subsidies for the dam.

In retaliation, Nasser nationalized the Anglo-French company that owned the Suez canal and barred the canal to ships sailing to and from Israel. He said the fees from the ships using the canal would finance the dam. Britain, France and Israel sent troops and captured the canal. Washington, which had the clout to do so, made them give it back to Egypt.

This should have earned the US some standing as a champion of ex-colonies and ex-protectorates like Egypt. But the US was also a friend of Israel, Britain and France. The friend of my enemy, the Arabs say, is my enemy. Nasser had proclaimed Egypt a one-party Socialist state and had himself elected president with 98 per cent of the vote, the sort of electoral victory Stalin used to arrange for himself.

Neither Washington nor Moscow understood that Nasser was no Socialist. He was a Muslim autocrat, head of a junta, a grand acquisitor playing the US against the USSR to get more aid from each, including weapons, to make himself the leader of the Arab world and to defeat Israel.

There were two more attacks on Israel by its Arab neighbours in 1967 and 1973. Israel won decisively both times.* The Muslims have felt unbearably humiliated ever since. They attribute their defeats to US support for Israel.

Can there ever be a solution that is fair and acceptable to the

---

* Israel also invaded Lebanon in 1982 to destroy Muslim guerrilla bases there. The Israelis did a lot of damage but did not accomplish their aim. The anti-Israeli guerrilla organizations survived.

Jews and not unfair to the Muslims? Conversely, can there ever be a solution that is fair and acceptable to the Muslims and not unfair to the Jews? The 'acceptable' part, unfortunately, applies to the religiously messianic on both sides: Muslims and Jews both prepared to die for a tiny piece of Jerusalem that is holiest to the zealots of both religions – a major obstacle to peace in Palestine. The other big obstacle is the so-called right of return: the right of those who fled Israel, and of their descendants, to return to their ancestral lands. Should that right be granted, Israel would have a Muslim majority. The Jews would never accept that.*

A 'possible' solution is often discussed:

> The Israelis withdraw from the territory called 'The West Bank' which they took from Jordan after the 1967 war – withdraw totally even from Jewish settlements in the West Bank and from the Gaza strip. The Muslims who fled Israel might forgo the right to return if they were given their own totally independent state in the West Bank and Gaza; and if they were given massive western aid to improve their prospects and standard of living. There would then be peace and the Israelis would no longer have to fear Muslim terrorism.

Would Washington be prepared to invest heavily to make a Muslim Palestinian state wealthy? Would other Middle East Muslim states go along with such a solution? It would certainly remove a major problem for the US, the Muslim–Jewish conflict in the Holy Land.

---

* Even Israeli historians now concede that many Muslims were deliberately frightened by the Israeli army, so they would leave. Their villages were then obliterated.

However, there are Muslims who want the US to have problems. The US was called 'the Great Satan' by Iran's Ayatollah Khomeini, because the culture represented by the US is the main enemy of Muslim culture and religion. With the globalized means of communication Muslims, especially young Muslims, are exposed to US culture and question Muslim social rules.

People like Osama Bin Laden, the Saudi multi-millionaire master of terrorists – and he is not the only master of Muslim terrorists – share the late Ayatollah's view that the US is the principal enemy of Islam as a way of life. Ordinary fundamentalist Muslims – and there are very many – share it too. Such master terrorists can always find men who will festoon themselves with sticks of dynamite, die blowing up US embassies, warships, fly planes into New York skyscrapers, and go to sexual heaven, to be for ever young with seventy virgin wives who are for ever young, beautiful and libidinous.*

Some Arab governments want no more wars. Egypt has signed a peace treaty with Israel. Jordan is always trying to broker an Arab–Israeli peace. The Syrians, however, will back no solution that will not give them back the Golan Heights. One third of Israel's water supply comes from the Golan Heights. Will Israel trust Syria's hand on the tap?

Iraq's Saddam Hussein is against Israel, of course.† Saddam took power in 1968 as the head of the Ba'ath party, which means the party of 'Renaissance Socialism'. There is neither Socialism nor renaissance in Saddam's Ba'ath. He is a sanguinary, autocratic tyrant who does not hide his ambition to

---

* See the teaching of Muhammad in Chapter 5.
† In June 1981, Israel bombed and destroyed an Iraqi facility capable of producing an atom bomb. Israel's ultimate guarantee against being overwhelmed by its Muslim neighbours is its capacity to destroy their cities and armies with nuclear weapons. Israel will not allow any Muslim neighbour to develop nuclear weapons.

unite all Arab states under his rule. It had been Nasser's ambition, and it didn't work. The various Muslim states are not anxious to unite, certainly not under Saddam.

Saddam nationalized Iraq's oil industry in 1972. In Iran, the Ayatollahs who took power in 1979 would have nothing to do with Saddam whom they accused of not being a sufficiently strict Islamist. They plotted to overthrow him. So Saddam's forces invaded Iran's oilfields.

The war between Iraq and Iran lasted eight years and the opposing armies ended where they had been at the beginning. The Americans sent help to Saddam, preferring him to the Ayatollahs, who had occupied the US embassy in Teheran, keeping its staff hostage. Saddam subsequently accepted tanks, rockets and other weapons from the USSR.

In 1990 Saddam occupied Kuwait, a small neighbour, rich in oil. A US-led coalition with a United Nations mandate destroyed the Iraqi army. US President George Bush the elder proclaimed a ceasefire on 28 February 1991. Saddam Hussein stayed in power.

Why did the 540,000 American troops massed against him not invade Iraq and overthrow him? One reason was the recent western reluctance to take casualties – US losses in the war: 281 dead, 458 wounded. Iraq losses: 100,000 soldiers killed, 300,000 wounded, 150,000 deserted and 60,000 taken prisoner, plus disputed numbers of civilians hit in air attacks.

Though kings, emirs and sheiks in the region oppose Saddam's expansionism (at their expense), their subjects feel sympathy and a certain admiration for him. He survived the war and a UN embargo; he foiled UN arms' inspectors on his territory; he did not fall despite renewed US air attacks in 1998 and 2001. In short, he made himself a role model for the ordinary Muslim believer who sees the US as the main mover of globalization, the cultural enemy of Islam.[5]

That Saddam is an autocrat does not seem to bother the ordinary Muslim. Islam as a religion makes no room for western democracy. Its leaders have never been democratic. They started in the seventh century as caliphs, 'successors' to the prophet Muhammad, temporal and spiritual leaders of all Muslims. The caliphate passed from the Arabs to the Turks and was not abolished until 1924. Turkey proclaimed itself a republic with a parliament, but run by army strongmen – just as the original Islamic caliphs were military strongmen. The military in Turkey have tried to make theirs a secular, westernized state, but they are losing ground to Muslim fundamentalists.

Will Islamic fundamentalism wane? Not for the foreseeable future. Muslims feel the rich, democratic, modern west does not want them. They fall back on the spiritual comfort they find in the teachings of Islam, including the promise of a sexual paradise for Muslims who die fighting against those they believe to be enemies of their faith. Muslim poor in the east are inundated with Palestinian propaganda which even recycles the old calumny of the Protocols of the Learned Elders of Zion, a fictitious document that purports to be a plan for world domination by the Jews.

Huge numbers of the world's poor are Muslims. They seem to think that the rich west does not care about them – that the west took land from poor Muslims and gave it to the Jews. These poor Muslims apparently listen to their mullahs who would lose power and influence if their flocks became secular, as the west largely is.* Osama Bin Laden expressed that feeling starkly when he called the 2001 American attacks against Afghanistan a war between the faithful and the unbelievers.

---

* In the Middle Ages, the 'mullahs' of the Catholic and Orthodox churches similarly fought against any reduction of their power.

Jacques Chirac, president of France, claimed on 15 October 2001, that we are not facing a clash of civilizations between the secular west and the religious Muslims. We shall have to see. The clash, if it develops, may also express the resentment of the Muslims at having been dispossessed of their historic power by Europeans (including Americans), and at the west having built its prosperity with oil bought at derisively low prices from Muslim lands.

In the twentieth century, could the US have done better in its relations with weaker, poorer countries, especially those that we call the east when we talk of an east-west discord? The US has solved none of the East-West problems it inherited after the Second World War. Did any other preceding empire do better? Not the British Empire, not the German, Austro-Hungarian or Russian Empires. Not the Ottoman, Byzantine or Roman Empires. Not the Babylonians, Assyrians, Persians. Not the Egyptians. The failures of the US are more apparent because they are flaunted before all eyes by global communications. The global corporations are more threatening to some, because they seem immune to the will of the people, which may be more true than in earlier times. But the instincts of the gazillionaires who run these corporations are no different from those of the robber barons, large landlords and other grand acquisitors who preceded them.

Will the US succeed in its fight against terrorism? To write history is not to write prophecy. When dealing with the future, one can only ask questions, and make observations on the past:

The US has not managed to stop foreign-grown drugs from infesting America with cocaine, heroin and crack.

The INS (Immigration and Naturalization Service) estimates that there are 6 million illegal immigrants in the US.

If illegal immigrants and drug traffickers have not been kept out, how are terrorists going to be stopped from entering the US, living hidden lives there for years, to emerge as human bombs?

But then, these terrorists are only modern, more technical versions of pirates and those who robbed stagecoaches. States survived the pirates and the robbers. The magnificent temple of Artemis at Ephesus, one of the Seven Wonders of the World, was burned by a fanatic called Herostratus in 365 BC. It was rebuilt. In 1871, the Communards in Paris rose against the rich and the state and burned the Tuileries Palace. It was rebuilt. What was destroyed by the terrorists on 11 September 2001, will be rebuilt – that much it is safe to prophesy.

EPILOGUE

In the fifth century BC, Thucydides, one of the greatest historians the world has known, said that it is in the very nature of humans to act in the future as they did in the past.[1] Have the last twenty-five centuries proved him right?

In this book, we have examined what the US military calls the rules of engagement for the war between society and the grand acquisitors – rules established by nine teachers: Moses, Solon, Plato, Jesus, Lao-tzu, Confucius, the brahmins, the Buddha, and Muhammad. Did their rules affect the grand acquisitors? Did higher forms of intelligence and self-interest such as compassion, forgiveness, generosity and respect for others become more frequent than in our sanguinary, predatory past?

The answer must examine two particular aspects: the citizen's relation with his state, and the relations of his state with other states.

As regards the citizen's relation with his state, within some progressive nation states the democratic rules of Solon have improved the lot of the individual citizen. Compassion and generosity have been legislated into practice. Respect for others is enforced by the courts. However, even in progressive states, not all have equality of opportunity, even if they have the physical and mental qualifications for success. Race, colour, restriction of rights can be handicaps. Inherited wealth or beauty are an advantage. In non-democratic states, the fate of the citizen is even more precarious, especially if he or she opposes established authority or doctrine.

As for relations between the states – and as for wars – the nine great teachers, or those who allegedly speak in their name, prescribed few rules.

For Jesus, clearly, all people were equal, whatever their ethnicity. He said that we should love our enemies, which would preclude war. Yet the churches created in his name never prevented war.

The Buddha was against war and thought all humans were equal. Yet, to give but one example, the Japanese, a warrior nation, managed to blend Buddhism with their traditional warlike religion.

Lao-tzu said one should avoid relations between nations. Yet there surely was war in his time; for the dominant ethnic group, the Han, conquered others and taught them its writing for their spoken word, so the Chinese people have one written language, but the same written word has at least seventeen different pronunciations.

Confucius would have seen war as disturbing the proper functioning of the state. Yet, as a high functionary, he would have administered the armed forces most competently.

Solon did not prescribe rules for relations between one state and another. He accepted war. He urged the conquest of the island of Salamis. The state, he said, would bring up children whose fathers died in war.

Plato went further. He provided for a warrior caste, as did Brahminism.

Moses went further still. He gave the Israelis the order to conquer the land promised by God to Abraham; so the concept of *jihad*, holy war sanctioned by God, appears first in the Old Testament.

Islam followed his lead. It is clearly a faith that prescribes war and conquest. Yet Muhammad did say: 'In a holy war, if those you defeat are prepared to convert to Islam, they must be spared.'

Subsequently, there have been efforts to make rules for relations among states and abolish war: the League of Nations after the First World War, and the United Nations after the Second World War. The UN has done laudable charitable work for children, for the hungry, against disease. Yet relations among states have not improved, nor has war been avoided. When a stalemate is reached, the UN serves as the keeper of the stalemate, no more.

There is, however, perhaps one faint beacon of hope. The European Community, itself a collective grand acquisitor quite capable of brutally blocking the recovery of poorer states by its import restrictions, has acknowledged the need for millenary enemies to stop fighting one another. Their states devastated one another century after century, culminating in two world wars. They have learned the lesson – and perhaps found an answer.

Possibly – just possibly – their answer might point the way ahead.

APPENDIX:
A Sobering Chronology

Wars between 1469 and 1679, as discussed in Chapter 10

1469–1502	England vs Scotland and France
1481–1512	Ottoman Danube campaigns
1494	Spain vs Portugal
1494–8	French invasion of Italy
1497–9	Poland's Moldavian war
1499–1500	French invasion of Italy
1500–23	Denmark vs Sweden and Norway
1500–01	French invasion of Italy
1500–13	Poland vs Russia
1502–03	Spain vs France
1502–03	French invasion of Italy
1508–10	French invasion of Italy
1511–15	French invasion of Italy
1511–43	England vs Scotland and France
1512–18	England vs France
1521–5	France vs Austria
1521–47	Ottomans vs Austria
1522–5	England vs France
1526–9	France vs Austria
1536–8	France vs Austria
1542–4	France vs Austria
1544–6	England vs France
1547–51	German wars of religion
1548	Spain vs England (the Armada)
1551–62	Ottomans vs Austria
1555–9	France vs Austria

1557–64	England vs France
1560–92	Sweden vs Russia
1561–9	Poland vs Russia
1562–3	Spain vs North Africa
1562–3	French wars of religion
1563–70	Sweden vs Denmark
1564–1630	England vs France
1564–1630	England vs Spain
1566–1648	Spain vs Netherlands
1567–8	French wars of religion
1568–70	French wars of religion
1569–72	Ottomans vs Venice and Catholic powers
1571	Spain vs Ottomans (Lepanto)
1572–3	French wars of religion
1573–81	Ottomans vs Austria
1574–6	French wars of religion
1577–82	Poland vs Russia
1577	French wars of religion
1580	French wars of religion
1585–7	England vs Spain in the Netherlands
1587–9	French wars of religion
1589–98	French wars of religion
1598–9	Spain vs France
1598–1603	Anglo-Irish wars
1598–1611	Sweden vs Poland
1610–19	Poland vs Russia
1611–13	Sweden vs Denmark
1614–17	Sweden vs Russia
1617–29	Sweden vs Poland
1618–23	Bohemian war*
1620–1	Poland vs Ottomans
1622–3	French wars of religion
1622–6	Spain vs France
1624–9	Danish war*
1627–30	England vs France
1627–31	Spain vs France
1627–9	French wars of religion
1630–5	Sweden in the Thirty Years War*
1632–4	Poland vs Russia
1635–48	France in Thirty Years War*
1642–6	English civil war
1644–6	Scots intervention in English civil war
1647–51	Scots intervention in English civil war

1648–9	Ottomans vs Venice and Catholic powers
1648–59	Spain vs France
1651–4	Anglo-Irish wars
1652–4	Anglo-Dutch war
1654–67	Poland vs Russia
1655–60	Sweden vs Poland
1657–60	Sweden vs Denmark
1664–7	Anglo-Dutch war
1671–6	Poland vs Ottomans
1672–4	Anglo-Dutch war
1675–9	Sweden vs Denmark

* Wars marked with an asterisk, were part of the larger are called the Thirty
Years War.

NOTES AND SOURCES

Chapter 1. Moses (c. 14th–13th century BC)

1. All dating of Moses is an uncertain approximation. See Will Durant, *The Story of Civlization*, New York: Simon & Schuster, 1980, vol. 1, pp. 301–2 (notes below text).
2. *Leviticus*, 18. The *Septuagint* translators, instead of coming right out and saying the word for sexual organs, use a euphemism, *aschemosyne*. The Oxford University's *Greek–English Lexlcon* (1961) says that aschemosyne is a euphemism for sexual organ.
3. *Deuteronomy*, 20: 13.
4. *Leviticus*, 25: 17.
5. *Ibid.*, 25: 28.
6. *Numbers*, 16: 31.
7. *Exodus*, 32: 25–8.
8. *Isaiah*, 3: 14–15; 5: 8; 10: 2.
9. *Numbers*, 31.
10. *Leviticus*, 19: 18.
11. *Numbers*, 31: 7–18.
12. *Joshua*, 8: 25.
13. *Genesis*, 12: 7.

Chapter 2. Solon (c. 630–560 BC)

1. John Burnet, *Greek Philosophy*, London: Macmillan, 1914, p. 9.
2. e.g. Homer, *The Iliad*, Book xxi, lines 383, 400, 424.
3. e.g. Hesiod, *Theogony*, 166, 736.
4. G. S. Kirk and J. E. Raven, *The Presocratic Philosophers*, Cambridge: Cambridge University Press, 1966, p. 172.
5. Aristotle, *Metaphysics*, London: Oxford University Press, 1966, A3, 983b6.
6. Mainly in Aristotle's *The Athenian Constitution*, and in Plutarch's *Solon*.
7. Plutarch, *Solon* xix, 1.
8. *Ibid.*, xx, 1.
9. *Ibid.*, xviii, 5.
10. *Ibid.*, xxi, 3.

11. *Ibid.*, xxiv, 1.
12. *Ibid.*, xx, 4.
13. *Ibid.*, xx, 5.
14. *Ibid.*, xx, 2. Classicists have generally sunk into prudishness when they translate this passage of Plutarch's *Solon* to mean that the sexually deprived heiress could 'marry another man from her husband's clan'. Plutarch did not say 'marry' another. He said 'copulate' with whichever man she fancied from her husband's clan; and that the impotent husband would thus be mortified.
15. *Ibid.*, xxiv, 2.
16. *Ibid.*, xxiv, 1.
17. Athenaeus, xiii, 25.
18. Aristotle, *The Athenian Constitution*, 10. Did the trading partners of Athens know they were being paid 30 per cent less silver? I have yet to find relevant historical evidence.
19. Diogenes Laertius, *Solon*, vii.
20. Plutarch, *Solon*, xv, 6.
21. *ibid.*, xv, 2.
22. For a lively discussion of Greek democracy, see W. G. Forrest, *The Emergence of Greek Democracy*, New York: McGraw-Hill, 1966.
23. Durrant, *The Story of Civilization*, vol. 2, p. 118.

Chapter 3. Plato (c. 428–347 BC)

1. Paul Shorey, Plato, *The Republic*, Cambridge, Mass.: Harvard University Press, 1963, p. xxxix.
2. In *De Civitate Dei*, viii St Augustine ranks Plato above all other philosophers and closest to Christianity.
3. Bertrand Russell, *A History of Western Philosophy*, London: Unwin Paperbacks, 1989, p. 444. Among Catholic philosophical thinkers there is much acrimony about the differing views of Plato and Aristotle, and therefore of St Augustine and Thomas Aquinas.
4. Gilbert Ryle, *New Essays on Plato and Aristotle*, New York: Routledge & Kegan Paul, 1965, p. 7.
5. Karl Raimund Popper writes: 'I shall not therefore attempt a serious treatment of Aristotle except in so far as his version of Plato's essentialism has influenced the historicism of Hegel, and thereby that of Marx.' *The Open Society and Its Enemies*, Princeton: University Press, 1966, vol. 2, p. 1.
6. Popper, *op. cit.*, vol. 1, p. 54.
7. Plato, *The Republic*, 335E–336A.
8. N. G. L. Hammond, A *History of Greece*, Oxford: The Clarendon Press, 1959, p. 443.
9. *Ibid.*, p. 444.
10. John Burnet, *Greek Philosophy* London: Macmillan, 1914 p. 208. See also the Introduction of Burnet's edition of Plato's dialogue, the *Phaedo*.
11. Plato, *The Apology*, 29.
12. *Ibid.*, 30.
13. Plato, *Crito*, 52.
14. Plato, *The Apology*, 42.
15. Plato, *The Republic*, 559.
16. James Adam, *The Republic of Plato*, Cambridge: Cambridge University

Press. 1965, vol. 2, p. 240. See also note on 559D–562. D–562 A; and note on 559.

17. Paul Shorey, *op.cit.*, p. xxxvii.
18. Plato, *The Republic*, 416, 417.
19. Was Plato a feminist? For a discussion of the contradictory evidence, go to the Internet.
20. Plato, *The Republic*, 459 E.
21. *Ibid.*, 460C.
22. *Ibid.*, 473.
23. Paul Shorey, *op. cit.*, p. xxxv; also Shorey's edition of *The Phaedrus*, Cambridge, Mass: Harvard University Press, 1963, 239.
24. Bertrand Russell, *op.cit.*, p. 134.
25. Plato's words quoted by Popper, *op. cit.*, p. 7.

Chapter 4. Jesus (c. 5/1 BC–AD 30/33)

1. *Matthew*, 10: 33.
2. *Luke*, 23: 34.
3. The earliest dating of the Gospels ranges from AD 40 to 55. Other dating ranges from AD 45 to 90.
4. See James Carrol, *Constantine's Sword, The Church and the Jews*, Boston: Houghton Mifflin, 2001.
5. *Matthew*, 19: 24.
6. *Matthew*, 9: 12.
7. Durant, *The Story of Civilization*, vol. 3, p. 566.
8. *Mark*, 12: 17.
9. E. T. Salmon, *A History of the Roman World*, London: Methuen & Co., 1968, p. 197.
10. *Isaiah* 61: 1–7.
11. *Ibid.*, 2: 4.
12. *Ibid.*, 11: 6.
13. *Ibid*, 7: 14.
14. *Ibid.*, 53: 4–5.
15. Durant, *op. cit.*, vol. 3, p. 575.
16. Paul, *Epistle to the Hebrews*, 11: 1.

Chapter 5. Brahminism, the Buddha, Lao-tzu, Confucius, Muhammad (3102 BC–AD 632)

1. On the Internet's Google search engine, consult 'religous population of the world' for the latest figures.
2. This quotation from the Hindu holy book the *Bhagavad Gita* it can be found in Juan Mascaro's *The Bhagavad Gita*, Baltimore: Penguin Books, 1962, Ch. 18, lines 41–4.
3. J. H. Hutton, *Caste in India*, Cambridge University Press, 1951, p. 223.
4. John Stackhouse, *Out of Poverty and Into Something More Comfortable*, Toronto: Random House, 2000.
5. See *The Buddha's Teachings*, edited in the original Pali text with an English translation facing it by Lord Chalmers, Cambridge, Mass: Harvard University Press, 1932. Buddhism has its sects which have philosophical and ethical differences; but it has texts accepted by Buddhists of all denominations.
6. *The Buddha's Dialogues*, iii, 154.

7. Sarvepali Radhakrishnan, *Indian Philosophy*, vol. 1, p. 275.
8. *The Buddha's Dialogues*, ii, 35.
9. *Ibid., ii*, 186.
10. Radhakrishnan, *op. cit.*, vol. 1, p. 38.
11. *Ibid.*, vol. 1, p. 356.
12. H. G. Rawlinson, *India*, London: Cresset Press, 1952, p. 80. On the Internet, see The Edicts of Ashoka at http://www.cs.colostate.edu//malaiya/ashoka.html and a *Profile of Ashoka* at http://www.itihaas. com/ancient/ashoka-profile.html.
13. James Legge, *The Sacred Books of China: The texts of Taoism*, London: Oxford University Press, 1927, vol. 1, xlix, 2; lxi, 2.
14. Legge, *op. cit.*, i, 4–5. See also Durant, *op. cit.*, vol. 1, p. 653.
15. Friedrich Hirth, *Ancient History of China*, New York: Columbia University Press, 1923, pp. 53–7.
16. Legge, *op. cit.*, vol. 2, lvii, 2–3; lxxx.
17. Legge, *op. cit.*, vol. 1, lxv, 1–2; vol. 2, lxxxi, 3.
18. See Durant, *The Story of Civilization* vol. 1, p. 659.
19. Legge, *op. cit.*, ix, 4. Also Legge, *The Chinese Classics Translated Into English*, vol. 1 *The Life and Teachings of Confucius*. London: The Clarendon Press, 1895.
20. Legge, *Life*, 83.
21. *Ibid.*, 67.
22. *Ibid*, p. 75.
23. *Ibid.*, p. 266.
24. Legge, *Chinese Classics*, xxii, 19; ii, 20.
25. *Ibid.*, x, 9.
26. *Ibid.*, xii, 7.
27. *Ibid.*, xv, 40.
28. *Ibid.*, xvi, 10.
29. *Ibid.*, xii, 2.
30. *Ibid.*, xiv, 36.
31. *Ibid.*, vi, 20.
32. See Jonathan D. Spence, *Treason by the Book*, New York: Viking, 2001.
33. Durant, *op.cit.*, vol. 1, pp. 675–6.
34. *Ibid.*, vol. 4, p. 163. See also Ali Tabari, *The Book of Religion and Empire*, a translation of a ninth century text, New York: Longmans, Green, 1922.

Chapter 6. The Decline of the Roman Empire (1st century AD)

1. Will Durrant, *The Story of Civilization*, p. 368.
2. Many references in this chapter are to the Latin text of Oxford's Clarendon Press 1907 edition of *The Annals of Tacitus*, which comprise several books (shown in roman numerals). Subdivisions of the book or chapters will be shown in Arabic numerals. References to material other than Tacitus' text in the Clarendon Press volume cited above will be to its editor, Furneaux.
3. *Tacitus*, iv, 53.
4. Footnotes on Suetonius refer to the biography of Caligula in the book *Suetonius*, vol. 1, pp. 405–97, London: William Heinemann, 1920. The Roman numerals in the references indicate the sections on which my narrative is based.
5. *Tacitus*, vi, 24.

6. *Ibid.*, vi, 50.
7. Furneaux, p. 5.
8. *Suetonius*, xxiv.
9. *Ibid.*, xxix.
10. *Tacitus*, iv, 75.
11. *Suetonius*, xxii.
12. *Ibid.*, xxiii.
13. *Ibid.*, xvi.
14. *Ibid.*, xxi.
15. *Ibid.*, xxvi.
16. *Ibid.*, xxvi.
17. *Ibid.*, xxvii.
18. *Ibid.*, xxxv.
19. *Ibid.*, xl.
20. *Ibid.*, xxxviii.
21. *Ibid.*, lviii.
22. Suetonius: '*primus Caesarum fidem militis etiam praemio pigneratus*'. see Furneaux, p. 10.
23. *Tacitus*, iv, 4.
24. *Ibid.*, xi, 12 and 27.
25. *Ibid.*, xi, 30–8.
26. *Ibid.*, xii, 53.
27. *Ibid.*, xii, 1.
28. *Ibid.*, xii, 3.
29. *Ibid.*, xii, 5.
30. *Ibid.*, xii, 7.
31. *Ibid.*, xii, 8.
32. *Ibid.*, xii, 7. My translation.
33. *Ibid.*, xii, 26.
34. *Ibid.*, xii, 27.
35. *Ibid.*, xii, 37, 42.
36. *Ibid.*, xii, 8.
37. *Ibid.*, xii, 25.
38. *Ibid.*, xii, 41.
39. *Ibid.*, xii, 52, 57, 59.
40. *Ibid.*, xii, 42.
41. *Ibid.*, xii, 64–65.
42. *Ibid.*, xii, 64.
43. *Ibid.*, xii, 65.
44. *Ibid.*, xii, 65.
45. *Ibid.*, xii, 66.
46. *Ibid.*, xii, 69.
47. *Ibid.*, xiii, 5.
48. *Ibid.*, xiii, 12.
49. *Ibid.*, xiii, 13.
50. *Ibid.*, xiii, 14.
51. *Ibid.*, xiii, 16.
52. *Ibid.*, xiii, 18.
53. *Ibid.*, xiii, 19.
54. *Ibid.*, xiii, 20.

55. *Ibid.*, xiv, 1.
56. *Ibid.*, xiv, 3–4.
57. *Ibid.*, xiv, 5.
58. *Ibid.*, xiv, 7.
59. *Ibid.*, xiv, 9.

Chapter 7. The Byzantine Empire (6th century)

1. Will Durant, *The Story of Civilization*, vol. 4, p. 107.
2. Edward Gibbon, *The Decline and Fall of the Roman Empire; The Great Books*, New York: Encyclopaedia Britannica Inc., 1952, vol. 40, p. 651.
3. Gibbon, *op. cit.*, p. 649.
4. Procopius, *The Secret History*, trans. by Richard Atwater, Ann Arbor: University of Michigan Press, 1961. I often paraphrased the text to make it more contemporary. I have also rearranged the sequence of the extracts.
5. Gibbon, *op. cit.*, p. 895, n. 81.
6. Gibbon, *op. cit.*, pp. 658–9.

Chapter 8. Islamic Incursions into Europe (711–1603)

1. Gregory of Tours, *The History of the Franks*, trans. with an introduction by O. M. Dalton, Oxford: Clarendon Press, 1927, ii, p. 42.
2. *Ibid.*, ii, 43.
3. *Ibid.*, iii, 1.
4. *Ibid.*, iii, 7.
5. *Ibid.*, iii, 8.
6. *Ibid.*, iii, 18.
7. *Ibid.*, v, 14, 18.
8. *Ibid.*, vi, 35.
9. Gregory, x, 3.
10. *Ibid.*, v, 20.
11. Norman Davies, *Europe*, London: Pimlico, 1997, p. 253.
12. Frederic Donner, *The Early Arab Conquests*, Princeton, NJ: Princeton University Press, 1981, ch. 6, Conclusions.
13. Ibn Abd-el-Hakem, *History of the Conquest of Spain*, trans. by John Harris Jones, Gottingen: W. Fr. Kaestner, 1858, pp. 21–2. Ibn Abd-el-Hakem was an Egyptian Arab historian who wrote more than a century after Tarik's invasion of Spain. He is not a wonderful source but he is all we've got.
14. Al Maggari, *Tarik's Address to His Soldiers*, AD 711, from *The Breath of Perfumes* in Charles F. Horne, ed., *The Sacred Books and Early Literature of the East*, vol. vi, *Medieval Arabia*, New York: Parke, Austin, & Lipscomb, 1917, pp. 241–2.
15. This account of events in Memphis and Alexandria is compressed from two books: (1) Al Baladhuri, *The Origins of the Islamic State*, New York: Columbia University Press, 1916; (2) Sawirus ibn al-Muqaffa, *History of the Patriarchs of the Coptic Church of Alexandria*, Paris: Firmin-Didot, 1904, vol. i.
16. Davies, *op. cit.*, p. 333.
17. The description of what happened at Lepanto is based on two books: (1) Angelos Bambakos, *The Battle of Naupaktos* (Naupaktos is the Greek name for Lepanto), Athens, 1974; (2) Jack Beeching, *The Galleys at Lepanto*, New York: Scribner, 1983.

18. This is a highly compressed account of the battle and its consequences. It is taken from the following three books: (1) Stewart Steven, *The Poles*, New York: Macmillan Publishing Co. Inc., 1982; (2) Oscar Halecki, *A History of Poland*, New York: Dorset Press, 1992; (3) Jan Wimmer, *The 1683 Siege of Vienna*, Warsaw: Interpress, 1983.
19. Davies, *op. cit.*, p. 255.
20. Durant, *op. cit.*, p. 430.

Chapter 9. The Crusades (1095–1204)

1. August C. Krey, *The First Crusade: The Accounts of Eyewitnesses and Participants*; Princeton: Princeton University Press, 1921, pp. 54–6.
2. Krey, *Ibid.*, pp. 257–62.
3. The text of what the Pope said can be found in documents listed by Gibbon, *op. cit.*, p. 738, note 26.
4. Durant, *The Story of Civilization*, vol. 4, p. 602.
5. Villehardouin *Memoirs, The Fourth Crusade*, trans. by Frank T. Marzials, London: J. M. Dent, 1908. Villehardouin's *Memoirs* are to the above Internet text. Villehardouin was a Fourth Crusade leader. To find the original Venetian text of the treaty containing Dandolo's demands for helping the Crusade, see Gibbon, *op. cit.*, p. 739, note 40.
6. Villehardouin, *op. cit.*, p. 16.
7. *Ibid.*, p. 20–21.
8. *Ibid.*, p. 21.
9. *Ibid.*, p. 21.
10. *Ibid.*, p. 26, 27.
11. Gibbon, *op. cit.*, p. 429.
12. Durant, *op. cit.*, p. 603.
13. Villehardouin, *op. cit.*, p. 24. The account of Villehardouin concords pretty well with that of Robert de Clari, another eyewitness and chronicler of the Fourth Crusade.
14. Robert de Clari in Dana C. Munro, 'The Fourth Crusade', *Translations and Reprints from the Original Sources of European History*, vol. 3: 1, Philadelphia: University of Pennsylvania, 1896, pp. 1–18.
15. Villehardouin, *op. cit.*, p. 17, 18.
16. *Ibid.*, p. 20–23.
17. *Ibid.*, p. 31.
18. *Ibid.*, pp. 32–48.
19. Robert de Clari, *op. cit.*, pp. 5, 6.
20. *Ibid.*, p. 7.
21. Villehardouin *op. cit.*, pp. 54–63.
22. Selected by the Internet Medieval Source Book, under the title The Sack of Constantinople, translated from *Alexii Ducae Imperium*, ch. iii-iv, in *Recueil des historiens des Croisades*, hist. grec., 1.
23. From the Internet's Medieval Source Book, translated from the Latin: Gunther de Pairis: *Historia Constantinopolitana*, ch. xix, in Riant: *Exuviae*, 104 ff.
24. Pope Innocent III, Ep. 136, *Patrologia Latina* 215, 669–702, trans. by James Brundage, *The Crusades: A Documentary History* Milwaukee: Marquette University Press, 1962, pp. 208–9.
25. See note 1, above.

26. Gibbon, *op. cit.*, p. 379.
27. Durant, *op. cit.*, p. 549.
28. Robert de Clari, *op. cit.*, p. 7.
29. Durant, *op. cit.*, p. 427.
30. Gibbon, *op. cit.*, p. 331.
31. *Ibid.*, p. 331–2.

Chapter 10. Conquering Latin America (1518–48)

1. The passage on the Hundred Years War is highly compressed from three books: (1) Clifford J. Rogers, *The Wars of Edward Three*, Rochester NY: Boydell Press, 1999; (2) J.J.N. Palmer, *Froissart, Historian*, Woodbridge, Suffolk: Boydell Press, 1981; (3) Auguste Bailly, *La Guerre de Cent Ans*, Paris: A. Fayard, 1943.
2. The sources for this very compressed account are: (a) William Prescott, *History of the Conquest of Mexico and the Conquest of Peru*, New York: The Modern Library, 1935; (b) John Hemming, *The Conquest of the Incas*, London: Macmillan, 1970; (c) Clements Markham, *A History of Peru*, New York: Greenwood Press, 1968; (d) Hugh Thomas, *Montezuma and the Fall of Old Mexico*, New York: Simon and Schuster, 1993.
3. Jared Diamond *Guns, Germs and Steel*, New York: Norton, 1999.
4. Diamond, *op. cit.*, p. 110.

Chapter 11. The Conception and Birth-pangs of Protestantism (1517–1610)

1. My main source for Wycliffe is John Stacey, *John Wyclif and Reform*, New York: AMS Press, 1980.
2. Compressed from Franz Lützow, *The Life and Times of Master John Hus*, London: J.M. Dent, 1909.
3. *Romans*, 8: 29–30.
4. What I write about Luther and Calvin is a hyper-compressed compendium from the following books: (1) Ronald Wallace, *Calvin, Geneva and the Reformation*, Grand Rapids, Michigan: Baker Book House, 1988; (2) James G. Kiecker, *Martin Luther and the Long Reformation*, Milwaukee: Northwestern Publishing House, 1992; (3) Charles Beard, *Martin Luther and the Reformation in Germany until the Close of the Diet of Worms*, London: Philip Green, 1896; (4) David Curtis Steinmetz, *Luther in Context*, Grand Rapids, Michigan: Baker Book House, 1995; (5) *Calvin's Theology, Theology Proper, Eschatology*, edited by Richard C. Gamble, New York: Garland Pub., 1992; (6) Randall C. Zachman, *The Assurance of Faith; Conscience in the Theology of Martin Luther and John Calvin*, Minneapolis: Fortress Press, 1993.
5. I give so compressed a version of events that traditional references to pages would be irrelevant. My sources on Julius II, Michelangelo, Raphael and St Peter's basilica are: (1) Emmanuel Rodocanachi, *Histoire de Rome; le pontificat de Jules II, 1503–1513*, Paris: Hachette, 1928; (2) Christine Shaw, *Julius II, the Warrior Pope*, Oxford: Blackwell, 1993; (3) Clemente Fusero, *Giulio II*, Milan: Dall'Oglio, 1965; (4) Emmanuel Rodocanachi, *La première renaissance; Rome au temps de Jules II et Léon X; la cour pontificale; les artistes et les gens de lettres; la ville et le peuple; le sac de Rome en 1527*, Paris: Hachette et Cie, 1912.

6. For those interested in more ample reading on the Calvinists in America, I recommend T.H. Breen. *The Character of the Good Ruler; A Study of Puritan Political Ideas in New England, 1630–1730*, New York: Norton, 1974; also Jon Butler, *The Huguenots in America*, Cambridge, Mass.: Harvard University Press, 1992.
7. This account of the St Bartholomew Massacre is based on De Thou, *Histoire des choses arrivées de son temps*, Paris, 1659, in J. H. Robinson, *Readings in European History*, Boston: Ginn, 1906, vol. 2, pp. 180–3.
8. There are a large number of books on Henri IV, whom the French call, rightly, Henri the Great. Three I have read are (1) Henry M. Baird's *The Huguenots and Henri of Navarre*, New York: AMS Press, 1970; (2) François Bayrou, *Le roi libre*, Paris: Flammarion, 1994; (3) Jean Pierre Babelon, *Henri IV*, Paris: Fayard, 1982. I also recommend highly the first 127 pages of Michel Carmona's *Richelieu*, Paris: Fayard, 1983.
9. Davies, *op. cit.*, p. 539.

Chapter 12. Where the Sun that Never Set, Did Set (1783–1865)

1. As I have said before, I compress. My passage on the Thirty Years War is compressed from the following sources: (1) Ronald G. Asch, *The Thirty Years War: the Holy Roman Empire and Europe, 1618–48*, New York: St Martin's Press, 1997; (2) *The Thirty Years' War*, edited by Geoffrey Parker, New York: Routledge, 1993; (3) Sir Edward Cust, *Lives of the Warriors of the Thirty Years's War*, Freeport, NY: Books for Libraries Press, 1972.
2. For the proportions and areas of the earth captured by various Europeans, see Mary Evelyn Townsend, *European Economic Expansion since 1871*, Chicago: J. P. Lippincott Company, 1941, p. 19, and A. Supan, *Die Territoriale Entwicklung der Euroaischen Kolonien*, Gotha, 1906, p. 254.
3. John Strachey, *The End of Empire*, New York: Praeger, 1964.
4. Francis Jennings, *Through Revolution to Empire*, New York: Cambridge University Press, 2000.
5. John W. Blassingame, *The Slave Community: Plantation Life in the Antebellum South*, rev. ed., New York: Oxford University Press, 1979.
6. Bruce Catton, *This Hallowed Ground*, New York: Doubleday and Co. Inc, 1959, p. 15.
7. Catton, *op. cit.*, p. 6.

Chapter 13. The French Revolution and its Aftermath (1789–1821)

1. For a good read, see Trevor Nevitt Dupuy, *The Battle of Austerlitz; Napoleon's Greatest Victory*, New York: Macmillan, 1968.
2. Méneval, Claude-François, baron de, *Memoirs of Napoléon Bonaparte*, New York: P. F. Collier, 1910, vol: 2, p. 563. Méneval was Napoleon's private secretary.

Chapter 14. Prometheus and the Pax Britannica (19th century)

1. Adam Hoschschild, *King Leopold's Ghost*, New York: Houghton Mifflin Company, 1998.
2. (a) Michael Sadler, *Hansard's Parliamentary Debates*, 8 March 1819. New Series, vol. 39, p. 901. (b) Lord Ashley's *Mines Commission of 1842*. Parliamentary Papers, 1842, vols. XV–XVII, Appendix I, pp. 252, 258,

439, 461; Appendix II, pp. 107, 122, 205. (c) Chadwick's *Inquiry into the Sanitary Conditions of the Labouring Population of Great Britain*. London, 1842, pp. 369–72.

3. I paraphrase Spencer. For those who may want his exact words, I recommend David Wiltshire, *The Social and Political Thought of Herbert Spencer*, Oxford: Oxford University Press, 1978, pp. 63, 122, 139, 143, 154.
4. *Romans*, 8. 29–30.
5. Ron Chernow, *Titan*, New York: Random House, 1998 p. 334.

Chapter 15. Three World Wars: Two Hot, One Cold (20th century)

1. Davies, *op. cit.*, London: Pimlico, 1997, p. 1,328.
2. *Ibid*.
3. *Ibid.*, p. 964.
4. There are two recent and excellent books on the subject of Mao: Philip Short *Mao, a Life*, New York: Henry Holt and Co. 2000; and Jonathan Spence, *Mao Zedong*, New York: Viking, 2000.

Chapter 16. The Global Village, (21st century)

1. Paul Johnson, *Ireland, a Concise History from the Twelfth Century to the Present*, London: Granada, 1981, p. 67. This is an excellent book, remarkably fair.
2. Alexander Somerville, English journalist, writing in the *Manchester Examiner*, 1847, 5 March.
3. The Koran, ix, 5. See also ii, 90; ii, 191 and 193.
4. Hervé Laurier, *Assassins au nom de Dieu*, Paris, Editions La Vigie, 1951.
5. Muslim views on relations between the US and Saddam Hussein can be found on the internet in numerous sites.

Epilogue

1. Thucydides, *The Peloponnesian War* Oxford: Clarendon Press, 1966, 1, xxii, 4.

BIBLIOGRAPHY

ABD-EL-HAKEM, Ibn, *History of the Conquest of Spain*, trans. by John Harris Jones, Gottingen: W. Fr. Kaestner, 1858.

ADAM, James, *The Republic of Plato*, Cambridge: Cambridge University Press, 1965.

AL-MUQAFFA, Sawirus ibn, *History of the Patriarchs of the Coptic Church of Alexandria*, Paris: Firmin-Didot, 1904.

ARISTOTLE, *Metaphysics*, London: Oxford University Press, 1966.

ARMSTRONG, Karen, *Buddha*, New York: Viking, 2001.

ASCH, Ronald G., *The Thirty Years War: the Holy Roman Empire and Europe, 1618–48*, New York: St Martin's Press, 1997.

ASHLEY, Lord, *Mines Commission of 1842*, Parliamentary Papers, 1842.

BABELON, Jean Pierre, *Henri IV*, Paris: Fayard, 1982.

BAILLY, Auguste, *La Guerre de Cent Ans*, Paris: A. Fayad, 1943.

BAINVILLE, Jacques, *Napoléon*, Paris: Balland, 1995.

BAIRD, Henry M., *The Huguenots and Henri of Navarre*, New York: AMS Press, 1970.

BALADHURI, Al, *The Origins of the Islamic State*, New York: Columbia University Press, 1916.

BAMBAKOS, Angelos, *The Battle of Naupaktos*, Athens, 1974.

BAYROU, François, *Le roi libre*, Paris: Flammarion, 1994.

BEARD, Charles, *Martin Luther and the Reformation in Germany until the Close of the Diet of Worms*, London: Philip Green, 1896.

BEARD, Charles A. and BEARD Mary R., *A Basic History of the United States*, New York: Doubleday, Doran & Company, 1944.

BEECHING, Jack, *The Galleys at Lepanto*, New York: Scribner, 1983.

BELLOC, Hilaire, *The Campaign of 1812 and the Retreat From Moscow*, New York: Thomas Nelson & Sons, 1924.

BERNARD, Jack F., *Talleyrand, a Biography*, New York: Putnam, 1973.

BERTAUT, Jules, *Napoleon in His Own Words*, Chicago: A. C. McClurg, 1916.

BLASSINGAME, John W., *The Slave Community: Plantation Life in the Antebellum South*, New York: Oxford University Press, 1979.

BODANIS, David, $E = mc^2$ *A Biography of the World's Most Famous Equation*, Toronto: Doubleday Canada, 2000.

BOORSTIN, Daniel J., *Teacher's guide to A History of the United States*, Lexington, Mass.: Ginn & Co., 1981.

BOSWELL, James, *Life of Samuel Johnson*, edited by Christopher Hibbert, London: Penguin, 1979.

BREEN, T. H., *The Character of the Good Ruler; A Study of Puritan Political Ideas in New England, 1630–1730*, New York: Norton, 1974.

BRINKLEY, Alan, *Liberalism and its Discontents*, Cambridge, Mass.: Harvard University Press, 1998.

BRINKLEY, Alan, *The Unfinished Nation: A Concise History of the American People*, New York: Knopf, 1997.

BROGAN, D. W., *Proudhon*, London: Hamish Hamilton, 1934.

BROWN, Anthony Cave, *'C' The Secret Life of Sir Stewart Menzies, Spymaster to Winston Churchill*, New York: Macmillan, 1987.

BROWN, Dee, *Bury My Heart at Wounded Knee: An Indian History of the American West*, New York: Henry Holt, 1991.

BROWN, Harrison, *The Challenge of Man's Future*, New York: Viking, 1954.

BRUCE, Evangeline, *Napoleon and Josephine: An Improbable Marriage*, New York: Scribner, 1995.

BRUNDAGE, James, *The Crusades: A Documentary History*, Milwaukee: Marquette University Press, 1962.

BRYANT, Arthur, *Makers of the Realm*, London: The Reprint Society, 1951.

BURY, J. P. T., *Thiers, 1797–1877: A Political Life*, Boston & London: Allen & Unwin, 1986.

————*Napoleon III and the Second Empire*, New York: Harper & Row, 1968.

BURNET, John, *Greek Philosophy*, London: Macmillan, 1914.

BUTLER, Jon, *The Huguenots in America*, Cambridge, Mass.: Harvard University Press, 1992.

CANTU, Caesar, *Cortés and the Fall of the Aztec Empire*, Los Angeles: Modern World Publishing Co., 1966.

CARLYLE, Thomas, *The French Revolution*, New York: AMS Press, 1974.

CARMONA, Michael, *Richelieu*, Paris: Fayard, 1983.

CARROL, James, *Constantine's Sword, The Church and the Jews*, Boston: Houghton Mifflin, 2001.

CATTON, Bruce, *This Hallowed Ground*, New York: Doubleday, 1998.

————*A Stillness at Appomatox*, New York: Doubleday, 1957

CHADWICK'S *inquiry into the sanitary conditions of the labouring population of great britain*, London, 1842.

CHALMERS, Lord, ed., *The Buddha's Teachings*, Cambridge, Mass.: Harvard University Press, 1932.

CHANDLER, David (ed.), *Napoleon's Marshals*, New York: Macmillan, 1987.

CHERNOW, Ron, *Titan*, New York: Random House, 1998.

CHURCHILL, Winston, S., *A History of the English Speaking People*, vol. 3., New York: Dodd, Mead and Company, 1957.

————*History of the Second World War*, London: The Reprint Society, 1950–2.

COUCHOUD, Paul-Louis and Jean Paul (eds), *Talleyrand-Périgord, Charles Maurice de, Prince de Bénévent, 1754–1838, Mémoires*, Paris: Plon, 1982.

CRANKSHAW, Edward, *Bismarck*, London: Macmillan; New York: Viking Press, 1981.

————*The Fall of the House of Habsburg*, London: Longmans; New York: Viking, 1963.

CUST, Sir Edward, *Lives of the Warriors of the Thirty Years' War*, Freeport, NY: Books for Libraries Press, 1972.

DARD, Emile, *Napoleon and Talleyrand*, translated by Christopher R. Turner, New York: D. Appleton-Century Company, Inc., 1937.

DAVIES, Norman, *Europe*, London: Pimlico, 1997.

DAVIS, John A. and Ginsborg, P., *Society and Politics in the Age of the Risorgimento*, New York: Cambridge University Press, 1991.

DEGLER, Carl N., *Neither Black Nor White: Slavery and Race Relations in Brazil and the United States*, New York: Macmillan, 1971.

DEUTSCHER, I., *Stalin, A Political Biography*, London: Oxford University Press, 1950.

DIAMOND, Jared, *Guns, Germs and Steel*, New York: W. W. Norton, 1999.

DODD, William, *The Factory System Illustrated in a Series of Letters to the Right Hon. Lord Ashley* . . . London: Cass, 1968.

DONNER, Frederic, *The Early Arab Conquests*, Princeton, NJ: Princeton University Press, 1981.

DRAPER, Theodore, *A Struggle for Power: The American Revolution*, New York: New York Times Books, 1996.

DUBOIS, Abbé, *Hindu Manners, Customs, and Ceremonies*, Oxford: Oxford University Press,

DUPUY, Trevor Nevitt, *The Battle of Austerlitz; Napoleon's Greatest Victory*, New York: Macmillan, 1968.

DURRANT, Will, *The Story of Civilization*, New York: Simon & Schuster, 1980.

EDWARDS, Stewart, *The Communards of Paris, 1871*, London: Thames & Hudson, 1973.

ENGERMAN, Stanley L. and GENOVESE, Eugene D., *Race and Slavery in the Western Hemisphere*, Princeton N.J.: Princeton University Press, 1979.

FARB, Peter, *Man's Rise to Civilization*, New York: E. P. Dutton, 1968.

FAY, Bernard, *Louis XVI ou la fin d'un monde*, Paris: Perrin, 1965.

FOOTE, Shelby, *The Civil War, a Narrative*, New York: Random House, 1974.

FORREST, W. G., *The Emergence of Greek Democracy*, New York: McGraw Hill, 1966.

FRAME, Robin, *Colonial Ireland*, Dublin: Helicon, 1981.

FREGOSI, Paul, *Dreams of Empire: Napoleon and the First World War, 1792 to 1815*, London: Hutchinson, 1989.

FURNEAUX (ed.), *The Annals of Tacitus*, Oxford: The Clarendon Press, 1907.

FUSERO, Clement, *Giulio II*, Milan: Dall'Oglio, 1965.

GALBRAITH, John Kenneth, *The Great Crash, 1929*, Boston: Houghton Mifflin, 1955.

GAMBLE, Richard C. (ed.) *Calvin's Theology, Theology Proper, Eschatology*, New York: Garland Pub., 1992.

GIBBON, Edward, *The Decline and Fall of the Roman Empire; The Great Books*, New York: Encyclopaedia Britannica Inc., 1952.

GREGORY OF TOURS, *The History of the Franks*, trans. with an introduction by O. M. Dalton, Oxford: Clarendon Press, 1927.

GUNTHER, John, *Inside Africa*, London: Hamish Hamilton, 1955.

HALECKI, Oscar, *A History of Poland*, New York: Dorset Press, 1992.

————*Inside South Africa*, London: Hamish Hamilton; New York: Harper & Row, 1967.

HAMILTON-WILLIAMS, David, *One Hundred Days: The Fall of Napoleon: The Final Betrayal*, New York: Wiley, 1994.

HAMMOND, N. G. L., *A History of Greece*, Oxford: The Clarendon Press, 1959.

HEMMING, John, *The Conquest of the Incas*, London: Macmillan, 1970; New York: Penguin Books, 1983.

HESIOD, *'Theogony' and 'Works and Days'*, trans by M. L. West, Oxford: Oxford Paperbacks, 1999.

HIRTH, Friedrich, *Ancient History of China*, New York: Columbia University Press, 1923.

HOFSTADTER, Richard, *The American Political Tradition and the Men Who Made It*, New York: Vintage Books, 1954.

HÖHNE, Heinz, *Canaris*, Paris: Balland, 1981.

HOMER, *The Iliad*, trans. by Robert Fitzgerald, Oxford: Oxford University Press, 1988.

HORNE, Charles F. (ed.), *The Sacred Books and Early Literature of the East, vol. Vi, Medieval Arabia*, New York: Parke, Austin & Lipscomb, 1917.

HOSCHSCHILD, Adam, *King Leopold's Ghost*, New York: Houghton Mifflin Company, 1998.

HUME, David, *The History of England: From the Invasion of Julius Caesar to the Revolution in 1688*, Indianapolis, Ind.: Liberty Classics, 1983–5.

HUTTON, J. H., *Caste in India*, Cambridge: Cambridge University Press, 1951.

INNES, Hammond, *The Conquistadors*, London: Collins; New York: Knopf, 1969.

JENNINGS, Francis, *The Creation of America*, New York: Cambridge University Press, 2000.

JENNINGS, Francis, *Through Revolution to Empire*, New York: Cambridge University Press, 2000.

JOHNSON, Paul, *Ireland: A Concise History from the Twelfth Century to the Present*, London: Granada, 1981.

KEE, Robert, *The Green Flag*, London: Quartet Books, 1976.

KEEGAN, John, *A History of Warfare*, London: Pimlico, 1993.

KENNEDY, Thomas C., *Charles A. Beard and American Foreign Policy*, Gainesville: University Presses of Florida, 1975.

KIECKER, James G., *Martin Luther and the Long Reformation*, Milwaukee: Northwestern Publishing House, 1992.

KINSEY, Dr Alfred, *Sexual Behaviour in the Human Female*, 1532.

KIRK, G. S. and Raven, J. E., *The Presocratic Philosophers*, Cambridge: Cambridge University Press, 1966.

KREY, August C., *The First Crusade: The Accounts of Eyewitnesses and Participants*, Princeton: Princeton University Press, 1921.

LACOUTURE, Jean, *De Gaulle*, Paris: Editions du Seuil, 1984.

LACROIX, Paul, *Les Femmes de la Révolution*, Paris: A. D. Delahays, 1854.

LAURIER, Hervé, *Assassins au nom de Dieu*, Paris, Editions La Vigie, 1951.

LEE, J. J., *Ireland 1912–1985: Politics and Society*, Cambridge: Cambridge University Press, 1989.

LEGGE, James, *The Sacred Books of China: The Texts of Taoism*, London: Oxford University Press, 1927.

———*The Chinese Classics Translated into English, vol. 1 The Life and Teachings of Confucius*. London: The Clarendon Press, 1895.

LEVY, Bernard-Henri, *La Barbarie à Visage humain*, Paris: Grasset, 1977.

LOCKHARDT, James, *Spanish Peru, 1532–1560. A Colonial Society*, Madison: University of Wisconsin Press, 1968.

LÜTZOW, Franz, *The Life and Times of Master John Hus*, London: J. M. Dent, 1909.

McCRAW. Thomas K. (ed.), *Creating Modern Capitalism: How Entrepreneurs, Companies, and Countries Triumphed in Three Industrial Revolutions*, Cambridge, Mass.: Harvard University Press, 1997.

McNAMARA, Robert S., *In Retrospect: The Tragedy and Lessons of Vietnam*, New York: Times Books, Random House, 1995.

McNEILL, J. R., *Something New Under the Sun*, New York: W. W. Norton, 2000.

McQUAIG, Linda, *Behind Closed Doors*, Markham, Ont., Canada: Viking, 1987.

MADARIAGA, Salvador de, *Hernan Cortés, Conqueror of Mexico*, Buenos Aires: Editorial Sudamericana, 1941.

MANCHESTER, William, *The Last Lion. Alone 1932–1940*, London: Michael Joseph; New York: Little Brown, 1983.

MARKHAM, Clements, *A History of Peru*, New York: Greenwood Press, 1968.

MASCARO, Juan, *The Bhagavad Gita*, Baltimore: Penguin Books, 1962.

MENEVAL, Claude-François, baron de, *Memoirs of Napoléon Bonaparte*, New York: P. F. Collier, 1910.

MICHELET, Jules, *History of the French Revolution*, Chicago: Chicago University Press, 1967.

MOKYR, Joel, *Why Ireland Starved: A Quantitative and Analytical History of the Irish Economy 1800–1850*, London: Allen & Unwin, 1983.

MONTGOMERY, D. H., *Leading Facts of American History*, Boston: The Atheneum Press, 1990.

MOOREHEAD, Alan, *The Russian Revolution*, New York: Harper & Brothers, 1958.

MORNER, Magnus, *Race Mixture in the History of Latin America*, Boston: Little Brown, 1967.

MUIR, William, *The Caliphate, Its Rise and Fall*, London: The Religious Tract Society, 1892.

MUNRO, Dana C., '*The Fourth Crusade*', *Translations and Reprints from the Original Sources of European History, vol. 3:1*, Philadelphia: University of Pennsylvania, 1986

NIETZSCHE, Friedrich, *Le Gai Savoir*, Paris: Gallimard, 1967.

OAKES, James, *The Ruling Race: A History of American Slave Holders*, New York: Knopf, 1982.

PALMER, J. J. N., *Froissart, Historian*, Woodbridge, Suffolk: Boydell Press, 1981.

PARKER, Geoffrey (ed.), *The Thirty Years' War*, New York: Routledge, 1993.

PLUTARCH, *Solon*,

PONTING, Clive, *Armageddon: the reality behind the distortions, myths, lies, and illusions of World War II*, New York: Random House, 1995.

POPPER, Karl, *The Open Society and Its Enemies*, Princeton: University Press, 1966.

POWER, John James, 'The Famine and its Aftermath', (dissertation) 2000.

PRESCOTT, William, *History of the Conquest of Mexico and the Conquest of Peru*, New York: The Modern Library, 1935.

PROCOPIUS, *The Secret History*, trans. By Richard Atwater, Ann Arbor: University of Michigan Press, 1961.

RADHAKRISHNAN, Sarvepali, *Indian Philosophy*, vol. 1

RAWLINSON, H. G., *India*, London: The Cresset Press, 1952.

RIEHN, Richard K., *1812, Napoleon's Russian Campaign*, New York: Wiley, 1990.

ROWSE, A. L., *The England of Elizabeth*, London: The Reprint Society, 1953.

ROBINSON, J. H., *Readings in European History*, Boston: Ginn, 1906.

RODOCANACHI, Emmanuel, *Histoire de Rome; le pontificat de Jules II, 1503–1513*, Paris: Hachette, 1928.

————*La première renaissance; Rome au temps de Jules II et Léon X; la cour pontificale; les artistes et les gens de letters; la ville et le people; le sac de Rome en 1527*, Paris: Hachette et Cie, 1912.

ROGERS, Clifford J., *The Wars of Edward Three*, Rochester, NY: Boydell Press, 1999.

RUSSELL, Bertrand, *A History of Western Philosophy*, London: Unwin Paperbacks, 1989.

RYLE, Gilbert, *New Essays on Plato and Aristotle*, New York: Routledge & Kegan Paul, 1965.

SADLER, Michael, *Hansard's Parliamentary Debates*, 8 March 1819. New Series, vol. 39.

SALMON, E. T., *A History of the Roman World*, London: Methuen & Co., 1968.

SCHLESINGER, Arthur M., *The Birth of the Nation; a Portrait of the American People on the Eve of Independence*, New York: Knopf, 1968.

SCHOM, Alan, *Napoleon Bonaparte*, New York: Harper Collins, 1997.

SCHWARTZ, Stuart B., *Sugar Plantations in the Formation of Brazilian Societies: Bahia, 1550–1835*, New York: Cambridge University Press, 1985.

————*Implicit Understandings: Observing, Reporting and Reflecting on the Encounters Between Europeans and Other Peoples in the Early Modern Era*, New York: Cambridge University Press, 1994.

SHAW, Christine, *Julius II, the Warrior Pope*, Oxford: Blackwell, 1993.

SHILLER, Robert J., *Irrational Exuberance*, Princeton, NJ: Princeton University Press, 2000.

SHOREY, Paul (ed.), Plato, *The Republic*, Cambridge, Mass.: Harvard University Press, 1963.

SHORT, Philip, *Mao, a Life*, New York: Henry Holt and Co., 2000.

SIMPSON, F. A., *Louis Napoleon & the Recovery of France*, Westport, Conn.: Greenwood Press, 1975.

SPENCE, Jonathan D., *Treason by the Book*, New York: Viking, 2001.

————*Mao Zedong*, New York: Viking, 2000.

STACEY, John, *John Wyclif and Reform*, New York: AMS Press, 1980.

STACKHOUSE, John, *Out of Poverty and Into Something More Comfortable*, Toronto: Random House, 2000.

STEINMETA, David Curtis, *Luther in Context*, Grand Rapids, MI: Baker Book House, 1995.

STERN, Fritz Richard, *Gold and Iron: Bismarck, Bleichröder, and the Building of the German Empire*, New York: Vintage Books, 1979.

STEWART, John B., *Opinion and Reform in Hume's Political Philosophy*, Princeton: Princeton University Press, 1992.

STEVEN, Stuart, *The Poles*, New York: Macmillan Publishing Co. Inc., 1982.

STRACHEY, John, *The End of Empire*, New York: Praeger, 1964.

STROUSE, Jean, *Morgan*, New York: Random House, 1999.

SUETONIUS, London: William Heinemann, 1920.

SUPAN, A., *Die Territoriale Entwicklung der Euroaischen Kolonien*, Gotha, 1906.

TABARI, Ali, *The Book of Religion and Empire*, a translation of a ninth century text, New York: Longmans Green, 1922.

TAYLOR, Edmund, *The Fall of the Dynasties*, New York: Doubleday, 1963.

THOMAS, Hugh, *Montezuma, Cortés and the Fall of Old Mexico*, New York: Simon & Schuster, 1993.

THUCYDIDES, *The Peleponnesian War*, Oxford: Clarendon Press, 1966.

TOCQUEVILLE, Alexis de, *L'ancien Régime et la révolution*, Paris: Gallimard, 1967.

————*Democracy in America*, New York: Vintage Books, 1990.

TOWNSEND, Mary Evelyn, *European Economic Expansion since 1871*, Chicago: J. P. Lippincott Company, 1941.

TUCHMAN, Barbara, *A Distant Mirror*, New York: Ballantine Books, 1979.

VILLEHARDOUIN, *Memoirs, The Fourth Crusade*, trans. By Frank T. Marzials, London: J. M. Dent, 1908.

WALLACE, Ronald, *Calvin, Geneva and the Reformation*, Grand Rapids, MI: Baker Book House, 1988.

WEHLER, Hans Ulrich, *The German Empire, 1871–1918*, translated by Kim Traynor, New Haven, Conn.: Dover, 1985.

WEST, Rebecca, *The Meaning of Treason*, London: Phoenix Press, 2000.

WILTSHIRE, David, *The Social and Political thought of Herbert Spencer*, Oxford: Oxford University Press, 1978.

WIMMER, Jan, *The 1683 Siege of Vienna*, Warsaw: International Press, 1983.

WOOD, Michael, *Legacy – the Search for Ancient Cultures*, New York: Sterling, 1994.

WOODHOUSE, C. M., *The Greek War of Independence: Its Historical Setting*, New York: Russell & Russell, 1975.

ZACHMAN, Randall C., *The Assurance of Faith; Conscience in the Theology of Martin Luther and John Calvin*, Minneapolos: Fortress Press, 1993.

ZOLA, Emil, *Germinal*, Oxford: Oxford Paperbacks, 1998

ZUCKERMAN, Larry, *Potato*, New York: Faber & Faber, 1998; London: Macmillan, 1999.

ZWEIG, Stefan, *Joseph Fouché*, New York: Blue Ribbon Books Inc., 1932.

INDEX